THE MASTER MUSICIANS SERIES

SCHOENBERG

Malcolm MacDonald

*With eight pages of plates and
music examples in text*

J. M. DENT & SONS LTD
LONDON

First published 1976
© Text, Malcolm MacDonald, 1976

Made in Great Britain
at the
Aldine Press, Letchworth, Herts
for
J. M. DENT & SONS LTD
Aldine House, Albemarle Street, London

This book is set in 11 on 12 pt Fournier 185

Hardback ISBN 0 460 03143 0
Paperback ISBN 0 460 02183 4

To David, Judy,
Lucy, Flora,
and Thomas

Whether to right or left, forward or
backward, uphill or downhill—you must
go on, without asking what lies before
or behind you. It shall be hidden; you
were allowed to forget it, you had to,
in order to fulfil your task!

                     (*Die Jakobsleiter*, 1915)

But there is nothing I long for more
intensely . . . than to be taken for a
better sort of Tchaikovsky—for heaven's
sake; a bit better, but really that's all.
Or if anything more, then that people
should know my tunes and whistle them.

                  (Letter to Hans Rosbaud, 1947)

Preface

Once, in the course of a long conversation with Schoenberg, I told him of my opinion that the 'twelve-note method' had been over-publicized and, in the process itself as well as in the controversy which resulted, had become greatly distorted in the minds of many people; and that this had led to strained and artificial attitudes towards the music itself. He replied, somewhat glumly, 'Yes, you are right, and I have to admit that it's partly my fault.' After a pause he recovered his animation and added, 'But it's still more the fault of some of my disciples.'

(Roger Sessions)

'Here! None of that mathematical music!'
Said the Kommandant when Münch offered Bach to the regiment.

(Ezra Pound, *Canto LXXX*)

Everyone seems to have problems with Schoenberg. Perhaps one reason is that none of the books written about this complex and crucial artist seem to take account of the ordinary music-lover who is not consumingly interested in mere matters of technique, yet wonders if there is a way to take Schoenberg's music, despite all its difficulties, to his or her heart. For that, as with all music that has something important to say, there is really no substitute for familiarity born of repeated listening to sympathetic performances. The most a writer may do is to place the music in perspective and give it a human context; from which, perhaps, its human *content* will emerge more clearly. That is what I have tried to do. The music will stand or fall independent of any commentary; but while it remains very partially performed, confusingly interpreted, and imperfectly understood, a simple guide like this may serve some modest purpose.

Schoenberg's posthumous reputation, like the man in life, is rich in paradox. His intense and many-sided creativity—as composer, teacher, theorist—assures his historical significance. For better or worse, he changed the face of music in our century and profoundly affected the development of its language. That has brought him some respect and honour throughout the Western world. Practically his entire *œuvre* is available on record, and certain of his scores are intensively studied by students. There are schools of thought which hold that his extension of the Austro-German musical tradition constituted the sole valid historically inevitable development out of the 'impasse' of late-Romanticism along the road to Webern, Stockhausen, Boulez and beyond.

But the acclaim is hardly universal. There are still composers and writers who honestly detest Schoenberg's music and deeply resent his influence. And his works—with a very few exceptions —have not yet gained a place in the general repertoire. The general public finds him difficult, even though music has since moved on into far stranger and murkier regions, and some of Schoenberg's most impenetrably 'modern' scores were written close on seventy years ago. Many people seem to have a mental picture of a musical *monstre sacré*, whose domed cranium broods among the twisted roots of modern music, hatching artificial systems of composition, like Frankenstein's monsters, by the sickly moonlight of Romanticism's decay. Yet few can actually claim familiarity with a true cross-section of his output, and his music is seldom presented to the public in a way that encourages interest. One suspects that listeners are too often advised to strive after the wrong *kind* of comprehension—a purely 'intellectual' response to a composer who maintained that the worlds of feeling and intellect are inseparable, and not to be sundered by such artificial distinctions.

In fact Schoenberg evokes as wide a range of attitudes as he has listeners. There are those for whom he is a godlike creative genius who could do no wrong; and those who regard him as a spiritual and emotional cripple who surrendered his power of inspiration to the strait-jacket of an arbitrary 'mathematical' system. For some he is the arch-bogeyman of tuneless modern music; and for others (among the musical *avant-garde*) he is really rather old hat—a parochial Viennese neo-Brahmsian pedant left over from the Art Nouveau era, who stumbled across a fruitful constructional principle which only attained full significance in the work of his more truly radical pupil, Webern. I know a twelve-note composer who thinks Schoenberg was a great inventive genius, but not a great creator; and a much more conservative composer who says that, though he would never wish to use his methods, he has always felt that everything Schoenberg did somehow *matters* very much indeed. And there are some (curiously enough) who simply love his music.

The fact that I belong with the last-named group perhaps unfits me to write; for one can only write out of personal experience, and whereas so many seem to have had problems with Schoenberg, I cannot remember a time when I found his music altogether strange. I must have been thirteen, and musically hardly literate, when I first heard the Piano Concerto, fourteen when I heard *Moses und Aron*. I did not imagine I 'understood' how the music operated. I simply knew that I liked the tunes in the Concerto and sensed the dramatic power of the opera; I liked the sounds the music made, sensed and approved something of its passion and high seriousness; felt a certain trust in the composer and a wish to know him better. Over the years I have come to know Schoenberg's works tolerably well, and though a few of them remain distant from me, I feel my trust has been amply repaid—and I have always proceeded from the basis of the simple experience of listening for enjoyment. Technical minutiae interest me less than the spirit which inhabits a work, and its audible, apprehensible motions and forms.

This book, therefore, sets out in the same spirit to explain and popularize Schoenberg—to present some basic information about him, to survey his music, to delineate the principal issues, and to ask some questions. If I do not always answer the questions, that is because there are some answers which are only to be found in the music, and I should like to create a readiness in the reader to go to the music once he puts down the book. My desire was to write a plain and easy introduction to a less than easy figure: if I have not altogether succeeded that is partly because I prefer to acknowledge the difficulties which many people confess, and explain too much rather than too little.

The biographical section could not, in a book of this scope, make any pretence at completeness: instead it gives a fairly impressionistic account of the composer's full and turbulent life, concentrated around certain salient events. For dramatic emphasis I have begun the story in the middle and only later sketched in the background. This is not meant to confuse—the reader will find a chronological summary of Schoenberg's life in Appendix A. Indeed both the Calendar and Personalia contain some biographical information for which no room was found in the main text. I have taken grateful advantage of the 'Master Musicians' series format to avoid the customary discussion of Schoenberg's works in chronological sequence—which so easily lends itself to false emphasis and a concentration on selected 'milestones' in the development of his musical language. I have endeavoured, instead, to give some account of practically every work he composed; for many of his most interesting pieces are among the least known, and my impression is that even comparatively few 'Schoenbergians' have a complete picture of the richness and variety of the output, which points not in one direction, but in many. I have no taste for exclusivity. Inclusiveness is a function of love and subverts orthodoxy: if the reader might be tempted by a few words about the cabaret songs or the *Christmas Music*, I feel it my duty to give them space.

Even if, at the end, the reader *still* cannot muster any liking for Schoenberg, I hope something will have been learned, and for my part I shall continue to whistle Schoenberg's tunes whenever they come into my head. I have written this book because I am interested not in demigods or sacred monsters, but in a man and his music. I do not imagine he would have approved of it; but I am sanguine enough to hope I have done him no injustice.

Grateful acknowledgments are due to the following publishers for their kind permission to quote from Schoenberg's works: Belmont Music Publishers, Los Angeles (Exx. 9, 28, 42, 51); Boelke-Bomart, Inc., Hillsdale, N.Y. (Exx. 13, 19, 37); Bote & Bock, Berlin (Ex. 18); Edition Wilhelm Hansen, Copenhagen (Exx. 34, 41); Edition Peters, London (Exx. 6–7, 21, 38); G. Schirmer Inc., New York (Exx. 10, 23–7, 36); B. Schotts Söhne, Mainz (Exx. 11*a*, 50, 52–5); Nathaniel Shilkret Music Co., Inc., Malverne, Long Island, N.Y. (Ex. 28); and Universal Edition (London) Ltd (Exx. 1–5, 11*b*, 12, 14–17, 20, 22, 29–33, 35, 39–40, 42–9), to whom acknowledgment is also made for the use of photographs and passages from Schoenberg's *Harmonielehre* and *Drei Satiren*. Extracts from *Arnold Schoenberg: Letters* and *Style and Idea* are made by kind permission of Faber & Faber, London and The St. Martin's Press, New York. Other photographic illustrations by kind permission of Universal Edition AG (Vienna), the Österreichische Nationalbibliothek, Vienna, and Mrs Roberto Gerhard, who has also allowed me to use the quotations from her husband's writings.

Many people have helped me with this book; too many properly to thank in such a short space. I must, however, pay tribute to Robert Simpson, no 'Schoenbergian' himself, without

Acknowledgments

whose kindness in bringing Messrs Dent and myself together in the first place the book might never have been written; and Ronald Stevenson, in whose company no one need lack for stimulating ideas, and whose interest, pertinent information and constructive suggestions have been most helpful. A special debt of gratitude is owed to O. W. Neighbour for allowing me access to Schoenberg's correspondence with Zemlinsky (passages from which are quoted in Chapters 3 and 8) and to his own article on Schoenberg for the forthcoming edition of *Grove*; also for the loan of material and for reading and commenting on my typescript at short notice. My thanks go to Sheila Stanton for drawing the music examples, to Sigmund Laufer for assistance in translations, and to David Drew, Graham Hatton, Paul Rapoport, Derek Watson and Eric Walter White for loan of material. Among those who have read parts of the manuscript and suggested improvements, and those who have helped me simply by their interest and encouragement, their conversation or their hospitality, I thank Bernard Benoliel, Paul and Liz Chipchase, Ann Measures, Bruce Roberts, Mike and Ruth Smith, and Roger Williams.

London—Edinburgh—Cambridge 1972–5   M. M.

Contents

Illustrations

1 Peripeteia (1908–13)

Personally I had the feeling as if I had fallen into an ocean of boiling water, and not knowing how to swim or get out in another manner, I tried with my arms and legs as best I could . . . it burned not only my skin, it burned also internally.

(Message to the American Institute of Arts and Letters, 1947)

'Scandal in the Bösendorfer Saal!' ran the Vienna newspaper headlines on 22nd December 1908, the morning after the famous Rosé Quartet, with one of the leading singers from the Court Opera, Marie Gutheil-Schoder, had given a recital in Ludwig Bösendorfer's concert-hall. The 'scandal' was the reception accorded a new string quartet with voice by a thirty-four-year-old composer and teacher already notorious for outrageous modernism—Arnold Schoenberg.[1] The whistling on door-keys, jeers, catcalls and angry confrontations between protestors and greatly outnumbered supporters were reported by the *Neue Wiener Tageblatt* in its 'crime' column, with the comment that the composer had 'already created a public nuisance with others of his products. But he has never gone so far as he did yesterday . . . it sounded like a convocation of cats'. Though a few more temperate critical voices were raised, the 'review' of the event in the *Neue Wiener Abendblatt* typified the general response:

. . . anxious to make the acquaintance of the composer Arnold Schoen-

---

[1] His name at this time and until 1933 was of course Schönberg; he adopted the anglicized form as soon as he settled in the U.S.A., used it consistently afterwards, and is now most widely known by it.

berg at last, we were completely cured by a String Quartet by that gentleman, allegedly in F sharp minor. . . . The caterwauling turned what should have been an artistic event into an event of quite another nature, by provoking an unparalleled scandal; similarly, the composition is not an aesthetic but a pathological case. Out of respect for the composer we will assume that he is tone-deaf and thus musically *non compos* . . . otherwise the Quartet would have to be declared a public nuisance, and its author brought to trial by the Department of Health. We cannot imagine in what way the subscribers of the Rosé Quartet concerts had sinned, to cause the leader of that group to programme such a worthless assault on their ears. The members of the Quartet and Frau Gutheil-Schoder, who affixed to the fiddled abominations two sung ones with turgid texts by Stephan [*sic*] George, have been punished enough.[1]

The overworked terms of abuse tell us precisely nothing about the music. What was so objectionable? A less affronted critic actually commented that the Quartet sounded rather tame for a Schoenberg work. With its four relatively short, clear-textured movements, it was certainly more easily assimilable than the huge one-movement Quartet in D minor which had been heard —and almost as violently disliked—the previous year. What *was* unsettling, however, was the way in which it undermined the listener's basic assumptions about the stability of key: its unheard-of rapidity in modulation plunged the audience into a half-familiar yet unsettling world. Disturbances began when, by the sixth bar, the music had already reached C major—the most remote region from the F sharp in which it had begun (Ex. 1).

The first movement was almost over-expressive, tense and feverish in character, with a strange air of unreality which momentary outbursts of energy were unable to dispel. Then came an even more unsettling scherzo, half-scurrying, half-

[1] Quoted in Ursula von Rauchhaupt (ed.), *Schoenberg, Berg, Webern. The String Quartets: a documentary study* (Hamburg, 1971), p. 145.

Ex.1

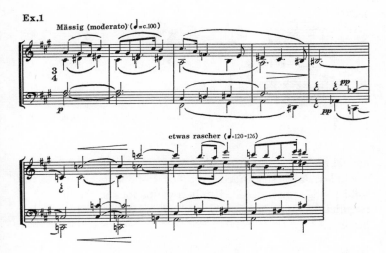

stumbling in gait, invaded at one point by a bizarre quotation from a well-known Viennese street-song, 'O, du lieber Augustin, alles ist hin!' (O, dear Augustin, it's all over), on second violin:

Ex.2

Then in the dark and tragic slow movement ('Litany'), the soprano sang a highly emotional prayer for spiritual renewal in the depths of weariness (see Ex. 3).

The finale, 'Entrückung' (Rapture), opened with an instru-

3

Ex.3

Tief___ ist die trau – er, die___ mich___ um dü – stert, ein tret ich wie – der

Herr!___ in dein Haus.___

('Deep is the sorrow which now surrounds me, once more, Lord, I enter thy house')

mental prelude of uncanny, ethereal beauty, in which key-feeling was at last almost suspended. To new, free-floating harmonies, the soloist sang words destined to become famous in the history of twentieth-century music: 'I feel air blowing from another planet.'

Ex.4

Quartet (con sord)

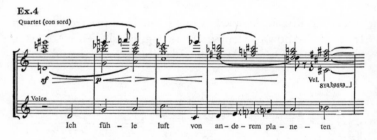

Ich füh – le luft von an – de – rem pla – ne – ten

And to many ears—nowadays at least—the music *does* float and soar as if suddenly lighter than air. There is a feeling of release, though release at a price, as the poem tells of loss of self and union with God; a triumphant climax blazes at the words 'I am an ember of the Holy Fire, am but an echo of the Holy Voice'. The Quartet touches earth again, very gently, with an epilogue that resolves its tonal difficulties into a pure F sharp major.

Curiously this finale—'the first piece of atonal music', as it is sometimes inaccurately called [1]—was received in relative silence at the Bösendorfer Saal; something, at least, of its affirmative spirit must have communicated even to that resentful audience, however strange the language. In fact the Second Quartet embodies a very characteristic Schoenbergian emotional progression: the experience and exploration of fear, disorientation, near-despair; the cry for strength to endure these trials; and then fulfilment—awakening from the nightmare, the tortured self emerges into mental clarity, consolation, union with God. It is the first work in which this pattern appears unmistakably. Though still not a 'popular' piece, it has gradually been accepted by many listeners as a beautiful and vital one; an important stage in Schoenberg's own musical and spiritual development, and a crucial document in twentieth-century music.

Such things do not happen in a vacuum. The Second Quartet was born in unusual personal circumstances. When Schoenberg began sketching it early in 1907, he seems to have been temporarily unsure of his direction. In the previous few years his artistic development had been confident and astonishingly rapid —far too rapid for most listeners. Its climax was the highly compressed, affirmative First Chamber Symphony of 1906. He immediately began a Second Chamber Symphony: but somehow found progress less and less easy. A tendency towards ever livelier contrapuntal activity, ever more exhaustive interrelationship of every part, and ever-wider expansion of the limits of conventional tonality, naturally raised ever greater problems of musical mastery. At the same time his personal position was equally difficult. The little money Schoenberg derived from

[1] 'Atonal': a vulgarism in worldwide circulation as the acceptable term for 'music without key'. I do not introduce it again except to damn it further (see below, p. 72), preferring for Schoenberg's music of the years 1908–17 the at least descriptive phrase 'totally chromatic'. The finale of the String Quartet No. 2 is, in fact, centred on F sharp, with a strong contrary pull towards D.

teaching and hack-work for publishers could hardly support his wife and children, especially after the birth of his second child, about the same time as he completed the Chamber Symphony. Apart from a small, loyal circle of pupils and disciples, such as Alban Berg and Anton Webern, and close artistic friends, such as his brother-in-law Alexander von Zemlinsky and Gustav Mahler, Schoenberg was practically isolated: composition is a lonely and unromantic activity. Mahler's departure late in 1907 to assume the conductorship of the New York Philharmonic was a severe blow, robbing him of the presence and active support of the man and musician of acknowledged prestige whom he admired above all others.

At the same time he began to feel the need to express himself through a second medium: that of paint and canvas. Perhaps there were some inspirations for which he could find no musical outlet. Certainly, like other artists of the period, he believed the immediacy and intensity of his ideas made it possible to embody them directly in any creative form. He lacked technical proficiency, however, and began taking lessons from a friend, the highly strung young painter Richard Gerstl, a forerunner of the Austrian Expressionists, who had rejected the prevailing style of Art Nouveau. Although Schoenberg never became as adept as Gerstl, his brushwork and approach to portraiture do show the latter's influence. Gerstl also painted portraits of Schoenberg and his family, and by early 1908 he occupied a studio in the same block in the Liechtensteinstrasse where the Schoenbergs had their flat.

Schoenberg's wife Mathilde also had lessons from Gerstl, and began to feel strongly attracted to the young man (nine years her husband's junior). In the summer, she deserted Schoenberg and went to live with Gerstl, and it was at this time that the bulk of the Second String Quartet was written. We may be sure that the experience finds some reflection in the music. Not only did Schoenberg dedicate the work 'to my wife' but—as a recent commentator [1] has pointed out—the weird episode in the scherzo, where the second violin intones the street-song ('it's all over'), contains plentiful musical anagrams of the initials A.S. and names Arnold, Mathilde, Richard and Gerstl. During the same period he began a song-cycle (*Das Buch der hängenden Gärten*) in an even more tonally unstable style, to poems by Stefan George that trace the progress and final extinction of a love affair.

Meanwhile, he tried to persuade Mathilde to return. Webern, of all Schoenberg's pupils the closest to his master, acted as an intermediary between them, begging Mathilde to come back, if only for the sake of their daughter and baby son. Eventually she gave in. Not long afterwards Gerstl killed himself. He was only twenty-five. Having thus tragically lost a friend, and the central basis of his marriage, Schoenberg's feelings at his Quartet's reception, only a month after Gerstl's suicide, can be imagined.

It would be impertinent, in the absence of information, to speculate on the character of the reconstituted marriage. Schoenberg, at the best of times, cannot have been an easy person to live with; nor was he, by nature, a particularly forgiving one. Unfortunately Mathilde Schoenberg, forever overshadowed by her forceful husband, remains a dim figure to biographers. The letters of Alban Berg seem to present her in her later years as a bit of a trouble-maker, taking at times an odd delight in fuelling her husband's explosive rages. But we should set this picture beside Schoenberg's own tributes to her memory after her death (see Chapter 3).

The first stages of the reunion were difficult enough on both sides. Mathilde was not unnaturally deeply depressed and taciturn. Moreover, the events of 1908 provoked in Schoenberg an emotional and creative upsurge of daunting intensity. The year 1909 was musically decisive for him: he found welling up in

---

[1] Michael Graubart, in *Tempo* 111 (December 1974), pp. 47–8.

himself a succession of works which drove deeper and deeper into perilous regions of feeling and language. He had always composed quickly, trusting to inspiration and the rightness of his inner ear; but never so fast as in the few short months which brought forth *Das Buch der hängenden Gärten*, the Three Piano Pieces Op. 11, and the Five Orchestral Pieces Op. 16. To judge from a letter he wrote to Richard Strauss, offering the Orchestral Pieces to Strauss to conduct, he now felt that his music was drawing close to the principles of contemporary painting. He described the pieces he had completed so far as 'absolutely not symphonic, quite the opposite—without architecture, without structure. Only an ever-changing, unbroken succession of colours, rhythms and moods'. Commentators nowadays do not find this music 'formless', but the forms were certainly new, freer and more intuitive than anything written before. Much more than the Second Quartet, the works of 1909 give the impression of rendering troubled psychological states directly in sound.

Schoenberg's approach to Strauss was unsuccessful. The older man's interest in him was rapidly cooling. Though his letters remained guardedly cordial, he remarked in private to Alma Mahler not long afterwards that he believed Schoenberg could only be helped by a psychiatrist—and would be better off shovelling snow than scribbling on music-paper. Schoenberg got wind of this comment, and the relationship with Strauss was abruptly and bitterly terminated.

The last work of 1909 was the most astonishing of all. Schoenberg asked Marie Pappenheim, a poet and medical student, to write him an opera-text. She produced (presumably with a detailed knowledge of Schoenberg's requirements) an extraordinary, dream-like, *angst*-ridden monodrama apparently influenced by the techniques of psychoanalysis: *Erwartung* (Expectation). The sole protagonist, a woman, wanders through a forest, seeking her lover, and finds only his dead body. She may have killed him herself; or the whole thing may be a hallucination of her disordered mind. Schoenberg took this text, and in the incredibly short space of seventeen days composed the entire work. Over half an hour's music, tighter packed with more extreme invention than ever before, embodies and underscores the emotional tumult laid bare by the lone woman's broken sentences. If ever the metaphor was applicable, this was composition at a white-hot pace; and it took him only three weeks more to score the whole monodrama for very large orchestra, in an instrumental style of dazzling and unprecedented virtuosity.

Erwartung had to wait fifteen years for its first performance. Beside it, the 'scandalous' Second Quartet appears a gentle, straightforward piece in a familiar, traditional style. Yet almost certainly they chart different aspects of the same experience. In all the works of 1909 (as well as the shorter, slightly more 'objective' near-monodrama *Die glückliche Hand*, which he began in 1910) Schoenberg was revolutionizing his own musical language not just because of the logic of his technical development, but because he was driven to work out his responses to his own emotional and spiritual turmoil. It was, in every sense, a personal crisis, which he mastered by transforming it into music: one reason why these works have such a powerfully disturbing effect even today.

Not that things necessarily improved once they were written. The effort of creating *Erwartung* seems to have produced a reaction, and for almost a year he found it very difficult to compose. From about this time has survived a shaky draft of a will that speaks of the paralysis of his creative powers and contemplates suicide. Instead, he plunged into the writing of his massive harmony text-book, *Harmonielehre*, and began to paint much more. Several of his best-known paintings date from 1910. The various 'Visions' and 'Gazes' seem to share the uncanny ethos of his recent musical works—disembodied portraits of

9

Christ, or Mahler, or nameless beings with enigmatic stares, denizens of some haunted dream-world. They are mostly, in the opinion of experts, clumsily done: but they radiate an almost frightening emotional intensity, a sense of acute distress.

At the same time he offered his talents for hire as a portrait-painter, for his financial position was getting steadily worse. He applied for a professorship of composition at the Vienna Academy of Music and Fine Arts, but accepted instead the much lowlier position of *privatdozent* (outside lecturer), which did not carry a regular salary. Mahler, who returned to Austria in the summer to compose his Tenth Symphony, supported Schoenberg's application in the warmest terms, describing him as 'one of those fiery spirits—of the kind bound to provoke opposition but just as certainly to add life and set things in motion'. But in August, when Mahler's own marriage was going through its severest crisis, Schoenberg was forced to write him a desperate letter.

I can scarcely tell you how awful it is for me to have to write this letter to you, of all people. But you cannot imagine what impossible things I have tried, but also what possible things, and it was all no use. . . . The fact is that I have no money and have to pay the rent. . . . I cannot tell you how unhappy it makes me to tarnish my relationship with you by bringing up such a matter. And I must say: I should not have done it on my own behalf; I can get over such a thing all right. But when one has a wife and children one is no longer the only person who counts . . . (Letter 264) [1]

The appeal did not go unanswered, and two days later Schoenberg could write a letter of heartfelt thanks. Apologizing if he seemed over-effusive, he concluded with a comment that gives a significant clue to all his creative activity of the period: 'Extrava-

[1] *Arnold Schoenberg, Letters,* a selection ed. Erwin Stein, translated by Ernst Kaiser and Eithne Wilkins (London, 1964). Citations of letters followed by a number refer to this edition throughout.

gant emotion is the fever that purges the soul of impurity. And it is my ambition to become as pure as yourself, since it is not permitted to me to be so great' (Letter 265).

It was clear that he could not go on living in this hand-to-mouth fashion. The lecture fees from the Academy were far too little on which to support his family, and public recognition as a composer was still denied him in his native city. Elsewhere, however, his reputation was growing; and after his symphonic poem *Pelleas und Melisande* received a highly successful performance in Berlin in October 1910, his thoughts began to turn in that direction. Events in 1911 helped impel him to such a move: above all the fact that, in May, Mahler returned to Vienna, dying of severe streptococcal blood infection. In his last rational hours the great man worried about what would happen to Schoenberg now—'If I go, he will have nobody left'. At midnight on 18th May, during a thunderstorm, his turbulent and unhappy life came to an end. Three days later Schoenberg attended the funeral, then went home to write the last and saddest of his *Six Little Piano Pieces*, Op. 19, with its melancholy alternation of two chords, like distant tolling bells. The *Harmonielehre*, completed in July, was dedicated to Mahler's memory.

Soon afterwards Schoenberg and his family left Vienna, to try his luck in Berlin as he had done a decade before. It was no smooth transition: they spent most of September stranded, penniless, near Munich. Eventually Schoenberg managed to reach Berlin in October and find some monetary support, as well as lodging for himself and his family in the south-western suburb of Zehlendorf. The Munich episode was not without benefit, however: he met the painters Wassily Kandinsky (with whom he had already been in correspondence) and Franz Marc at Murnau, and three of his paintings were accepted for inclusion in the first *Blaue Reiter* Exhibition—the second great showing of Expressionist Art, which opened in December and subsequently toured Germany. He also contributed an essay to the famous *Blaue Reiter* Almanac, and his new song *Herzgewächse* was reproduced there in facsimile.

In Berlin his circumstances improved: he lectured at the Stern Conservatoire, was able at long last to complete the *Gurrelieder*, the huge cantata whose scoring he had abandoned nine years before, and gained new composition pupils, notably the Englishman Edward Clark and Eduard Steuermann. The latter was recommended by Busoni, who was already Steuermann's piano teacher. The two composers had corresponded over the years, and there now arose a reserved cordiality between them. Despite Busoni's large-minded tolerance, their artistic aims were far apart; Schoenberg was privately (and unfairly) contemptuous of some elements of Busoni's musicianship. But he was grateful for the older composer's interest and genuine desire to help, and confessed himself deeply moved ('I have done him an injustice') when he heard Busoni's *Berceuse Elégiaque*. One fruit of their association was a recital of Schoenberg's music given in Berlin's Harmoniumsaal in early 1912, with three of the Five Orchestral Pieces performed in an eight-hand piano arrangement by pupils of Schoenberg and Busoni. The latter contributed a sympathetic, impressionistic review of the occasion to the periodical *Pan*:

Seated at the two keyboards, four men with refined, characteristic heads; almost touching, to see how they place their young intellects at the service of what is still inexplicable, with devotion and efficiency. At the back of the small podium two eyes glimmer restlessly, and a baton makes short, nervous movements. One sees only Schoenberg's head and hand, communicating with his four champions, infecting them more and more with his own fever. An unusual picture which, together with the unusual sound, exerts its own fascination. In any case, different from that of a sonata-evening by two royal professors.

To judge by eyewitness accounts of the Schoenberg household that winter—the composer holding forth to his guests, Mathilde listening, comfortably wrapped in a shawl, on the sofa, the children running about—the marriage had regained a certain stability. Schoenberg was restless to begin new works, but in a less fevered spirit than before. Commenting on this restlessness in his diary he wrote, 'I know now where it comes from. Spring is always my best time. Once more I feel ready for the motion inside me. In this I'm almost like a plant. Every year the same. In the spring of the year I have to compose something.' Then the actress Albertine Zehme sent him a text—Otto Erich Hartleben's translation of Albert Giraud's poetic cycle 'Pierrot Lunaire'—and a commission to compose music to which it could be recited. It was just what Schoenberg needed. A twenty-one number cycle, for *Sprechstimme* (pitched speaking voice) and an ensemble of five players handling eight instruments was set down in a very short space of time—most of the numbers took a single day each to write.

Pierrot Lunaire is really an ironic epilogue to the works since 1907. Pierrot, the violent, moonstruck clown of Bergamo, is partly a minor bogeyman of the Expressionist vision, partly a parody of the artist helpless in the grip of that vision. The verses, for all their surface *fin-de-siècle* decadence, are tightly organized, and so are the miniature forms of Schoenberg's settings. In this sense it is the most 'classical' music he had written for several years, and its bizarre humour and fleeting beauty (which does not exclude the awareness of pain) suggest that he was now able to view his own upheavals in a more detached, sardonic perspective. It is not the music of a madman, as was often the criticism in the first few years of its existence, but the work of a very sane one who knows he may have been near madness. This is one reason why the final number ('O ancient scent of far-off days'), which ends the 'moonlit' melodrama in daylight with something curiously like traditional E major tonality, can still seem so moving. The bad dream is over, and we breathe again a morning air which, nevertheless, is not quite the air of yesterday—the 'other planets' still float overhead.

After a private performance at Busoni's house, Schoenberg himself conducted the first public performance in October 1912, at which Albertine Zehme wore a Columbine costume and the specially trained ensemble (who had been coached through more than forty rehearsals) was hidden behind dark screens. During the next year he toured with these performers throughout Germany and Austria, sharing the conducting with the young Hermann Scherchen, who now became a convert to his music. *Pierrot Lunaire* was anathema to the critics—but, for once, a success with the public; and ever since, despite its curious ensemble, great technical demands, and uncomfortably ambiguous character, it has remained one of Schoenberg's most frequently performed works. With its completion, he seems to have felt able to direct his imagination outwards again, to see his struggles in the perspective of humanity at large; and he began to sketch an enormous symphony for soli, chorus and orchestra in which he intended to deal with the spiritual problems of contemporary man. The first movement was to depict 'A Change of Life (looking backwards, looking to the future)'; there was to be a grand scherzo celebrating the 'Joy of Life'; settings of poems by Tagore and Dehmel, a critique of the bourgeois idea of God, and passages from the Bible; leading at last to 'the union of objective, sceptical consciousness of reality with faith'. This was indeed a massive task—had it ever been carried out, the result would be by far the largest symphony ever written.

Meanwhile his fame was still spreading. He visited Prague (where Zemlinsky was now in charge of the New German Theatre) twice in 1912, to conduct *Pelleas und Melisande* and to give a moving lecture in memory of Mahler. He conducted *Pelleas* again in Amsterdam and St Petersburg, where it was well received; while in London, Henry Wood gave the world première of the Five Orchestral Pieces to an astonished Queen's Hall audience. Many years later, paying tribute to Wood's 'great artistic and personal courage' in arranging this performance,

Schoenberg recalled with some amusement his first experience of London orchestras:

Struggling with the little English I had been taught at school, I had tremendous difficulties to present my ideas, demands or suggestions to the orchestra. I have today a fairly correct idea how funny my pronunciation must have sounded at that time. In recollection I still hear myself addressing the orchestra: 'Bliss, tchentlemen, nember fiffffe', whereupon Sir Henry Wood in his softest dolcissimo con sordino, with the most delicate pronunciation of the 'G' and the 'V', and a long extended 'I' would repeat: 'Please, gentlemen, number fi-eve.' Though I understood the lesson and appreciated the fine manner in which it was given, I could not profit from it at once. There was a passage of fast notes to be played by six horns. It was tremendously difficult because of some intricate intervals, and in spite of repeating it over and over it never came out faultlessly. In desperation I turned to Mr Wood: 'This should perhaps be played by eight horns.' 'My God, no; there would only be more false notes,' he replied and we both laughed heartily.[1]

The greatest triumph, however, came in Vienna, on 23rd February 1913, with the first performance—thirteen years after its inception—of the *Gurrelieder*, conducted by Franz Schreker, with Schoenberg's cousin Hans Nachod singing the part of Waldemar. Many Viennese came to jeer, bringing their house-keys to whistle louder with. They stayed spellbound. Schoenberg's gigantic early masterpiece, from whose expansive romantic lyricism and brave pantheistic faith in the essential rightness of natural order he must by now have felt impossibly far removed, disarmed all scoffers. This was music they understood! When— after the long Wagnerian love-tragedy had been enacted, the wild ride of the ghostly hunters sent on its way, and the Summer Wind's riotous breezes invoked by the speaker—the music

[1] From a contribution by Schoenberg for *Homage to Henry Wood, a World Symposium* (L.P.O. Booklets No. 1, London, 1944), edited by Miron Grindea; reproduced here with Mr Grindea's permission.

15

gained the blazing C major that opens the final Hymn to the Sun—then the entire audience, in a kind of dumbfounded concession to their own astonishment, rose to their feet and remained standing for the last five grandiose minutes.

It was a magnificent success. There was tumultuous applause, and rapturous shouts of 'Schoenberg! Schoenberg!'. The composer was eventually discovered sitting grimly in an inconspicuous seat, and very unwillingly was led on stage. There he bowed to Schreker and the performers, but pointedly ignored the audience that was applauding him so enthusiastically. 'For years,' he said afterwards, 'these people have refused to recognize me. Why should I thank them for appreciating me now?' A graceless attitude, no doubt, but he had good reason to be bitter. Shortly before the performance, the father of an early pupil, pursuing a debt which Schoenberg understood to have been paid on his behalf by the pupil long ago, sent bailiffs to seize his personal effects and deprive him of part of the money for his return fare. To get back to Berlin after the concert, he had to borrow from friends. Nor was the acclamation anything but a passing mood: at a concert of music by Schoenberg and his associates in Vienna a few weeks later the barracking was worse than ever.

2   The past (1874–1907)

.. our loathed and beloved Vienna
(Schoenberg to Mahler, 1910)

The Vienna into which Schoenberg was born, and which so readily abused him, enclosed a society of unsettling paradoxes. Time has rubbed smooth its rough edges and bestowed a lustre that in some respects the city really deserved—glittering capital of the Austro-Hungarian Empire, cultural and commercial crossroads: the prosperous, stable, easy-going, infinitely leisured high-summer realm of the log king Franz Joseph I and the waltz king Johann Strauss II. Yet the colourful surface often concealed disillusionment and despair, and the cross-currents of social spite, growing antisemitism and political and intellectual ferment. Since the Austro-Prussian War firmly demoted Austria from its position of European political predominance, Viennese society had become hamstrung by an inert paternalistic bureaucracy whose incapacity, moral hypocrisy and political corruption became progressively more evident as the nineteenth century drew to a close. As its collapse began to seem possible, and so less possible to contemplate, so did attitudes harden against new ideas. Yet the ambiguous city exercised an uncanny fascination on even its most mistreated sons.

In artistic circles there was a gradually heightening awareness of social stagnation, of all-pervasive double standards in life and thought, and a sense of imminent disintegration, vividly recalled in the essays and stories of Stefan Zweig, the plays of

Hugo von Hofmannsthal and the novels and plays of Schoen-berg's friend Hermann Bahr. While these writers, aware of their own powerlessness, responded to the situation with a melancholy masked in more or less bitter scepticism, there were others who tried to combat it with a positive ethical opposition founded on the traditions of European humanism. Their efforts drove them, during the last decade of the nineteenth century and the first of the twentieth, into an extreme position where a radical rethinking of the language of their various disciplines was vitally necessary to maintain their validity. Insofar as this was not escapism, but a response to social pressure, their attitude might be summed up as the belief that a determined critique of the various idioms in which a society expresses itself is a critique of the society itself. They saw turn-of-the-century Vienna's predilection for *Schmuck* (ornament, decorative effect) and cliché as concealing a real poverty of life, thought and artistic substance. Under this broad banner, if no other, we may link the names of the polem-ical satirist Karl Kraus, the psychoanalyst Sigmund Freud, the painter Oskar Kokoschka, the architect Adolf Loos, the philo-sopher Ludwig Wittgenstein, and—the composer Arnold Schoenberg.

Schoenberg was born on 13th September 1874 at 57 Obere Donaustrasse in the Second District of Vienna, the first of the three children of Samuel Schoenberg and his wife Pauline (*née* Nachod). The family belonged to the poorest level of the Jewish petit-bourgeoisie: Samuel owned a small shoe-shop, and had worked his way up in the trade from boy apprentice. Both parents hailed from the Eastern parts of the Empire—Pauline from Prague and Samuel from the polyglot city of Pressburg (now better known as Bratislava) where Austrian, Czech, Slovak and Hungarian cultures mingled. The marriage seems to have been rather an attraction of opposites. Samuel was a romantic, idealistic freethinker of a combative, iconoclastic cast of mind, while Pauline was conservative, practical, deeply attached to the old Jewish beliefs. Arguments were not infrequent, with Pauline's brother Fritz (father of the singer Hans Nachod) taking part on Samuel's side—so the young Arnold must have been aware quite early in life of the contrary pulls of faith and scepticism. In the struggle to reconcile the reverence for Jewish tradition he inherited from his mother with the critical outlook derived from his father, we see the earliest of the many dichotomies that shaped his intellectual development.

Neither parent was particularly interested in music, although Samuel, once a member of a choral society, used to sing Slovak folksongs to his young son, while Pauline's family had provided synagogue cantors in Prague for generations. Samuel's hope was that Arnold would one day become an engineer. But the boy's musical gifts became evident as soon as he was given a chance to show them. He began learning the violin at the age of eight or nine and immediately, without any tuition, started producing violin duets of his own. He used as models the works he played with his violin teacher, and the fact that he was thus able to bring his childish compositions to his lessons and play them over must have been a valuable stimulus. At first these little works progressed only as fast as his violin technique improved; but soon, after reading a life of Mozart, he was inspired to emulate him and compose without the aid of an instrument.

Real progress came when he entered Realschule (secondary school without classics) at the age of eleven, and met there a boy named Oskar Adler, who was to become a lifelong friend. Adler gave Schoenberg some tuition in elementary harmony and ear-training. With one of Arnold's cousins they formed a trio of two violins and viola, and arranged for this combination whatever music they could lay hands on. Arnold wrote many original pieces, too, some of which have survived: polkas, marches, *ländler* and so forth—quite endearing efforts in the popular style of the day. A somewhat larger attempt was a '*Romance* (Ré mineur) pour deux violons et alto par Arnaude Schönberg, op. 1': the Frenchified title probably shows the influence of his uncle Fritz Nachod, the nearest thing to an intellectual in the family, who taught Arnold French and kindled an interest in poetry and drama, especially Schiller.

In time, the trio became a quartet; Schoenberg graduated to the viola, then to a substitute-cello (a viola fitted with zither strings) and finally to the cello itself, which remained his principal instrument afterwards. His actual playing, though never technically wonderful, is said to have had great character and intense musicality; and the experience of playing all four roles in a string quartet was valuable grounding for the future composer of so much chamber music. Not surprisingly, as soon as he had found out from an encyclopedia article how to construct a sonata-form movement, string quartets began to flow from his pen. It hardly mattered that his formal training was still non-existent: in later years he often said that Art is not a matter of 'can' but 'must'; and the 'must' of music impelled him from the start.

Samuel Schoenberg died of influenza when Arnold was fifteen. To help support Pauline and her other children, the boy had to leave school (where he had been a cocky, irrepressible, unwilling pupil of average scholastic ability) and start work as a clerk in a small private bank. He hated it. Music, however, continued to be his absorbing interest, whether composing or playing or just walking in the Prater with friends like Oskar Adler and David Josef Bach (later a linguist and mathematician) listening to a military band playing Wagner excerpts—a stocky, cheerful, argumentative, rather bumptious youth in a yellow overcoat, already trenchant in his opinions, already balding on the domed cranium that was to be his most distinguishing physical feature. About this time he was hopelessly in love with a fourteen-year-old cousin, Malvina Goldschmeid, to whom he wrote letters casting a revealing light on his youthful convictions (he claimed to be an 'Unbeliever', but felt that the Bible was the foundation of all things—an early instance of his penchant for paradox). He also composed in her honour a nocturne for orchestra: the touchingly clumsy piece survives in a piano arrangement under the alternative title *Lied ohne Worte*.

In 1893 the gifted young composer-conductor Alexander von Zemlinsky took over the weekly rehearsals of the amateur orchestra 'Polyhymnia' and found, at the only cello desk, a striking young man 'fervently ill-treating his instrument'. It was Schoenberg: and here began a lifelong friendship. Zemlinsky, conservatoire-trained and a protégé of Brahms, gave Schoenberg his only real instruction in the principles of composition—though before long the pupil's prodigious capacity for learning had actually reversed their respective roles. Zemlinsky was able to broaden Schoenberg's musical horizons: he was one of the first of the younger generation to cut across the Brahms-Wagner axis that had long divided the musical world into opposing camps. Schoenberg, whose sympathies had so far lain with Brahms, began to appreciate Wagner's music, and by the end of the 1890s he had heard all the major operas several times. He came to appreciate Bruckner, too, and is known to have heard him lecture at the Vienna Academy. His own compositional efforts began to attract attention: 'Polyhymnia' awarded him a prize for one work, and in 1894 the blind organist-composer Josef Labor, hearing part of a string quartet by Schoenberg, urged him to devote himself entirely to music.

The opportunity swiftly arrived. According to one story, one day in 1895 Schoenberg came home and announced joyfully: 'My boss has gone bankrupt—nobody will ever get me inside a bank again!' Now, he would work only at music. Naturally his family did not take to the idea at all: relatives blamed him for unnecessarily worrying his mother; there were quarrels and determined efforts to get him to return to banking. Only Fritz Nachod, the romantic uncle, supported his stand. But Schoenberg had made up his mind. With the help of the socialist music-

21

teacher Josef Scheu he secured a post as conductor of a metal-workers' choir in Stockerau, twelve miles from Vienna (walking there and back when he could not afford the fare). Later he took charge of similar choirs in the villages of Meidling and Mödling. It was satisfying work, and he found himself in sympathy with the workers' political aspirations (they knew him as 'Comrade Schoenberg')—but it brought little money. He thus began, in addition, many years' drudgery of scoring operettas and making piano arrangements of other composers' works.

His own compositions continued unabated, with songs, quartets and piano pieces. In the summer of 1897, partly under Zemlinsky's tutelage, he wrote a String Quartet in D major. This, the latest of several essays in the form, was his first piece to be publicly performed: it was heard twice in concerts in 1897–8, and its warmly melodious style was well received. Even Eduard Hanslick, the all-powerful, arch-reactionary critic of the *Neue Freie Presse*, was pleased enough to comment: 'It seems to me that a new Mozart is growing up in Vienna.' But Schoenberg was not wholly satisfied with the quartet, and it was neither played again nor published during his lifetime.

Eighteen ninety-eight was the year in which under the influence of a friend, the singer Walter Pieau, he abandoned the Jewish faith altogether and was converted to Protestantism. Little is known of the circumstances: we can only say that the conversion marked the end of the first stage in a lifetime of spiritual restlessness and searching. He was writing much music, but few works reached completion. However, in September 1899, in the space of a mere three weeks, on holiday with Zemlinsky in Payerbach, he composed a string sextet which infused chamber music with characteristics of the symphonic poem: *Verklärte Nacht* (Transfigured Night) after a poem by Richard Dehmel.

Zemlinsky, recognizing a work of unusual mastery, submitted

it to the Wiener Tonkünstlerverein, who had arranged for the performance of the D major Quartet. This time the reaction was far less favourable: Schoenberg had advanced astonishingly in two years, and the jury found themselves confronted with 'modern' music which went beyond Wagner in chromatic intensity. 'It sounds as if someone had smeared the score of *Tristan* while it was still wet!' commented one disgusted judge, and the work was eventually rejected because it contained a chord which nobody could find in the textbooks.

Soon afterwards, the Tonkünstlerverein announced a competition for a new song-cycle. Schoenberg resolved to enter, and set some poems from the 'Songs of Gurre', a verse-cycle by the Danish novelist and poet Jens Peter Jacobsen. Then, fired with a much larger conception, he went on to set the entire *Gurre-lieder*, on a huge scale, for solo voices, speaker, choirs and a vast orchestra, bigger than anything any composer had hitherto asked for. Parts I and II of this immense undertaking were composed in short score by the middle of 1900, but work had to be abandoned for almost a year while Schoenberg earned sufficient to live on—scoring other people's operettas. One evening, after a party with his Mödling choral society, he climbed the nearby Anninger mountain and watched the sunrise over the forest—a sight that gave him the inspiration for the great Hymn to the Sun that closes the *Gurrelieder*. In mid-1901 the whole work—one of the summits of late Romantic music— had been drafted, and Schoenberg was able to order music-paper of an unheard-of size (forty-eight staves) on which to score it.

In October of that year, his bonds with Zemlinsky became even closer: for he married the latter's sister Mathilde. He had been in love with her since at least 1899, but we know next to nothing of the progress of the romance. A simple correlation of dates, however, suggests that Mathilde must have been six months pregnant at the time of the wedding: and this, together with the fact that Schoenberg's musical chances in Vienna remained slim, may have helped prompt the move to Berlin which the young couple made in December. He had been offered a vague 'musical directorship' in the *Überbrettl*—an early form of cabaret—at Ernst von Wolzogen's Buntes Theater. Wolzogen's idea was to bring art into the convivial atmosphere of the music-hall, and the *Überbrettl* was the venue for a group of writers including Frank Wedekind and Otto Julius Bierbaum, who had recently published a volume of *Deutsche Chansons*: light-hearted, satirical poems suitable for turning into popular songs. Schoenberg, who loved good light music, had set a few of the *Chansons* to music as *Brettl-lieder* (perhaps a reaction from the very different *Gurrelieder*) and a chance meeting with Wolzogen in Vienna in the summer of 1901 led to the invitation.

But once in Berlin, Schoenberg's life seems to have continued in the dreary furrow of arranging others' music. He seems to have gained little satisfaction from his activities at the Buntes Theater. It is not known that he did any conducting in the *Überbrettl*: of his own *Brettl-lieder* only the curious 'Nachtwandler' is known to have had a single performance, and was then withdrawn because the trumpet part was found too difficult.

Fortunately he came into contact with Richard Strauss, who at the age of thirty-eight had already completed his major symphonic poems and was recognized as Germany's leading composer. Strauss saw the draft of the *Gurrelieder* and was deeply impressed. Seeing Schoenberg's dire financial straits (there was now a baby daughter to support, as well as his wife) he gave him copying work and arranged for him to receive the 1902 Liszt Scholarship (the income of the Liszt Foundation, annually awarded to a gifted musician). This helped when the contract with Wolzogen expired in mid-1902. Moreover, at Strauss's recommendation, Schoenberg secured a teaching position at the Stern Conservatoire, one of the most respected music schools in Berlin. This kind of work was much more to his liking (perhaps he now began to discover his unique talents as a teacher).

Strauss gave Schoenberg arstistic encouragement, too, at a time when he was writing little (he had laid aside the orchestration of the *Gurrelieder* owing to pressure of hack-work). Turning Schoenberg's attention to Maeterlinck's drama *Pelléas et Mélisande*, Strauss urged him to attempt on opera on that subject.[1] Instead, Schoenberg composed a huge symphonic poem, one of the most dauntingly contrapuntal scores anyone had written up to that time. Completed in early 1903, this *Pelleas und Melisande* was the main artistic fruit of his first Berlin sojourn.

Financial worries continued to make life hard, and in July 1903 the Schoenbergs returned to Vienna. There, at least, something of a reputation now preceded Arnold: *Verklärte Nacht* had been performed for the first time the previous year. There had been much hissing and restiveness among the audience, but some took note of the composer who could pour such concentrated emotion and advanced harmonic content into the confining mould of chamber music. The battle-lines between conservatism and radicalism, in music as in the other arts, were now clearly drawn, and Schoenberg was not unwilling to enter the fray.

He first planned, with Zemlinsky, to set up a kind of 'free conservatoire'; and in the autumn of 1903 the philanthropist and educationalist Dr Eugenie Schwarzwald, who had been introduced to Schoenberg by their mutual friend Adolf Loos, made available classrooms for that purpose in the girls' school she ran in Vienna. The project was not well supported, and lasted for only a year; but several students from the Institute of Music History at Vienna University attended the classes, encouraged by the Institute's director, Guido Adler, who was sympathetic to new ideas and friendlily disposed towards Schoenberg. When Schoenberg began to take private composition pupils in 1904, these formed the core of his circle of young

[1] He apparently discounted the existence of Debussy's masterpiece, recently performed in Paris! (See Appendix A.)

disciples. Among the first was a certain Anton von Webern; and soon afterwards a young civil servant called Alban Berg abandoned his career to study with Schoenberg. These were the first, and among the most important, of the many notable composers Schoenberg was to teach in coming years; but others who would make their mark in different ways, such as Erwin Stein and Egon Wellesz, also came to him in these early years. Soon he would be likened by critics to Socrates—not as a compliment: as a 'seducer of the young'.

His position was morally strengthened by the fact that he received support from the one man in Vienna whose uncompromising musical idealism matched his own and who was, moreover, in a position to encourage younger composers—Gustav Mahler, conductor of the Court Opera. They were introduced at a rehearsal of *Verklärte Nacht* in 1903 and Mahler, greatly impressed, became a staunch and generous defender of Schoenberg, unselfishly associating himself with music which, as the years progressed, even he had difficulty in understanding. For his part, Schoenberg idolized the great composer-conductor. Their relationship was nevertheless often a difficult one, particularly in its early stages, as Alma Mahler has recounted:[1]

[Schoenberg and Zemlinsky] used to come in the evening. After one of our devastatingly simple meals, all three went to the piano and talked shop—at first in all amity. Then Schoenberg let fall a word of youthful arrogance and Mahler corrected him with a shade of condescension— and the room was in an uproar. Schoenberg delighted in paradox of the most violent description . . . Mahler replied professorially. Schoenberg leapt to his feet and vanished with a curt good-night. Zemlinsky followed, shaking his head. As soon as the door had shut behind them, Mahler said: 'Take care you never invite that conceited puppy into the house again.' On the stairs Schoenberg spluttered: 'I shall never again cross that threshold'. But after a week or two Mahler said: 'By

[1] In her *Gustav Mahler: Memories and Letters* (3rd ed., London, 1973), p. 78.

the way, what's become of those two?'[1] I . . . lost no time in sending them an invitation; and they, who had only been waiting for it, lost no time in coming.

In March 1904 Schoenberg, with Zemlinsky, Bruno Walter and other young musicians, founded a Society of Creative Musicians 'to give modern music a permanent home in Vienna, where it will be fostered'. Mahler was induced, with Guido Adler's aid, to become Honorary President and conductor-in-chief. The Society operated for only one season, but in that time it presented, among other recent works, Mahler's *Kindertotenlieder*, Strauss's *Sinfonia Domestica*, and the première of Schoenberg's *Pelleas und Melisande*. This last took place in January 1905, under the composer's baton. Rehearsals went badly: he was given a rough ride by the orchestra until Mahler appeared at one rehearsal, score in hand, to make sure they took their task seriously. The performance itself was hardly a popular success—sections of the audience left in droves—but others were convinced on this occasion of Schoenberg's individual genius, including Alma Mahler, who noted in her diary that her friend Zemlinsky's music, for all its distinction, lacked Schoenberg's strength and originality.

Schoenberg had settled down to a life of private teaching in his suburban flat, combined with hack-work for the recently founded Viennese music-publishers Universal Edition, who became his own publishers for the next twenty years. He had some hope of better things: it appears that the progressive Guido Adler was proposing to the government a radical re-organization of the Vienna Conservatoire, with Mahler as

[1] Mahler actually called them 'that Eisele and Beisele' after comic-strip characters of the time. The conjunction of the short, bald, bullet-headed Schoenberg with the even shorter, gnome-like, sharp-featured Zemlinsky was indeed a richly caricaturable one (see, for instance, the drawing by Emil Weiss among the illustrations in this book).

director and Schoenberg and Zemlinsky on the staff—and that the plan was not definitely dropped until Mahler's departure for the U.S.A. in 1907.

Schoenberg concentrated on composition only in the summer months. In September 1905, holidaying at Gmunden in the Traunsee, he completed the huge String Quartet in D minor (which he numbered as his First)—a work that aspired to the scale, and something of the profundity, of Beethoven's late quartets. In the following summer, while staying at Tegernsee, he finished the First Chamber Symphony, whose fifteen-piece orchestra showed he had turned away decisively from the huge forces of the *Gurrelieder* and *Pelleas*. He was reshaping the harmonic vocabulary of late-Romanticism into a new and purposeful polyphonic language. It was a difficult task, but life and Vienna were not to make it any smoother as time went on. The stupefied incomprehension which greeted the D minor Quartet at its première in early 1907 was a foretaste of the struggles to come. The 'scandal in the Bösendorfer Saal' was only a year away.

3　Consolidation (1914–33)

This was the time when everybody made believe he understood Einstein's theories and Schoenberg's music.

('How One Becomes Lonely,' 1937)

A summer's day near Traunkirchen in the Salzkammergut, towards the end of July 1921. Two men are taking a stroll in the country: Schoenberg, and Josef Rufer, one of the new generation of pupils that had come to him after the war. During the course of their walk Schoenberg turns to Rufer and declares: 'Today I have discovered something which will assure the supremacy of German music for the next hundred years.' It is a famous moment: he is referring to the 'method of composing with twelve notes related only to each other' employed in the Suite for piano on which he is working. A means of ensuring structural coherence in music within a totally chromatic idiom, its external features are simple and easily grasped but its implications far-reaching and easily misunderstood; to this day it remains the chief stumbling-block for his opponents, while mesmerizing many of his most fervent supporters. It is what the name 'Schoenberg' signifies to the public at large, even now: not so much a composer as the 'inventor' of a technique. And he was hardly one to deny the significance of that. Yet 'assure the supremacy of German music'? That has an oddly sinister ring; and it is, in any case, a strange desire for an Austrian Jew, even one so deeply involved with Germanic musical tradition.

In fact, the closer one looks at his life in the years following the *Gurrelieder* première, the stranger it becomes. They had been unsettled, unsatisfying years with, apparently, little to show for them.[1] Work had been interrupted time and again by the demands of teaching, touring and conducting, by ill-health, and most of all by the great upheavals of World War I. The war turned artistic life in Germany upside down. Schoenberg detested the surrounding atmosphere: he was convinced that art had no place in the prevailing lunacy. He wrote to Zemlinsky in October 1914:

My colleagues ignore me more than ever. They hold patriotic artistic soirées in C major and 'still know factions'. What do you say to Maeterlinck? I feel that all this palaver of the so-called spiritual leaders of the people is highly superfluous because it is dilettantish and therefore trivial. Now the only language one can use is that of the gun and those who are unable to use this language should crawl into a corner and try to be inconspicuous . . .

The Schoenbergs had returned to Vienna in the summer of 1915, when Arnold was ordered to report for an army medical examination there. In December he was called up, and served the best part of an unhappy year in garrison duty. By all accounts he did his best to remain 'inconspicuous'. When asked by an officer if he was 'that controversial composer', he gave the famous reply: 'Somebody had to be, and nobody else wanted to, so I took on the job myself.' The war's effect on him was deep, but did not find overt artistic expression. His own role in it must have seemed frustrating in the extreme. His health declined, he suffered from asthma attacks, and in October 1916, after a long wrangle with the Ministry of Defence in Budapest in which he was possibly aided by Béla Bartók,[2] he secured a release from

[1] The reader is reminded that many biographical details omitted here will be found in Appendix A.

[2] As Schoenberg's father had come from Bratislava (Hungarian Poszony, Austrian Pressburg), he inherited Hungarian nationality for administrative purposes, which became Czech when Czechoslovakia was formed in 1918.

military duties. Yet the following year he was called up once more—with disastrous effect on his major work of the period, the oratorio *Die Jakobsleiter* (Jacob's Ladder)—only to be discharged as physically unfit in December 1917.

As the war staggered to a close, there were the inevitable money worries, the necessity of earning a living by teaching: in 1919 Schoenberg was taking fourteen pupils (including Hanns Eisler, Rudolf Kolisch, Paul Pisk and Karl Rankl) individually in composition, harmony, counterpoint and analysis five or six days a week from 8 a.m. to 6 p.m. Then there was the problem of revivifying Viennese musical life, into which he threw himself with his customary energy. In November 1918 he founded a *Verein für musikalische Privataufführungen*: a Society for Private Musical Performances. This notable organization drew the core of its performers and membership from his circle of pupils and friends, and gave weekly concerts of chamber music featuring contemporary works in thoroughly prepared performances (fifty hours' rehearsal per work was not unusual!) by the finest players and singers. To ensure the audience's maximum comprehension, unfamiliar works were usually repeated two, three or more times in a season; participation by young artists was encouraged; programmes were not made known in advance; all applause, or expression of disapproval, was forbidden; and music critics were excluded.

Schoenberg, as the Society's President, was closely involved in all its activities and wielded absolute dictatorial powers. Gossip named it the 'Vienna Schoenberg Society'—yet in the first season he forbade performance of any of his works. Catholicity of taste was one of the Society's guiding principles. Its four years of existence (December 1918–December 1922) saw the production of over 150 different works, including pieces by composers as diverse as Bartók, Berg, Busoni, Debussy, Dukas, Hauer, Kodály, Korngold, Mahler, Milhaud, Pijper, Ravel, Reger, Satie, Franz Schmidt, Schreker, Scriabin, Stravinsky,

Josef Suk, Webern, Wellesz and Zemlinsky—in fact whoever, in Schoenberg's words, 'had a real face or name'. Quite apart from the direct educational effect on audience and players, awakening interest in new musical ideas, the Society helped to re-establish with other countries musical links that had been broken by the war. It was a forerunner of the more ambitious Modern Music organizations which grew up in Europe and America in the later 1920s; and to some extent it provided them with a model.

Yet all these upsets and activities cannot entirely explain the fact that, in the years since *Pierrot Lunaire*, apart from a few occasional pieces, Schoenberg had completed only one new work: the *Vier Orchesterlieder*, Op. 22, lasting about ten minutes in all, which had taken him nearly four years. He had, of course, composed much more than that, but the substantial completed portion of *Die Jakobsleiter* had been the fruit of a few feverish months—months of hardship, with money desperately short and little food or fuel to cook it, part of the time spent trailing from one cheap lodging-house to the next. All such aggravating factors apart, Schoenberg must have been finding composition itself more difficult; he knew the direction he wanted to take, but had not found the means by which to move onwards. The basis of this difficulty is examined more fully in Chapter 6. For the meantime, we may simply suggest that in 1908-9 he had arrived intuitively, and largely involuntarily, at a radically new kind of music in a bewilderingly short space of time; and that since the spiritual and emotional conditions which drove him then no longer obtained, he needed to provide a 'logical' basis, a conceptual framework, for what he had created, before he could extend it further.

He found it (or thought he had—the result is the same) in the twelve-note method,[1] where every theme, harmony or accompaniment is related to a particular succession of the twelve notes

[1] For the essentials of which see Chapter 6.

of the chromatic scale; to create, in effect, a continuous process of variation on the distinct configuration provided by the twelve-note row. He had taken steps in this direction as early as 1915, in the long-abandoned sketches for the choral symphony; and again in *Die Jakobsleiter*, which had grown out of that project—but clearly he had not recognized their full significance. Other influences helped to nudge him further along the path. One was the younger composer and theorist Josef Matthias Hauer, of whom he must have become aware about 1917. Hauer evolved another (and much more complicated) way of using a succession of the twelve chromatic notes as a work's structural basis, from quite different premises, and some of his works were performed by the *Verein für musikalische Privataufführungen*. Another influence, perhaps (and if so, more in attitude than example), was Anton Webern: Schoenberg's oldest pupil and one of his closest friends, no whit less strong-willed and as uncompromising in his ideals as his master. Their relationship was close but often strained: Schoenberg called him 'a very Hotspur', the spiritual leader among his pupils, but was dismayed at Webern's willingness to accept and apply his teacher's every idea, almost before he himself had fully formulated it. Webern was to be the first disciple to embrace Schoenberg's method.

It is beyond doubt, however, that the discovery of the method had a liberating effect on Schoenberg. He found himself able to bring works to completion; he could see his way forward; it did not cramp his invention; he felt freer to follow his fantasy than he had in years. 'So far,' he wrote to Hauer in 1923,

I have found no mistake and the method keeps on growing of its own accord, without my doing anything about it. This I consider a good sign. In this way I find myself positively enabled to compose as freely and fantastically as one otherwise does only in one's youth. (Letter 78)

They had been years of spiritual difficulties, too. Still officially Lutheran, his Christian beliefs had not lasted. Under the strain of

33

the crisis of 1908–9 and then the events of the war, religion had indeed become a major solace, but it was an extremely personal kind of religion—what he called 'the Faith of the Disillusioned' —with a Judaeo-Christian background modified by his reading of Strindberg and Swedenborg. The metaphysical poem *Totentanz der Prinzipien* (Death-dance of the principles), completed in 1915 and originally intended for setting in the choral symphony, examines the course of human existence and finds it wanting, material considerations 'leaving the spiritual eye blind'. In *Die Jakobsleiter*, the text of which was begun shortly after completing the *Totentanz*, Schoenberg depicts people at different stages of spiritual growth, being judged in the after-life and prepared for reincarnation into the turmoil of the world.

Nor, he found, was he ever able to forget his Jewishness: he was hardly allowed to. The virulent criticism to which his musical activities were always subjected in the Vienna press began, even before the war, to take an undisguisedly antisemitic tone. Mahler before him had experienced the same thing. The double paradox of being an apostate among Jews, but a Jew among Gentiles, must have increased Schoenberg's sense of spiritual isolation, yet magnified his feelings of solidarity with his own race.

In June 1921, following a 'merry evening' of Strauss waltzes at the *Verein*,[1] Schoenberg went to Mattsee, near Salzburg, to spend the summer. He was in good spirits, and felt at last near the solution of his compositional problems. He looked forward to a summer's hard creative work—perhaps even completing *Die Jakobsleiter*. But after only a few days, he was visited by a deputation from the town council. Jews, he was informed, were no longer welcome in Mattsee; but of course, if Herr Schoenberg

---

[1] The waltzes were specially arranged by Berg, Webern and Schoenberg, all of whom took part in performing them (Schoenberg as second violin) along with Steuermann, Kolisch and others. The manuscripts of the arrangements were then auctioned to raise money for future concerts.

could give proof of Christian baptism . . . He could, but refused
to demean himself by producing it. He left Mattsee immediately,
and eventually found accommodation in Traunkirchen. So it was
here, soon afterwards, that he told Rufer of his discovery which
would 'ensure the supremacy of German music'; and by his
own admission (in an important Letter [64] to Kandinsky, of
May 1923) he was, to say the least, rather bitter at the time:

Must not a Kandinsky have an inkling of what really happened when
I had to break off my first working summer for five years, leave the
place I had sought out for peace of mind to work in, and afterwards
couldn't regain the peace of mind to work? Because the Germans will
not put up with Jews!

A question-mark, at least, ought to remain over the phrase
'the supremacy of German music'. Could not Schoenberg's
remark have had an ironic dimension? He had lighted, in his
searchings, on a highly versatile compositional device, germane
to his own creative needs, which any other real composer might
take, leave or adapt at will. But his awakening re-identification
with the Jewish race enabled him to view dispassionately his own
deep Austro-German culture. He may have recognized that in
the Germanic mind, with its love of system and authority, this
device was fatally easy to misinterpret as a law to be obeyed
rather than a tool to be applied: as a magic formula which could
take the place of hard and true creative work.

The possibility (which is all it is) is worth bearing in mind. It
would help to explain why Schoenberg never formulated a
detailed theory of twelve-note music; why, though he gave a
few lectures on its application in specific works, he refused to
teach it to his pupils and did not care how they composed, as
long as the result was musical and craftsmanlike; why he was so
touchy about musicians and writers outside his immediate circle
handling the idea, referred to it jokingly as 'purely a family
affair' and made curious attempts to have it recognized as his own

'intellectual property'. After all, in a few years' time he was to apply the method in an opera (*Moses und Aron*) about the difficulty of communicating the essence of an idea, when people are so willing to be satisfied with superficial details. Fortunately, he was to gain a position where he could influence at least the preliminary stages of the revolution in musical technique which began as soon as his new method became known.

Before that happened, however, his circumstances showed no great improvement. He suffered, as all suffered, during the raging inflation that overtook Austria in 1922–3, though he laboured mightily to assist friends in need in any way he could. He saw no abatement in the anti-Jewish mood of the times and by 1923 was already aware of the danger represented by Hitler, against whose demagogy he explicitly warned Kandinsky in the letter already quoted. In October 1923 another blow fell: after a short, painful illness Mathilde Schoenberg died. Whatever tribulations the marriage had been through, a moving letter written to Zemlinsky on 16th November leaves no question of the tenderness of Schoenberg's feelings towards her, nor of his sense of loss.

I was very sorry that you did not come to the funeral: I cannot tell you how sorry. But I fully understood, because I remembered your agitation when you saw Mathilde for the last time. On the contrary, I still have to thank you many times for your dear and friendly words. ... We are gradually beginning to settle down. This, of course, does not come to pass smoothly. Mathilde's arrangements were so clear and simple, she knew how to solve complicated difficulties with a few words, and always virtually without a sound. Trudi, of course, is still far from being equal to this task although she is really very capable and good and has the best will in the world. ... Görgi too is very good. I am sure that Greissle [1] too is a kind and good human being. They are

[1] The composer Felix Greissle, husband of Schoenberg's daughter Gertrud ('Trudi'). 'Görgi' is Schoenberg's seventeen-year-old son Georg.

all trying very hard to make things easy for me. However, it may be that I am very irritable and it is not always easy therefore to get on with me. Moreover, Mathilde always knew how to restore peace by mollifying him who was easiest to mollify, without regard to justice. Perhaps I need someone who, at the right moment, will dare to tell me that I am in the wrong even when I am in the right. However, no other human being will ever again wield this authority. Now one has to think about many things the existence of which one was not previously aware of. So one gradually loses this human being, whom one hitherto merely ('merely!') regarded as the person to whom one was attached for inexplicable reasons, also as a value. This is less painful and also has the good point that one is frequently reminded of her.

It was to Zemlinsky, too, that Schoenberg wrote first on 21st August 1924, when he decided to remarry—to Gertrud, sister of his pupil the well-known violinist Rudolf Kolisch: a beautiful, talented girl half his age. He himself seemed a little bewildered by the turn of events, after a year in which, as we know from several sources, Mathilde's death had left him deeply depressed.

.. Need I tell you that I myself do not understand how it is possible that I can love another woman after Mathilde? And that I torture myself with the thought that I am disparaging her memory? Will you understand me and be indulgent with me? I know that you are too magnanimous not to realize that it is perhaps precisely because I loved Mathilde so very much that this gap must somehow be filled, and that I shall certainly never cease remembering her and shall never forget what she meant to me and what I owe to her.

They were married on 28th December. It was to prove a happy and productive union. There was, however, some initial friction—his son and daughter naturally found it difficult to accept Gertrud's role. It was probably with a certain relief that Schoenberg, for the third time in his life, moved to Berlin in January 1926—a move very different from the preceding ones. He had been appointed director of the Masterclass in Composition at the Prussian Academy of Arts, succeeding Busoni, who had died the previous year. It was very much an 'advanced' course, in which an acknowledged master imparted his knowledge and experience to a small circle of young but already proven composers. By this appointment, Berlin was recognizing the fifty-year-old Schoenberg as a figure of international eminence, both as composer and teacher.

The third sojourn in Berlin (1926–33) was maybe the happiest period of Schoenberg's life; it certainly provided the best conditions of work. The city was at this time one of the chief centres of European music. Hindemith taught at the Hochschule, Furtwängler conducted the Berlin Philharmonic, Klemperer was active at the Krolloper. At the Academy, Schoenberg found the atmosphere congenial enough, with composers such as Franz Schreker on the staff. As a Senator of the Academy he had, and took, a hand in its general administration. In his own field he was allowed sole responsibility for the way he ran his courses, and with Josef Rufer taking over the more mundane tasks, he was able to devote his time to the finer compositional problems in which he was particularly able to help his students. Moreover, he was required to teach for an average of only six months per year. His rate of composition naturally increased and he was able to secure performances for nearly all his new works, though the receptions accorded to such major scores as the Orchestral Variations (1926–8) and the comic opera *Von heute auf Morgen* (1928–9) were very mixed. He had a pleasant social life which included such old friends as Adolf Loos; and he and his wife were able to indulge his new-found passion for tennis.

Vienna pupils such as Rufer, Roberto Gerhard and Winfried Zillig followed Schoenberg to Berlin; there he found others, among them Walter Goehr, the Americans Adolf Weiss and Marc Blitzstein, the Rumanian Norbert von Hannenheim, and the Greek Nikos Skalkottas. His teaching centred on the work of the classical masters. He did not teach the twelve-note method;

on the other hand he did not stop pupils using it—or any other idiom—so long as the results were musical. At least one pupil found his first steps in serialism criticized for being too stiff, and 'corrected' by the master's hand with blatant disregard for the supposed 'rules' of the method! He also encouraged them to discuss and criticize each other's scores before coming to him— to cultivate the same uncompromising honesty of judgment he used with himself and towards them.

Much of his free time was consumed in travelling, conducting and lecturing; a process which aided his growing reputation abroad. He had visited Denmark, Holland and Italy in the early 1920s; now he moved further afield, to Britain, France, Spain and Switzerland. His old pupil Edward Clark, now head of the music department of the B.B.C., was a valuable champion in Britain, and persuaded Schoenberg to come to conduct the British premières of the *Gurrelieder* and *Erwartung*. On the former occasion (January 1928) he was in his most relaxed form, and made an excellent impression: not least on a composer about his own age, Havergal Brian, who reported on the rehearsals in glowing terms for the journal *Musical Opinion*: [1]

Schoenberg's merry black eyes pierce like an eagle—they are mirrors of his mind. He misses nothing in his vast orchestral apparatus at rehearsal. In a *tutti* passage he will detect a mistake on a particular instrument, and loses no time in correcting it in excellent English. He has a droll sense of humour, as was shown . . . when the four Wagner tubas failed to enter, he jokingly shouted 'Good morning!'

Another activity in which he engaged was radio broadcasting, especially for Berlin Radio, on which he gave several talks, mainly but not exclusively about his own music. He was an excellent broadcaster, able to use a wealth of musical illustration to demonstrate formal subtleties, eschewing jargon or abstruse

---

[1] 'Schönberg: Triumph at the B.B.C. National Concerts', *Musical Opinion*, March 1928, pp. 597–9.

discussion of technique in favour of direct, concrete, everyday images that the common listener could understand. He was much interested, too, in the possibilities inherent in films, and wrote an 'imaginary' soundtrack, the *Begleitungsmusik zu einer Licht-spielszene,* which showed how well the twelve-note method could depict changing emotions and situations. Nearly all his works during this period show a confident exploration of the possibilities and broadening of the expressive range of the method: in the relaxed 'classical' style of the String Quartet No. 3, the male-voice sound-world of the Choruses Op. 35, and the progressively larger structures of the Orchestral Variations, *Von heute auf Morgen* and—biggest of all—*Moses und Aron.* This opera, begun in 1930, was the largest piece of music yet based on a single series of twelve notes, and a dramatic parable of his own situation. Like the play *Der biblische Weg* (The Biblical Way) of 1926–7, a drama of the search for a new Palestine, it marks another stage in Schoenberg's rapprochement with Jewish traditions.

Only failing health curtailed his manifold activities. He found it necessary to spend longer and longer periods in the south. This tendency culminated in the Schoenbergs' staying in Barcelona from October 1931 to May 1932 as guests of Roberto Gerhard and his wife. It was a very happy period, one of the few in his life where he was able to unbend completely. He played much tennis, and was warmly received by Catalan musicians, notably Pablo Casals, for whom he later wrote a Cello Concerto. Here, in Barcelona, he composed much of Act II of *Moses und Aron.* He never required quietness to work—indeed, he preferred to hear people round about him—and it is odd to think that he wrote some of the deeply tragic final scene of Act II at a window overlooking the sunlit city, one ear cocked to the gossip of his wife and Mrs Gerhard chatting in the room behind him, always ready to take part if he felt inclined. The sojourn was crowned by the birth of Gertrud's first child, their daughter Nuria.

But this comparative idyll had to come to an end—Schoenberg's presence in Berlin was urgently requested by the Academy, and he must have realized he was losing ground there in the worsening political climate. He returned north, therefore, when he was declared fit enough to travel; and though the cold Berlin climate affected him as usual he decided to fulfil his contractual obligations by remaining there through the following winter. He watched the deteriorating political situation with grim interest; but after the general elections gave the Nazi Party a majority in the Reichstag, the writing was on the wall. On 1st March 1933, the President of the Academy, Max von Schillings, announced in its Senate that the Führer had resolved to 'break the Jewish stranglehold on Western music'. Schoenberg, treating this as an immediate dismissal, stormed out, shouting: 'This sort of thing you don't need to say to me twice!' There was never any doubt that he would openly declare himself against the régime: he is reported to have said to the philosopher Adorno about this time, 'Today there are more important things than Art.'

On 30th May the Prussian Ministry of Culture revoked its contracts with Schoenberg and Schreker, violating an agreement supposed to last till 1935. Schreker, in poor health, died a broken man in Berlin the following year. But Schoenberg had already left the city. He made his way first to Paris, where he looked for a publisher for his recent works, and conducting opportunities—without luck. On 24th July—no doubt partly as a display of solidarity with his increasingly endangered race, but more significantly as the natural outcome of his spiritual development throughout the last twenty years—he was received back into the Jewish faith, at a modest ceremony witnessed by the painter Marc Chagall. 'Religion,' commented one newspaper editorial in his native Vienna, 'has once again been defiled.'

In these circumstances he completed his Concerto for String Quartet and Orchestra after Handel, a *tour-de-force* of high good humour; but publishers and concerts refused to materialize.

Finally he accepted the offer of a teaching position at a small conservatoire in Boston, believing that in the U.S.A. he would be better placed to further the schemes that now occupied his unfailingly fertile brain—plans for a United Jewish Party, and a newspaper to mobilize opinion against Fascism. On 25th October Schoenberg, now in his sixtieth year, set out by sea for the U.S.A. with his wife and baby daughter. He was never to return to Europe.

4 In the wilderness (1933-51)

Schoenberg's years of exile in America saw the creation of some of his finest works: but otherwise they set no crown on his career. He was never as financially secure as he had been in Berlin, and he found the whole atmosphere alien to him. He was used to being a prophet without honour in his own country, but now he found himself accorded little more honour in his country of adoption, let alone elsewhere in the world.

The first year in the U.S.A. was a trying one. The Malkin 'Conservatoire' in Boston proved to be just a few rooms in a house, with only a few pupils—and Schoenberg was required to teach both in Boston and New York, with wearisome journeys in between. In December his health took an immediate turn for the worse; in January he became so ill that his first conducting appointment (*Pelleas und Melisande* with the Boston Symphony Orchestra) had to be postponed for two months. The New England climate was, if anything, worse than the Berlin one, and he suffered severely from asthma and heart trouble. In these circumstances his ideas for a political party and a newspaper crumbled.

After March 1934 he ceased to visit Boston, and as soon as the contract with the Malkin Conservatoire expired he moved to Chautauqua in western New York State to recuperate. There negotiations began with the large and prestigious Juillard School of Music in New York, who were willing to offer him a post. But Schoenberg doubted his ability to survive another New York winter; in search of a climate that would suit him, he decided to move to the west coast. In autumn 1934 the family therefore settled in Los Angeles—in whose immediate vicinity, apart from trips and short holidays, Schoenberg was to spend the remainder of his life.

Here his health and finances began to improve. He found private pupils. In 1935 he lectured at the University of Southern California, and in the following year he was appointed Professor at the larger University of California at Los Angeles (U.C.L.A.). He was now sixty-two, but the University's normal retiral age of sixty-five was extended to seventy in his case.

Schoenberg was thus more fortunate in his experience of exile than many Europeans who fled to America (for example, Bartók). But he was never prosperous, and was seldom performed. He was safe from the mounting danger in Europe, but he felt its shadow nonetheless, threatening the fate of his friends, relatives and disciples. He must, too, have felt he had abandoned a battlefield for a backwater: an underlying worry of his American years was that he might slip into total obscurity. Nevertheless, he gradually acclimatized himself to the new environment—a process which must have been helped by the raising of his thoroughly Americanized young family. He struggled to improve his grasp of the English language, writing and speaking it as much as possible; and in time he made it almost as flexible and vivid (if somewhat idiosyncratic) a medium of self-expression as his German.

It was difficult to adjust to the very different educational situation—above all, the fact that he had now to teach students who lacked even the basic familiarity with classical music which he considered essential:

Although in Europe I was almost unfailingly very dissatisfied, I did usually find that there was at least a certain fairly extensive knowledge of the works of the masters. This indispensable basis for teaching appears to be in the main lacking here. I attribute this to two circumstances: above all to the high price of printed music, which for most students makes it impossible to own the rudimentary little collection of something like 200 volumes that all but the very poorest had in Austria; and secondly to the excessively high price of tickets for concerts and operas, and the social style in which they are got up . . . (Letter 165)

Writing to the composer Ernst Krenek in 1939, Schoenberg made it clear that his sympathies lay with his students as victims of an inadequate educational system:

It's a great pity that the grounding is so bad. Actually I was not very enthusiastic about German teaching either, because [of] the mechanical methods . . . But American young people's intelligence is certainly remarkable. I am endeavouring to direct this intelligence into the right channels. They are extremely good at getting hold of principles, but then want to apply them too much 'on principle'. And in Art that's wrong . . . musical logic does not answer to 'if —, then —', but enjoys making use of the possibilities excluded by if-then. (Letter 183)

Schoenberg was, in fact, a popular figure with his students at U.C.L.A. He taught all kinds of classes, from elementary counterpoint to advanced musical theory—his teaching based as always on specific examples provided by the great classical composers. His chief protégés at this period included composers like Gerald Strang and Leonard Stein, who became his assistants in later years. He also taught John Cage privately, asking no fee 'as long as he would devote his life to music'. At the other end of the scale he had many students who took music only as a second subject, or even mere 'musical appreciation'. Far from finding such laymen beneath his dignity as a teacher, he contrived to instil in them the basic skills with which to compose music of their own. He believed this was the best way to encourage appreciation of 'the fine points of the game', and an understanding of form and musical development—even if the students never wrote another note of their own in later years. It is a tribute to his teaching prowess that these courses in 'Eartraining through Composing' were a complete success; and he went on to write a textbook on the subject, *Models for Beginners in Composition*.

Composers of film music, too, came to Schoenberg during his early days in Hollywood, hoping to learn some 'modern' tricks of the trade: but soon made their exit when he tried to teach them counterpoint and harmonization of chorale-tunes. He himself was approached by the M-G-M producer Irving Thalberg to write the score for the film of Pearl S. Buck's novel *The Good Earth*. However, negotiations were quickly broken off when Schoenberg stated his terms: 50,000 dollars and the assurance that not a note of his music would be tampered with once he had completed it. The money was not the problem; but the idea that a mere composer could think his score should be sacrosanct was outrageous, unheard-of! [1]

Following his appointment to U.C.L.A., Schoenberg settled in Brentwood Park, Hollywood. A near neighbour was George Gershwin, and a friendship soon sprang up between the composers of *Rhapsody in Blue* and *Pierrot Lunaire*. Both were keen tennis players, and Schoenberg used to take part in matches held once a week on a private court at Gershwin's house. But they also admired each other's music, and shared a common interest in painting: in April 1937 Gershwin made a fine portrait of Schoenberg in oils. Less than three months later he was dead. Schoenberg, whose feelings for the younger composer had been almost fatherly, was deeply affected, and broadcast a radio tribute affirming his belief in Gershwin's greatness as a composer. Later, in lectures and essays, he frequently referred to him in the same breath as Johann Strauss and Offenbach.

His own compositions of the immediate pre-war years were varied in character but unfailing in vitality. The Violin Concerto

[1] Such a guarantee would have been very necessary, considering the mutilation by 'rewrite men' of, for example, Kurt Weill's score for *You and Me* at about the same time.

(1935–6) and String Quartet No. 4 (1936) were highly sophisticated twelve-note works. With the Suite for Strings (1934) and the setting of the Hebrew *Kol Nidre* (1938) he developed the continuing interest in traditionally tonal music shown in the Cello and String Quartet Concertos. In 1939 he finally completed the Chamber Symphony No. 2, more than twenty years after he last laid it aside. It is one of the few works to which Schoenberg gave an overtly tragic ending: and though that may be a last musical reference to the emotional turmoil that followed the work's inception in 1906, it could as easily reflect his mood now that the Second World War had broken out in Europe.

The war was no surprise to him, but his distress at the course of events was as deep as that of the many other Austrian and German exiles (including Alma Mahler, her husband Franz Werfel and the novelist Thomas Mann) who were gathering in California. Though he assumed American citizenship in 1941, Germany's corruption and subsequent long, bitterly fought defeat could not fail to arouse his fascinated sorrow, quite apart from the blows he received through the loss of friends and relatives. His brother Heinrich, long an opera-singer under Zemlinsky in Prague, was killed by a poison injection in a Nazi hospital; his cousin, Arthur, died in a concentration camp; several of his pupils met violent deaths, including the gifted Hannenheim, killed in an air-raid, the Pole Joszef Koffler, murdered by the Gestapo in Warsaw, and Viktor Ullmann, who perished in Auschwitz. Just after the war came the tragic death of Webern, shot by mistake by an American sentry. And Zemlinsky, a shadow of his former self, died in New York in 1942, never having attained the recognition Schoenberg felt was his due.

His reaction to events can doubtless be sensed in the upheavals which wrack the *Variations on a Recitative* for organ (1941) and the Piano Concerto (1942); it is overt in the setting of Byron's *Ode to Napoleon Buonaparte* (1942) which, by implication, is a

47

passionate indictment of Hitler and of tyranny in any age. But it was after the war that he made his most crushing protest, in *A Survivor from Warsaw* (1947), an affirmation of the indestructibility of the human spirit in the midst of Nazi atrocities.

Nineteen forty-four marked a final downturn in his personal fortunes. In February of that year his health deteriorated markedly. His asthma got worse, as did an optical disturbance which had affected him for some years: it prevented him writing music except on specially lined paper with large spaces between the staves. He also experienced bouts of giddiness and fainting, and was found to be suffering from diabetes. He had long toyed with the idea of changing countries yet again (perhaps to New Zealand) but that was now out of the question. Only a few months later, on his seventieth birthday, he was compelled by statute to retire from U.C.L.A. Retiring professors received a pension according to their years of university service; which, in Schoenberg's case, meant he received an income of thirty-eight dollars a month on which to support himself, his wife and three young children. He had no desire to quit the post in any case— his inbuilt compulsion to communicate his ideas to young people was as strong as ever, and he knew himself to be, in mind at least, as lively as ever. On the other hand, the pittance on which he was pensioned off denied him what should have been the chief advantage of retirement—uninterrupted leisure for creative work. He was forced to take several private pupils—a much more time-consuming business. In January 1945 he applied to the Guggenheim Foundation for assistance, because 'I feel my life-task would be fulfilled only fragmentarily if I failed to complete at least those two largest of my musical, and two, perhaps three, of my theoretical works' (Letter 200). He requested a grant specifically to enable him to finish *Die Jakobsleiter*, *Moses und Aron* and three important textbooks. It was refused: only one textbook, the short *Structural Functions of Harmony*, was ever completed.

On 2nd August 1946, at his home, he suffered a violent heart-attack; a 'fatal' one, he afterwards called it in jest, for his heart-beat and pulse ceased, and he was only revived from certain death by an injection made directly into the heart. Although he recovered to some extent, the last years of his life were those of an invalid. Not a musical invalid, however: less than three weeks after his 'death' he began composing the String Trio, Op. 45—one of the finest and most concentrated of all his works, and one which in some way reflects that grim experience.

Schoenberg had seen Thomas Mann frequently since 1943: the novelist had approached him more than once to ask advice on points of detail for his work in progress—the famous novel of modern music and the corruption of twentieth-century Germany, *Doktor Faustus*. His chief mentor in musical matters, however, had been Berg's pupil Adorno, of whose views Schoenberg strongly disapproved. Schoenberg's relations with Mann, however, had remained cordial, and he had composed for Mann's seventieth birthday one of the finest and most ingenious of his occasional Canons.

But when *Doktor Faustus* was published, Schoenberg was outraged to find that Mann had ascribed to his fictitious composer-hero Leverkühn the invention of the twelve-note method, under the stimulus of meningeal syphilis and a pact with the Devil. Moreover, Mann gave a partial and externalized account of this 'twelve-tone goulash' (as Schoenberg called it), and used it to air his (and Adorno's) reservations about the nature of contemporary music. An acrimonious correspondence developed, and the friendship was not resumed until 1950. Quite apart from feeling that Mann had encroached on his 'intellectual property', Schoenberg feared an even wider dissemination of the superficial ideas about his music which he had always fought, and one which by its literary context could be used as a weapon against him. He also feared that his own role in musical development might be forgotten; for most of his time in America he felt isolated and bypassed by the musical world, little performed and little understood in a comparative cultural backwater. In his last years, however, interest in his works began to revive, especially among the younger generation of composers.

An exile still, his thoughts turned increasingly to the new state of Israel, the Promised Land whose creation he had foreseen in his play *Der biblische Weg*. His last works (apart from the brilliant *Phantasy* for violin and piano) are vocal, with philosophical or religious texts, concerned with the need to reaffirm the historical and ethical traditions of Judaism and make the new Israel not a narrow nationalist creation but 'an example of the old kind that can make our souls function again as they must if mankind is to evolve any higher' (Letter 257). In 1950 he began a collection of 'Modern Psalms' in prose, summing up his religious beliefs. He started to compose a setting of the first Psalm, for speaker, chorus and orchestra, but left it unfinished. The texts, however, occupied him into his last days.

They were days dogged by illness. The recurrent ill-health of so many years had taken a grim toll. The last photograph taken of Schoenberg before his death is almost shocking: the face hollow-cheeked and skull-like, the skin taut and shrunken. He resembles the emaciated, unreal being depicted in his painting 'Red Gaze': physically hardly present any more, except that the eyes are still intensely alive and disturbing. But in the death-mask which Mahler's daughter Anna was to make a few days later, the burning eyes are closed and the face, though that of a very weary man, has a serene repose, even a spirituality, that almost always eluded it in life.

Schoenberg grew progressively weaker in mid-1951. All his life he had been fascinated by number symbolism, and felt a cabbalistic dread of the number thirteen. The 13th, the date on which he had been born,[1] was also his unlucky day of the month

[1] The very number under which the birth was registered—8023—can be added up to 13.

(especially if a Friday); it was, too, the page on which things would go wrong in sketching a new work, or the bar he would forget to number, throwing out his calculations (when he did remember, he sometimes preferred to call it '12A'). Now aged 76 (7 + 6 = 13), he seemed to fear the approach of Friday, 13th July 1951, with especial anxiety, and for the preceding fortnight was sunk in deep depression. On the day itself he took to his bed; he slept, then woke at night and asked the time. It was 11.45 p.m.: he seemed encouraged that the day would soon be past. Shortly afterwards he murmured 'Harmony, harmony . . .', and, as if slipping back into sleep, he died: thirteen minutes before midnight, leaving an artistic legacy whose real complexities the commentator should not obscure by mere playing with numbers, and whose intense significance continues to fill much of the musical world with profound distrust, and not a little discomfort.

5 Heart and brain

Why were we not given a sense
For the intuition of unspoken laws—
An eye, that then could see?
An ear, that then could hear?

('One Wrestling', in *Die Jakobsleiter*)

'Schoenberg', said Alma Mahler, 'delighted in paradox of the most violent description.' It must have come naturally to him, for a whole series of interlocking paradoxes—historic, spiritual and artistic—structured his life. He was a Jew, irevocably committed to the Austro-German cultural tradition at a period when the two became incompatible; his heartfelt reverence towards tradition was in conflict with a freethinking, sceptical, iconoclastic intellect; a passionate man, he struggled to believe himself one whose heart was firmly in the domain of the head; a self-taught, exploratory creative artist, he became a great pedagogue. His difficulties were those of a supremely 'intuitive' composer who continually felt he must provide a logical, 'intellectual' basis for his achievements; of a man whom one biographer has called the 'conservative revolutionary'—but should it be the 'revolutionary conservative'?

Such real or apparent contradictions make it impossible to sum him up in a few words. Nor should we try: over-simplification is always a lessening of truth. People are complex. It is nonsense to criticize as inconsistent someone who strives to embrace opposing impulses, or to presume one set of impulses 'right' and the other 'wrong'. Such struggles are the essence of artistic creation—itself a highly paradoxical activity. Naturally, when the opposites are embraced with the passion that was Schoenberg's most consistent quality, the price of creation may be correspondingly high.

Passion was indeed the keynote of his life, so it is a cruel irony that—because much of his music sounds fairly complex, and because he is known to have 'invented' a 'system' of composition—he should be popularly stigmatized as too 'intellectual'. Certainly he had a powerful intellect, was unashamed of the fact, and used it to the full. That is not, alas, the implied sense of 'intellectual', too often nowadays a pejorative term signifying 'cold, divorced from life, concerned with barren abstraction' and so on. Nothing could be further from the truth. This fiery-tempered, hoarse-voiced, chain-smoking, bald-headed little man, this dynamo of nervous energy, was the battleground of barely governable emotions. He felt and thought with extraordinary intensity. His character was in no sense a 'comfortable' one; no-one would deny it had unattractive elements; but there are positive factors to compensate for the negative ones, and for these he is seldom so readily given credit.

A certain passionate self-confidence and enthusiasm seem to have been Schoenberg's chief character-traits in early life. Coming as he did from an undistinguished social background, this was all to the good, for it allowed nothing to deter him in his pursuit of musical knowledge, even though in the quest he was largely thrown on his own devices. Such textbook learning as he acquired, and the advice of friends such as Adler and Zemlinsky, could not change the fact that he was, in the truest sense, an autodidact. His consciousness of this achievement, and a conviction that such a process of personal discovery should operate in all aspects of life and intellectual experience, helped shape his fundamental outlook and attitudes. In 1902, Zemlinsky summed him up thus: 'He knows more than I do now, and what he does not know, he feels. He has a brilliant and inquiring mind. And he has the greatest amount of sincerity.'

Quite how far the 'inquiring mind' ranged is not often realized. Schoenberg was not just a composer, teacher, theorist and conductor; he was also at least an original painter, a poet, a considerable artist in prose—even an inventor. The latter activity, if the least important, indicates the fertility of his interest in various aspects of everyday life. His inventions (none of which he ever bothered to patent) included a music type-writer and an instrument for performing eye operations with a magnet. He devised a combination-ticket for use on buses, trams and subways, and a scheme for regulating the flow of traffic in big cities by means of freeways, He developed a form of chess with 100 squares instead of 64, and two new pieces (he carved his own set himself, just as he bound his own books); and invented a system of symbols to represent the various moves in tennis, so that a game could be 'taken down' and studied afterwards. He proposed a new notation for chromatic music which reduced the number of ledger-lines and dispensed with accidentals. As early as the first decade of the century he was interested in the possibilities of radio and pre-recorded sound; anticipated the great advances in films and television; foresaw the development of electronic instruments; and in his play *Der biblische Weg* (1926–7) already saw the possibility of a man-made holocaust like the atom bomb.

It is sometimes said that Bruckner had found God, while Mahler always sought but never found Him. We might complete the trinity by saying that Schoenberg had to invent God for himself, to have a big enough opponent to wrestle with. His religious life was certainly a difficult one, never finally resolved into a single coherent body of doctrine. He claimed never to have lacked religious instincts, and the need to believe in a higher power, beyond but sustaining and justifying human existence, was clearly strong in him. Most of all, we may surmise, in the years when he first broke away from traditional tonal forms and was really working blind, with no one's full understanding. As we have seen, he was raised in the Jewish traditions, but by a free-thinking father, and he came to find the Jewish religion wanting by late adolescence. His conversion to the Lutheran church was probably partly a means of strengthening his attachment to Western European cultural traditions; but there were surely many elements in Christian—and especially Protestant—thought and ethical conduct to which his moral idealism would respond strongly. However, the more necessary religious solace became, the less he was satisfied within the confines of the Church. Organized Christianity finds it difficult to offer a role to the intelligent, critical layman. The religion expressed in *Die Jakobsleiter* is a personal one—the faith of the disillusioned man who, to believe in himself, still needs to pray to an outside source. His long-meditated return to Judaism in 1933 was based on the realization, at least ten years previously, that his racial heritage was inescapable. With the rise of the Nazis it also became a moral imperative, so that he could take up an unmistakable position on the opposing side. But he remained to the end of his day a searcher, both less and more than an orthodox Jew. His final literary work, the *Modern Psalms*, is among other things a critique of various aspects of Judaism.

He confessed once that he was almost wholly lacking in political sense. He appears to have come to believe that basic human aspirations were unrealizable by political means, and the wise man should therefore leave the subject severely alone. In his youth he had been sympathetic towards socialism and workers' cultural movements; he had little reason at any time to feel much affection for decaying bourgeois society. But any faith he may have harboured in the reformation of this world seems to have been effectively shattered by the Great War, 'the overturning of everything one has believed in', as he put it. As his religious feelings intensified, so did his political scepticism.

55

He was merely irritated by the Marxist ideals of his pupil Hanns Eisler, who in this domain at least was certainly a better theorist than his master. Schoenberg's own view is set forth in the much-quoted letter to Kandinsky of May 1923:

Trotsky and Lenin spilt rivers of blood (which, by the way, no revolution in the history of the world could ever avoid doing!), in order to turn a theory—false, it goes without saying (but which, like those of the philanthropists who brought about previous revolutions, was well meant)—into reality. It is a thing to be cursed and a thing that shall be punished, for he who sets his hand to such things must not make mistakes! But will people be better and happier if now, with the same fanaticism and just such streams of blood, other, though antagonistic theories, which are nevertheless no more right (for they are of course all false, and only our belief endows them, from one instant to the next, with the shimmer of truth that suffices to delude us), are turned into reality? (Letter 64)

Such political opinions as he expressed in later life were hardly progressive, whether on the issue of constitutional monarchy for Germany or an idea for a 'United States of Europe'. But he was not therefore politically unaware. He foresaw the menace of Hitler fully ten years before the Nazis came to power, and recognized the shifts in social structure that were taking place in post-war Germany. His scheme hatched in exile for a 'United Jewish Party' was again politics on a narrow base, this time a nationalistic one. But his writings on collaboration with the Nazis, and on the U.N. Charter of Human Rights, show a broadening outlook. He certainly did not lack a sense of belonging to a broad community of mankind, as he shows in the poems on the mass-instinct and human obligations which he set in the *Six Pieces for Male Chorus* of 1929–30. But a conviction that the individual and the personal ethic can achieve more than the mass is the cornerstone of his political, or rather a-political, thinking. Perhaps his crucial dictum was, 'I believe in the right of the smallest minority.'

These concerns are reflected in the philosophy of *Der biblische Weg*, his principal poetic works *Totentanz der Principien*, *Die Jakobsleiter* and *Moses und Aron*, and the *Modern Psalms*. These form perhaps the lesser part of his literary achievement, however. Except in *Moses* the religious and philosophical themes with which he deals are seldom given vital expression through language and imagery. Too often they can read like tracts of half-digested Schopenhauer and Swedenborg. But it must be remembered that they were all originally conceived for musical setting: and thus, however absorbing, are artistically incomplete—perhaps only *Moses* can stand on its own as a dramatic poem.

More significant are his prose works. Many of them remain unpublished, but in the published essays, lectures, pedagogic textbooks and letters Schoenberg's prose style assumes its full, flexible strength. To some extent he modelled himself on Karl Kraus, who greatly influenced a whole generation of Viennese writers in his attempts to purify language. Schoenberg's style is accordingly almost bare of adjectives, terse, apophthegmatic, full of word-play and double meanings, eminently suited to aphorism and quotation; and (despite understandable awkwardnesses) he carried over many of these qualities when he switched from German to English.

By far the most important of his textbooks (a full list is given in Appendix B) is the vast *Harmonielehre* (first published 1911, expanded 1922): not just for a thorough exposition of the accumulated lore of harmonic practice up to about 1910, but also for its countless creative insights into all aspects of music. It reflects his own teaching methods—and not just in its famous opening sentence ('I have learned this book from my pupils'). He demanded that his students, even in their harmony exercises, think as artists and craftsmen at once: he also taught them the virtue of trial and error, and to discover musical possibilities for themselves as he had before. His role, as he saw it, was to help them cultivate whatever innate musical gifts they had by thinking through their problems logically.

Some find the word 'logic' has a chilling sound when applied to art; but not Schoenberg. Writing to Hauer in 1923 he summed it up concisely—'behind the term "logical" there is, for me, a complex that says: logic = human thinking = human music = human ideas of nature and law . . .'. He was not, therefore, seeking any kind of barren mathematical perfection, but a mode of human conduct. Most of us will admit, at some time, that the world is not a particularly logical place; but on the whole we try to live our lives as if it is. Perhaps that is all we can do, and certainly in the *Harmonielehre* Schoenberg does not claim to be doing more: '. . . the teacher must have the courage to be wrong. His task is not to prove infallible, knowing everything and never going wrong, but rather inexhaustible, ever seeking and perhaps sometimes finding. Why desire to be a demigod? Why not, instead, be a whole man?'

The idea of the 'whole man' informs his attitude towards his own creative work—for instance, in this aphorism of 1910:

Art is the cry of distress uttered by those who experience at first hand the fate of mankind. Who are not reconciled to it, but come to grips with it. Who do not apathetically wait upon the motor called 'hidden forces', but hurl themselves in among the moving wheels, to understand how it all works. Who do not turn their eyes away to shield themselves from emotions, but open them wide, so as to tackle what must be tackled. Who do, however, often close their eyes, in order to perceive things incommunicable by the senses, to envision within themselves the process that only seems to be in the world outside. The world revolves within: what bursts out is merely the echo—the work of art! [1]

This credo, of course, applies most strongly to the first totally-chromatic compositions of 1908–9; but though in later years

[1] Quoted in Willi Reich, *Schoenberg: a critical biography*, translated by Leo Black (London, 1971), pp. 56–7.

Schoenberg might have rephrased it, the idea of art as an exploratory human activity, a way of coping with life, underlies all his work. It is an ethical rather than an aesthetic ideal, though Schoenberg's proud conception of himself as a priest or prophet of art derives from the example of the more extreme Romantic composers (above all Wagner and Mahler). It is an attitude often deplored in modern times as arrogant—and there was a strong streak of arrogance in Schoenberg's nature. But he managed to escape the most vicious results of the attitude: he never felt better for being scorned by a greater number of people. He was an unwilling élitist, as he made clear in a moving lecture delivered in 1937, entitled 'How One Becomes Lonely'. He knew that comparatively few people would understand his music in his own time, and desired none of the isolation and abuse that were the inevitable result. But since an inner compulsion drove him beyond the bounds of the familiar, his artistic conscience would not allow him to renounce the new territory thus gained; it demanded that he consolidate and extend it. He took every opportunity to instruct his audience and encourage gradual appreciation; but he would not compromise the quality or the integrity of his ideas.

There was also a more down-to-earth side to his creativity, an attitude that stems more from Brahms than Wagner. As he once wrote, 'I do not attach so much importance to being a musical bogeyman as to being a natural continuer of properly understood good old tradition!' He certainly felt that he stood in a special relationship to the Austro-German tradition. Perhaps *too* special a relationship, for his interest in music outside that orbit was minimal, and his thinking scarcely admitted the possibility of the alternative structural and melodic resources afforded by other traditions and cultures. He was not even always able to see the merits of those who tried to develop the same tradition in different ways—he was blind, for instance, to the genius of Kurt Weill.

But his insight into the works of the great masters—Bach, Mozart and Brahms especially—was undeniably profound; his writings should be read by all students of these composers. And because he felt that a tradition dies when it ceases to develop, he believed that he had a moral obligation to honour and preserve that tradition—and his own place in it—by continuing to work out the implications he felt to be latent in the work of his predecessors. So he was both prophet and craftsman, an explorer of the unknown backed by the disciplines of a cultural tradition. The first role demanded, above all, faith; for the second he had to exercise his mental gifts to find an intellectual justification.

The two impulses frequently provoked inner conflict. The radical advances represented by *Erwartung* and other works resulted because he staked all on his inspiration. Yet the further he progressed, the more he needed some framework within which to operate, or even to understand his achievements to date. The loneliness and urgency of this need should not be underestimated. It led him, eventually, to develop the twelve-note method. Unable to intuit a natural law for his music, he had, instead, to invent one and then make a leap in the dark—to have faith, not in an abstract principle, but in his ability to control the principle he had originated. We may compare his remark that, if God did not exist, the accumulated faith of generations would eventually summon Him into being.

The struggle scarred his personality. The youthful resilience and high spirits gradually turned to suspicion and over-defensive pugnacity, an almost pathological tendency to look for and expect difficulties and opposition in every situation. He suffered from a kind of persecution-mania, for the good reason that he and his music were persecuted, and he belonged to a race whose very survival was threatened. Since he had to believe himself, he imputed righteousness to his own views and lent them the unlovely colour of fanaticism. Obsessively aware of his own worth, he was egocentric and often arrogant, overbearing and dictatorial in manner. Touchy, impatient with misunderstanding, he never attempted to suffer fools gladly, and made many bitter enemies—far more than, in calmer moments, he would have wished. 'It is very wrong, really,' he wrote in 1924. 'For we human beings are far too much in need of tolerance for any thoroughgoing honesty to be helpful to us. If only we could manage to be wise enough to put people on probation instead of condemning them, if only we could give proven friends such extended credit!—I am speaking of my own defects . . .' (Letter 82)

Partially, then, he acknowledged and regretted his temperament and tried to curb it. But even so he seems hardly to have realized the implications of his oft-repeated dictum that 'only he can bestow honour who himself has a sense of honour and deserves honour'; how off-putting it was even for people well disposed to him. But at least he was no respecter of persons, was ready to stand up against the leading conductors, performers and administrators of his day, never tried to curry favour with anyone for personal advantage, and exposed his feelings honestly, with devastating bluntness. Since he wore his aggression turned outwards, as a defensive carapace, it was the aspect of him with which most people came into contact, and as much of him as many ever saw. As Roberto Gerhard recalled, 'Even in repose, the burning eyes in that ascetic face and the faint expression of disdain in the peculiar shape of his mouth had an extraordinary power of intimidation.' Stories of his graceless egomania are legion, but we must remember that a fair proportion are filtered through the teller's own hurt pride.

Busoni—who of course did not know him well—said that Schoenberg had the heart of a dragon. We might also recall Nietzsche's dictum that he who fights with dragons becomes a dragon himself. Whatever fires burned in Schoenberg were stoked by real adversity: he was not always so. There remained a quite different side to his character, seen by his family and friends, and continually glimpsed, alongside his less ingratiating qualities, in his voluminous correspondence. The quickness, passion and spontaneity of his thought and feelings must compel admiration, linked as they were to a ruthless personal honesty and idealism, a strong (if predominantly ironic) sense of humour, unflinching loyalty to his friends and pupils, a real gaiety of spirit at the infrequent good times in his life, and, in adversity, the quality he claimed as his only virtue—the dogged persistence and refusal to give up. The closer one becomes acquainted with his paradoxical personality the more admirable and curiously attractive it seems, in spite of all : and if this is true of the letters, it is even truer of the music, for the paradoxes make the music live.

6 Style . . .

Ah yes, style! To listen to certain learned musicians, one would think all composers did not bring about the representation of their *vision*, but aimed solely at establishing a style—so that musicologists should have something to do. ('Why no Great American Music?', 1934)

You cannot expect the Form before the Idea,
For they will come into being together.
(Aaron in *Moses und Aron*, Act 2)

When Schoenberg was asked why he no longer composed music like *Verklärte Nacht*, he used to reply: 'I still do, but nobody notices.' On another occasion he commented: 'My music is not modern, it is merely badly played.' In 1945 he wrote bluntly to the musicologist René Leibowitz: 'I do not compose principles, but music.' Many commentators have yet to receive the message. Twenty-five years after its composer's death, Schoenberg's music certainly enjoys an enormous reputation (which does not necessarily betoken understanding) in certain critical, academic and performing circles. But among the general listening public its stock is considerably lower. Simple enjoyment and even love are less uncommon than at one time, but still confined to a minority. Much more widespread attitudes range from bewildered, uncomfortable respect to frank dislike—a dislike, be it noted, shared by many supporters of more *avant-garde* musical trends.

Here we re-encounter a form of the Schoenbergian paradox. He summed up these attitudes himself in the essay 'How One Becomes Lonely': he was too dry and too sweet, a 'constructor' and a romanticist, an innovator, and yet old-fashioned. His most famous pupils, the more conservative Berg and the more obviously radical Webern, have both won greater acceptance—though from differing audiences, for they were smaller, more limited composers. Their separate achievements, and much more besides, were only made possible by his larger one. He was an innovator *and*, in the best sense, a conservative: he spans the distance between his pupils and includes them both. He is less easy to pigeon-hole, so he is easily diminished by a partial or partisan view. But the large view is always the best, and it is by no means impossible.

The main stumbling block has been that of style and technique, and specifically Schoenberg's 'innovatory' methods. He did not set out to be an innovator: as we shall see, his musical language developed almost instinctively as he strove to express, with ever greater precision, the results of a search for truth in personal and artistic experience. Technique was never more than a means to an end. Yet by a ghastly irony it was the technique that attracted attention: Schoenberg, the passionate upholder of the 'idea' in music, is associated in most people's minds with a question of style. The world, as usual, has preferred Aaron's craft to Moses' message.

Yet Schoenberg's stylistic development is, after all, vital and integral to his achievement. What follows may help readers with the descriptions of individual works in Chapters 7 to 14. But there is no real substitute for listening—listening in no special way, but bringing to Schoenberg's works the same kind of response as one brings to any music whatever. From the first, one can discover passages of intense beauty and vitality which will invite further hearing. The music will often demand complete attention and a quickness of mind to match its own, but with a little familiarity it will begin to establish itself in the listener's imaginative universe. Its tensions and roughnesses will not disappear—they are part of its essence—but their expressive function will gradually become clear. A century and a half, after all, has not rendered the sound of the *Hammerklavier* Sonata or the *Grosse Fuge* exactly ingratiating; and it is mere evasive action to plead that Schoenberg is not a Beethoven. Neither he is; but his sights are set as high. Let us take heart, and recall the wise words of his contemporary Franz Schmidt,[1] who said he could not understand a note of *Pierrot Lunaire,* but felt that the composer of *Verklärte Nacht* and the *Gurrelieder* had earned a certain amount of trust.

As we have seen, Schoenberg was virtually self-taught: the process of independent discovery shaped his habits of mind, made him highly receptive to new ideas, gave him faith in his own judgment and mistrust of mere codified 'rules' of composition. His earliest musical development was one of 'imitating everything he saw was good' and working on and extending it until he gained mastery. In short, he learned composition from the only fruitful source: the example of previous masters. His 'teachers' in this process, he liked to say, were Bach, Mozart, Beethoven, Wagner and Brahms. Like Brahms himself, he had the kind of subtle, speculative mind well able to grasp and draw inspiration from the manifold unorthodoxies of the great classical composers. So, naturally, he built not on the norms of previous tradition, but on its most adventurous manifestations. For instance, the gigantic and daring multi-level forms of Beethoven's *Grosse Fuge,* the finales of the *Hammerklavier,* the *Eroica* and the Ninth Symphony, must have had a profound influence on his structural thinking.

In the earliest stages of his career, however, Brahms and Wagner were most important. Characteristically, they repre-

---

[1] Austrian composer (1874–1939), pupil of Bruckner and a fine symphonist in the Bruckner-Mahler tradition. He later came to understand *Pierrot* well enough to conduct his own students at the Vienna Conservatoire in a performance in 1929 which Schoenberg declared one of the best he ever heard.

sented opposing forces which he combined. On the one hand Wagner, especially in *Tristan* and *Parsifal*, provided the richest possible range of chromatic harmony, one which already strained conventional ideas of tonality; also extreme emotion, relative freedom of form and ways of continually metamorphosing themes for expressive effect. Brahms offered an essentially contrapuntal, classically based art, which stressed coherence between themes and motives, unified wide-ranging structures and expressed, if more austerely, an emotional world hardly less intense.

It was probably from Brahms and Wagner that Schoenberg derived two general and interdependent concepts which can be traced throughout his mature output. One is 'the unity of musical space': the idea that the constituent parts of a composition—melody, accompaniment, harmony, rhythm—being expressions of the same idea in different dimensions, should bear an intimate and apprehensible relationship to one another. The whole work should be mirrored in its smallest units, and achieve thereby a new degree of internal unity and consistency. The other is the principle of 'developing variation'. In classical sonata-form the development section, originally a quick survey of the harmonic horizon and a dash for the home key, had become a vehicle for transforming and combining themes and, from the first movement of the *Eroica* onward, assumed prime significance in the structure as a means of exploring the harmonic and melodic universe. Schoenberg took the process to its logical conclusion: though elements of exposition and recapitulation still function, his movements are all essentially developmental (whether sonata-like throughout or not). Thematic development inevitably entails variation, and as a general rule variation takes the place of repetition in Schoenberg's music—so concentrated listening is all the more necessary. Moreover, perpetual variation is enshrined in, and demanded by, the twelve-note method. Despite this the music, with a few exceptions, remains basically traditional in layout. Themes are recognizable, the proportions of the movements are familiar, the rhythmic pulse often classical in feeling (too much so for some tastes). The works have shape, direction, a sense of climax and release, and arguments that are clinched in often very traditional ways—an instance is Schoenberg's fondness for recalling themes from various sections of a piece at its very end. These are not negligible points: you cannot separate form and content in music, and structure is itself a part of the expression.

Schoenberg's sudden advance to mastery in his mid-twenties, from the D major Quartet of 1897 to the *Gurrelieder* (finished in draft in 1901) was as long a stride as many composers achieve in their whole lives. The Quartet is a pleasant, talented work, clearly derivative though not without original touches. In the far more individual *Verklärte Nacht* (1899) the Brahms and Wagner influences are fully assimilated with a sure command of the most advanced musical language of the day. The *Gurrelieder* then confidently extends this command over a far wider emotional range on the largest possible scale and, especially in Part III, gives a foretaste of the future.

Schoenberg might have stopped there and capitalized on this rapid progress for years. But the creative impetus impelled him onward, to work out the implications of his style; and so began his voyage in search of the unknown. He was not the only explorer. Mahler, Reger and Strauss were all attempting to revitalize the Austro-German musical tradition out of the legacy of Brahms and Wagner; while composers like Busoni, Debussy and Scriabin were contributing new resources from other traditions. If Schoenberg forged on furthest ahead, that was because he tried to broaden musical experience in many directions at once. His chief compositions of this period, up to 1906, are *Pelleas und Melisande*, the Eight Songs, Op. 6, the First String Quartet and the First Chamber Symphony.

These works, relatively easy to appreciate now, were thought 'incomprehensible' when first performed. The problems listeners experienced were not (as was popularly supposed) chiefly the result of the dissonant harmony, though Schoenberg certainly took full advantage of post-Wagnerian harmonic strategy in delaying the resolution of cadences until the 'delaying tactics' became more the point of the music than the resolutions so postponed. The difficulties stemmed rather from his wish to endow each work with the maximum substance in the shortest possible time. In *Pelleas und Melisande* the features of a four-movement symphony are fused into a single vast movement; the First Chamber Symphony manages the same feat in half the space. The melodies in these multi-character structures become more and more diverse; they combine in counterpoint, each individual voice asserting its identity to a previously unknown extent. It is to this end that the melodies become so angular, conveying expressive tensions by wide leaps and irregular phrasing. To elucidate the complex textures thus created, Schoenberg aimed, after *Pelleas*, at the maximum clarity of scoring, using each instrument as a soloist, turning away from the plush sonorities of the late-Romantic orchestra and seeking a clearly etched, chamber-musical style. Combination and superimposition of themes made it possible, too, for him to move the musical argument along more swiftly: and (though many insensitive, hard-driven, beat-counting performances do not help matters) the sheer quickness of mind that his scores display remains one of the chief problems for the unprepared listener. If Schoenberg possesses an actual vice of style, it is precisely that his passionate urge to communicate sometimes swamps his message through the very vigour of delivery. But to have too much enthusiasm rather than too little would seem to be a fault in the right direction.

The compact, ebullient Chamber Symphony No. 1 in E major, for fifteen instruments, represented his ideal at this period. In addition to the above-mentioned features, it raises hitherto

Ex.5

'inadmissible' harmonic resources to cardinal positions in the structure: for instance the horn-call of ascending fourths (Ex. 5*a*) from which such previously unimaginable cadences as Ex. 5*b* may be constructed; and the whole-tone main theme, Ex. 5*c*. Ex. 5*d* shows a characteristic contrapuntal texture from the main development section. The parts move very freely despite the typical use of canons; the melodic richness is remarkable, but it pulls strongly against the simple key-sense of D minor suggested by the first chord. The passage gains its sense of direction from the strongly defined rhythms of the various strands: but such an inherently unstable fabric needs a master hand to hold it together.

Schoenberg felt that in this work he had attained a settled, mature style—where he would much have preferred to remain. Events proved otherwise. Under the pressure of inner compulsions at whose full nature we can hardly guess—for the Gerstl affair is no more an explanation than are the inherent harmonic instabilities of the Chamber Symphony—an extreme situation arose which demanded extreme, even traumatic expression. To cope with it Schoenberg had to make a sudden leap in the dark—and so must the listener, coming for the first time upon the radically new kind of music which was the result.

The works in question (virtually there are only ten, Opp. 11, 15–22 and *Die Jakobsleiter*) are often referred to as forming Schoenberg's 'Expressionist' phase, and they do suggest certain parallels with the work of the Austrian and German Expressionist painters, among whom Schoenberg himself must be numbered. The Romantic ideal of conveying urgent subjective emotion directly, without interposing formal conventions, attains here a dark epiphany. The music strives to externalize states of mind, to voice feelings too strange or elemental for words—to be a music of the subconscious. Its constituent parts are tested in the furnace to reveal those that remain essential. To this end Schoenberg employs harsher dissonance, greater areas of harmonic ambiguity, melodies and phrase-lengths so asymmetrical they approach a kind of 'musical prose'. He also required freedom to introduce more abrupt contrasts and transformations on the one hand, and to concentrate on wholly static elements with unprecedented determination on the other.[1]

---

[1] The really 'revolutionary' feature in the finale of the Second Quartet, for instance (which forms a transition to this period), is not

Almost inevitably, he came to feel that the procedures and proportions of the traditional tonal forms, dedicated as they are to
precisely the kind of humane order whose temporary loss he
wanted to convey, afforded him insufficient scope. This was no
'historical mission' to destroy those forms; they were simply, at
this stage, irreconcilable with the pressure of his creative needs.
He wanted to loosen their framework, to rearrange their elements; and in this context the so-called 'dissolution of tonality'
was, for Schoenberg, an unavoidable by-product.

Ex.6

primarily harmonic; rather the way in which the structure is made to
accommodate disruptive elements such as an immobile, ticking
ostinato which propels the harmony in no special direction.

The opening of the fourth of the Five Orchestral Pieces, Op. 16, shown above, is an eloquent example of the creative outcome. Such music is popularly described as 'atonal', a term Schoenberg abominated as semantic nonsense, since it implies 'music written without tones'. One might as well speak of writing without words! In fact the probable originator of the word, the Austrian song-composer and critic Joseph Marx (1882–1964), seems to have used it as a carefully specialized term: he thought Schoenberg's works were no longer music in the accepted sense, but a different art-form entirely. But then Hauer, less clear a thinker than Schoenberg, willingly adopted the term 'atonality' to describe *his* style. Soon it became a useful missile of critical abuse, hurled first at Schoenberg and his school and then more and more indiscriminately, wherever a critic's ears were outraged by too uncomfortable an amount of dissonance in Bartók, Milhaud, Prokofiev, Britten. . . . So wide did it spread that it gradually lost its pejorative sting, crept into dictionaries, and finally attained respectability as the word in popular and scholarly use that supposedly describes 'music without a key'. But it is still a nonsense-word, and completely misrepresents the works to which it is so blithely applied. There is plenty of key-sense— though often of a limited or localized nature—in Schoenberg's works of this period. Even in Ex. 6 the key of D (major or minor would be too fine a distinction) can be felt as the centre of operations. Moreover, the term makes no distinction for twelve-note music, whose tonal organization is of a different, subtler and perhaps more far-reaching kind.

I prefer to call these first 'atonal' works just 'totally-chromatic'—implying simply that most or all of the twelve notes of the chromatic scale occur with extreme frequency and a consequent saturation—but not necessarily immobilization—of harmony. The stylistic progression, therefore, is not from 'tonality' to 'atonality' (with the veiled implication of 'from sense to nonsense') but from the classical conception of tonality as founded on the seven-note diatonic scale (centred on the major or minor triad) to a more extended view in which the five chromatic notes become equally important.[1] 'Tonality' is not, after all, a compositional preference; it is, for any composer who works within the confines of the tempered scale, the first fact of life. As Schoenberg wrote in the 1921 edition of *Harmonielehre*:

The expression 'tonal' has itself been wrongly used, exclusively instead of inclusively. It can mean only this: everything that results from a series of tones, whether its cohesion is the result of a direct relationship to a single tonic or from links of a more complex kind, forms tonality. . . . A piece of music will always have to be tonal at least insofar as, from one tone to the next, there is bound to be a relationship by which all the tones, successive or simultaneous, produce a progression that can be recognized as such.

This is no prescription for chaos: tonality is here seen as an all-embracing principle capable of different kinds of presentation. Diatonically-based tonality, with its powerful clarification of the hierarchy of relationships, is one of them: total chromaticism is another. But the hierarchies do not disappear in the latter—they cannot, and the real composer must work with, not against them. The *sensation* of relationships between tones, of functional differences arising from these relationships, of the tonic, the leading-note, and cadential movement—these are habitual to all Western listeners, and in no sense theoretical abstractions. What changes is their frame of reference.

In total chromaticism 'consonance' and 'dissonance' are not antithetical. Schoenberg contended in *Harmonielehre* that con-

[1] The principle that the chromatic scale provides the basic unit of tonality, adumbrated in the 1922 edition of *Harmonielehre*, is independent of the 'twelve-note method' as such; it had been partially anticipated by, among others, Busoni and the theorist Bernhard Ziehn (1845–1912). Several music examples in the last section of Schoenberg's *Harmonielehre* are virtually identical with examples in Ziehn's *Harmonie- und Modulationslehre* (1888).

Schoenberg

sonances (the simplest harmonies) derive from the nearer,
dissonances (more complex harmonies) from the more distant
overtones of their fundamental note: therefore all exist, at least
potentially, in nature. This idea—which he called 'the emancipa-
tion of the dissonance'—provided the theoretical sheet-anchor
for the procedures of his totally-chromatic works. Their harmonic language, therefore, tends to avoid the most obvious
tonal references (sevenths and ninths replace octaves, fourths and
tritones are as common as thirds, triads are augmented to span a
diminished sixth, anything approaching a perfect cadence is
virtually unknown), but continues to exploit the effects of
tension and release that give harmony its expressive force and
sense of movement, albeit the tension is fiercer and the release
more equivocal. This is essentially an extension, not a negation,
of the ear's previous musical experience. And behind the ear lies
the heart's ability to sense the expressive reality composed into
the music, and the brain's resourcefulness in perceiving, with
patience and application, the infinite variety of relationships
which, on the largest scale, make up each work's 'tonal' integrity.

Schoenberg, intending no permanent break with the past, took
care to limit the potential chaos of total chromaticism in every
way that could aid his music's comprehensibility. This is most
obvious where a background of diatonically-based tonality can
still be sensed, as at the opening of the second Op. 16 Orchestral
Piece (significantly entitled 'The Past')—anchored to a strongly
implied D minor.

Ex.7

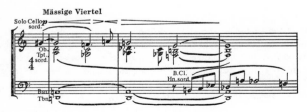

Schoenberg could prolong pedal-points like that in Ex. 7 to create a harmonic centre, or at least a fixed point of reference— as in the first piece of Op. 16, where a three-note chord implying, again, D is held continuously by bassoons or trombones for 106 of the 128 bars. Also themes and motives, after their first appearance, could be restated always at the same pitch, to aid their recognition despite variation (the first Op. 16 Piece illustrates this tendency also): indeed 'thematicism' now became for him the main structural agent.

The very need to keep as many chromatic notes in circulation as possible began to suggest some new but basic harmonic procedures: as Schoenberg tentatively remarked in the *Harmonielehre*, the sequence of chords seemed to be governed by the tendency to introduce in each chord the tones not included in the previous one; conversely, it began to seem 'out of style' to repeat too many tones before introducing all twelve. An extract from the Piano Piece Op. 11, No. 2 well illustrates the harmonic consistency of such totally-chromatic chord-progressions:

Ex.8

Far from being 'without form' as Schoenberg claimed while working on the Orchestral Pieces, the totally-chromatic works have mostly simple, clear-cut basic designs, however complex the details. The patterns of exposition-plus-development, a ternary A-B-A form, or some extension thereof, are the commonest. Moreover, despite the rapidity of events (indeed, because of it) most movements are short and can be grasped as a totality—the longest purely instrumental movement (Op. 11,

No. 2) lasts a mere seven minutes. In instrumental music the drive to encapsulate a state of mind in a self-contained musical utterance tended, in fact, to encourage the epigrammatic proportions we find in the *Little Piano Pieces*, Op. 19, and the tiny pieces for chamber orchestra of 1910.[1] The problem was to write *extended* forms which corresponded to the new freedom of musical discourse. Up to a point, in vocal works, the text helped shape the flow of events. But even in *Das Buch der hängenden Gärten* the forms tended to be simple and brief. The third of the Op. 11 Piano Pieces and the fifth of the Op. 16 Orchestral Pieces, with their open-ended, onward-moving, quasi-improvisatory forms, are both attempts in a new direction, however: Schoenberg, having found how to present states of mind, seems in these pieces to be trying to compose a musical 'stream of consciousness'.

He succeeded in the monodrama *Erwartung*, Op. 17, the last and in every respect the most extreme of the works of 1909. It is the supreme product of his creative *instinct*—for only an explosion from the unconscious could have allowed him to create, in seventeen days, this intensely emotional, highly complex score without developed themes, extensive motivic work, of analysable form, which runs in an unbroken stream of invention, with constant renewal of ideas, for a full half-hour. (Considering that almost all previous music had depended to some extent on structural repetition, those thirty minutes represent a quite gigantic stretch of time.) However difficult the commentator finds it to enter *Erwartung*'s nightmarish emotional world—so daunting is such creativity in the raw—he cannot but be staggered at the fact of its having been created at all. Attempts have been made to rationalize its structure: by tracing the growth of motivic germs or recurring chords; by theorizing about the use of 'sets' of notes with dual melodic and harmonic properties; by graphing the course of the vocal line, and so on. All have failed. No

[1] And which we encounter much more consistently, of course, in the music of Webern.

'explanation' explains more than a haphazard selection of details; none shows why or how the music proceeds from one point to the next, nor why its emotional unity is so powerful. It is instructive, though, to follow each suggested critical approach to the point where it collapses, if only the better to appreciate Schoenberg's truly torrential spontaneity. It is no diminution of his achievement to say, simply, that *Erwartung* is the most astonishing written-out improvisation in the history of music.

By its very nature, however, it was an unrepeatable success. That kind of inspirational frenzy takes hold of an artist at most once or twice in a lifetime. The *conscious* impossibility of developing large-scale forms without constraints remained. The works which followed *Erwartung*, slowly and over several years, show a gradual 'classicizing' tendency, a longing for recognizable structural supports. The symbolist opera *Die glückliche Hand* is more consciously a formed and rounded whole than *Erwartung*, with actual recapitulation of some of the opening music towards the end, symmetrical arrangement of the action, the tonal areas more clearly stabilized by *ostinato*-patterns and extended pedal-points. Most of the numbers in *Pierrot Lunaire* are still more firmly structured, the internal repetitions within each poem determining the recurrence of musical material in several cases; while the work is an extraordinarily rich compendium of intricate contrapuntal form-building devices which look back to the practices of the Baroque masters, and beyond. 'Nacht' is a particularly tightly organized passacaglia on a three-note motif and its transpositions. 'Der Mondfleck' is a *ne plus ultra* of self-contained polyphonic ingenuity: the instrumental portion consists of a palindrome canon between violin and cello (i.e. they repeat their lines in reverse once they pass the mid-point of the piece);[1] a simultaneous palindromic imitation between

---

[1] Commentators habitually refer to this as a 'crab-' or 'mirror-canon'; inexplicably, as these two terms mean different things, and neither applies in the present case.

piccolo and clarinet, not strictly canonic in pitch, but rhythmically exact; *and* a fugal piano part, the notes of whose principal voices correspond exactly to those in piccolo and clarinet, but with the rhythms augmented to fill twice the space—so that the piano fugue ends just as the other instruments have returned to the start of their canons. Although this pattern-making relates symbolically to the recited text (Pierrot turns round to look at himself from behind) we can hardly be intended to hear such intricacies consciously. They are rather a sign of Schoenberg's obsessive concern to provide his music with a strong, self-sufficient constructive basis.

The search for that basis took another ten years, during which few works saw the light of day. In previous totally-chromatic pieces he had worked sporadically with 'sets' of a few notes which always preserved the same mutual relationship whether employed in melody or chords—the passacaglia 'Nacht' is a simple example. In 'Seraphita', one of the richly fascinating Four Orchestral Songs, Op. 22, a quite large form is created by concentration on the melodic development of a few germinal motifs and salient intervals. Moreover, the first fourteen notes of the opening melody for six clarinets contains all twelve pitches of the chromatic scale. The abortive plan for a Choral Symphony went even further in this respect; the Scherzo was to open with an *ostinato* theme consisting of just the twelve chromatic notes. *Die Jakobsleiter*, which grew out of the Symphony, opens with a presentation of all twelve notes—six as a *basso ostinato*, six as a chord building above it.

Ex.9

78

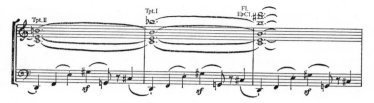

The aim was to fashion all the work's themes out of the notes of the *ostinato*, though not in any fixed order: a procedure close to that of Hauer. Schoenberg extended this technique in the Op. 23 Piano Pieces and the *Serenade*, Op. 24—the notes of the basic figures began to be tied to a fixed order, appearing in a particular series in both melody and harmony, forming 'rows' of varying lengths (anything up to fourteen notes). Thus was born the general principle of 'serialism'; though Schoenberg called his method, soberly enough, 'working with tones of the motif'. We have already noted how motives gained importance over harmonies in articulating his musical structures. But what if motives, themes and harmonies were to spring from an identical source?

Only gradually did Schoenberg come to accept as logical the direction in which these developments were tending: that the most rational and fruitful way to harness the disruptive forces of total chromaticism was to give each complete work a 'serial' basis on a single note-row of all twelve chromatic notes. This he achieved for the first time in the Suite for Piano, Op. 25. Yet logic and inspiration are different things. A compositional method, in the abstract, is valueless; its only justification lies in the specific musical outcome. Schoenberg, of all people, was unlikely to confuse this issue, since he placed an enormous premium on spontaneous inspiration—without it, he said, he was incapable of writing ten bars. But his artistic conscience *demanded* logic to justify the results; and a belief in the 'logic' of the twelve-note method seems to have been the crucial act of creative irrationality which enabled his inspiration to flow.

What, then, is the fearsome 'twelve-note method'? In essence, it is a simple device for ensuring complete structural unity in the spheres of melody and harmony. It affirms the unity of musical space and the relationship of all ideas in a work to each other and to their overall context. It starts from a simple, fundamental premise which is surely shared by every real composer, whatever his methods: namely that one does not create themes, motives, rhythms and harmonies; one composes the *whole piece* of which these features are but the individual details. Some vision of the work as an entity precedes the composition of its tiniest cell. Here I can speak from personal experience, and the experience of every composer with whom I have ever discussed the matter: one scarcely ever begins with a chord or tune, but with an idea of a work that slowly assumes a distinctive size, shape, colour, internal motion and character according to its inborn expressive intention. Like a ship at night, or an iceberg through the fog, its bulk looms into the composer's mind. Then, in his head, 'the working-out in breadth, length, height and depth begins . . . I hear and see the picture as a whole take shape and stand before me as though cast in a single piece, so that all that is left is the work of writing it down'. The words are not Schoenberg's, but Beethoven's;[1] yet Schoenberg's own descriptions are very similar.

Twelve-note music depends on the composer's ability to study 'the picture as a whole', form a precise notion of its necessary melodic and harmonic qualities, and extract from it the binding essence of its ideas, expressed in the form of a succession of the twelve pitches of the chromatic scale. From this 'note-row' the realization of the whole work will draw its material. Each pitch should appear once before any of the twelve is

[1] In Thayer's *Life of Beethoven* (London 1964, ed. Forbes), Vol. II, p. 851.

repeated. Pitches may be sounded in succession, as a melody; simultaneously, as chords; or different segments of the row may combine as melody and accompaniment. At the precompositional stage the pitches do not relate to a key-note: each is defined by its relationship to the series as a whole. Thus the intervals between them remain constant (except for transposition to different octaves) and the series is impervious to the kind of chromatic alteration that occurs in diatonically-based tonality through the changes between major and minor.[1] The twelve-note series takes four equally important forms: the original; the original inverted, so that each interval falls instead of rising and *vice versa*; the retrograde (the original series played in reverse); and the retrograde of the inversion. Each form can be transposed to begin on any of the twelve chromatic pitches, so that the original series generates forty-eight variants of itself (in Schoenberg, however, a much smaller number usually suffices for a whole composition).[2]

[1] It is also impervious to enharmonic alteration: for example, the notes B-natural and C-flat are presumed to be identical in pitch, and so on throughout the scale—something which, in practice, is really only true of keyboard instruments. Schoenberg admitted, in this regard, that 'the method' could thus be said to be a direct product of the tempered scale; from which it follows that it is fundamentally instrumental, rather than vocal, in origin. This area of ambiguity has never been satisfactorily resolved. But, then, neither is it resolved in the music of the preceding centuries, from Bach onwards; Schoenberg is hardly to be blamed for not providing a solution to a problem which the weight of European musical tradition has, perhaps, made actually insoluble.

[2] Though 'the method' grew out of Schoenberg's immediate creative concerns, it could be said to develop certain elements latent in music of previous times. Something approaching a 'serial' use of pitches is found intermittently in some works of the Classical masters. See 'Strict Serial Technique in Classical Music' (*Tempo* 37, Autumn 1955) by Hans Keller, who adduces a rare instance of such 'classical serialism' in the context of all twelve notes, in Mozart's E flat String Quartet K.428—a work Schoenberg is known to have played as a boy.

These are the fundamental rules of twelve-note music; or rather, they *would be* 'rules' if such things had any jurisdiction in art. Critics, composers and listeners who cannot distinguish between an inflexible commandment and a useful guiding principle are liable to come to grief here. I repeat: a method, *in itself*, has no magic properties. That depends on the composer who wields it, and what use he makes of it—whether as a pair of crutches or of seven-league boots. Schoenberg, we have seen, felt himself able once again to compose with almost youthful freedom. And from the beginning he allowed some modification of basic principles. Thus notes may be repeated as soon as they are sounded; and two or more may be alternated in trills, *ostinati* and similar formations. At first he avoided creating triadic harmonies or doubling lines in octaves, but later relaxed this practice, commenting that, after all, every note naturally contains its own octave doubling, in the first partial of the overtone series. We shall encounter further 'bending' of the 'rules' at every turn as we proceed.

A few simple examples are now in order. Ex. 10 shows some passages from a highly developed twelve-note work: Schoenberg's Violin Concerto. Ex. 10*a* is the main theme of the slow movement—a melody of such refined beauty that the listener need hardly worry that it enunciates a twelve-note row, with liberal relaxations of the 'rules' governing note-repetition. From it we can deduce the series which binds the work: Ex. 10*b* sets it out in its original form (starting on A rather than the E of Ex. 10*a*), with its inversion. The actual opening of the Concerto is shown in Ex. 10*c*: here we see the series split up in an intimate dialogue between the soloist and the orchestral cellos. By bringing notes 3 and 5 to the top of the cello chords, Schoenberg makes them echo the violin's own phrase. Finally Ex. 10*d* quotes a pawky, dance-like tune from the finale. Again the row is split between soloist and orchestra, and this time two forms are used to make the complete theme, providing two related halves like the antecedent and consequent in a classical melody. The rise and fall of the accompaniment gives the passage a perfectly natural propulsive force.

Ex.10

(a)

(b)

(c)

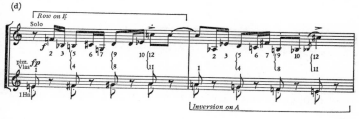

(d)

Ex. 11 shows two more twelve-note melodies. Ex. 11*a*, the main theme of one of Schoenberg's last compositions, the chorus *Dreimal Tausend Jahre*, manages to retain a certain hymn-like quality (the words are 'It is thrice a thousand years since I saw you, Temple in Jerusalem, Temple of my grief'). Schoenberg splits the note-row into two halves, and repeats the six notes of each half in reverse order before proceeding to the next. The same thing seems to happen in Ex. 11*b*, a tipsy waltz-tune that emerges in the first movement of the Op. 29 Suite for seven instruments; here Schoenberg employs only six notes, and in the last three bars seems blithely to rearrange their order. But, in fact, he has switched to a different form of the row at a different transposition—one that uses the same six notes and so helps maintain the definitely C-major/minor-ish tonal feeling.

These themes illustrate the practice of dividing the note-row into two complementary six-note segments or 'hexachords'

for separate treatment. As we see in Ex. 11*b*, Schoenberg was very fond of constructing his row so that the first hexachord, when inverted and transposed by a particular degree, would produce the same pitches (though in a different order) as the *second* hexachord of the original, and make possible new combinations and interrelationships of the twelve tones. A particularly fine case occurs in one of the classics of twelve-note music (and one of Schoenberg's greatest works), the *Variations for Orchestra*, Op. 31. A mysterious Introduction, a tidal ebb and flow of *ostinato* patterns, very gradually builds up the series, and its inversion a minor third lower, as two parallel currents of steadily accumulating pitches. As shown in Ex. 12*a*, these two forms are complementary in the manner described. The logic of their combination emerges after thirty bars: they attain a defined form with Ex. 12*b*—the basic statement of the romantically lyrical Theme (the original) and its accompanying harmonies (the inversion).

Ex.12

(a)

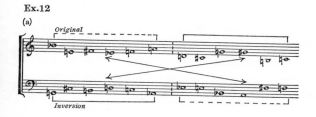

(b)

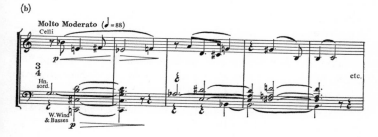

By now it should be obvious that there is nothing in 'the method' that relieves the composer of responsibility for every note he writes. Rhythm, dynamics, register, texture, part-writing, large-scale form—in fact all *composition* proper—is left, as before, to his own skill and judgment.[1] So, it must be stressed, are melody and harmony: these are simply channelled in certain directions by the use of the series. Moreover, the composer must still provide recognizable themes whose developments will be audible and comprehensible. The note-row will not do this for him, though it does make possible a certain consistency of material at all levels. Schoenberg liked to call this kind of relationship 'subcutaneous'—i.e. more than skin-deep—but in fact it is positively molecular. The note-row is, in fact, the DNA molecule of twelve-note music: the agent which stamps every bar, every theme, every chord, as belonging to a single, unique work. Almost an abstraction, it exists only at a primordial level, before tonality, before rhythm, before the articulation that makes music possible. But it is produced *via* the work's basic ideas, and not the other way round. Schoenberg always maintained that the rows presented themselves to him in the form of melodies; and there are several sketches extant which show how he composed, reshaped and refined the themes of his major works, altering the note-row at every step to follow suit.

Unfortunately, it is on the primacy of the essentially abstract note-row, rather than the conjunction of the composer's imagination with the actual *sounds* of which his music is composed, that a whole pseudo-scientific tradition of serial analysis has been established over the past thirty years. It now holds sway throughout half the world, particularly in academic institutions. At its simplest it operates by various ingenious means of counting notes; but long ago it reached a remarkable degree of sophistica-

[1] At least as far as Schoenberg is concerned. Certain later composers have attempted to extend serial principles into the other areas as well, with, on the whole, results which are less than enthralling.

tion in seeking various forms of quasi-mathematical logic within the operation of the serious itself. To this end, the works of Schoenberg and his pupils have become laboratory specimens for dissection. Theories of their structural organization, sometimes wildly at variance with the ordinary listener's experience of what he can *hear*, are erected with the support of charts, tables and diagrams and often expounded in a jaw-breaking 'technical' jargon which successfully obfuscates the author's discourse to the point of incomprehensibility.

There is nothing necessarily heinous in that. It might be maintained that such analysis stems from a humble conviction (akin to Wittgenstein's delineation of the limits of language) that the notes and their internal relationships are the only things in a piece of music that we are equipped to describe: any idea of expressive or personal significance is 'transcendent' and therefore beyond the possibility of useful discussion. That would be an honourable view, though I do not share it: and at that level, some interesting and valuable work has been done. But far too much writing on serialism and 'atonality' seems arrogantly to deny the very idea that music could have any reality except as a pseudo-mathematical logical construct: the approach is frigid, its 'objectivity' false, infinitely far removed from the 'heart and brain' which forged those works in the heat of inspiration. To some extent, this whole analytical approach must bear responsibility for many dead Schoenberg performances and much dead post-Schoenbergian music, let alone dead responses on the part of the general willing music lover who wants a little *help*.

Notes on paper are not, in themselves, music. Once a composer begins writing, whether he uses the twelve-note method or not, he must descend from the realms of theory and involve himself with physical reality—with sounds that exist as vibrations and have harmonic consequences that will not tamely fit any predetermined scheme. He must compose with, not against, this simple fact. No wonder Schoenberg hated too theoretical an approach to his music. His warnings against it were frequent and pungent. Perhaps his most definitive statement comes in a letter to Rudolf Kolisch of July 1932:

You have rightly worked out the series of my string quartet [No. 3] . . . You must have gone to a great deal of trouble, and I don't think I'd have had the patience to do it. But do you think one's any better off for knowing it? . . . This isn't where the aesthetic qualities reveal themselves, or, if so, only incidentally. I can't utter too many warnings against overrating these analyses, since after all they only lead to what I have been dead against: seeing how it is *done*; whereas I have always helped people to see: what it is! I have repeatedly tried to make Wiesengrund [Adorno] understand this, and also Berg and Webern. But they won't believe me. I can't say it often enough: my works are twelve-note *compositions*, not *twelve-note* compositions. . . . You may wonder at my talking about this at such length. But although I'm not ashamed of a composition's having a healthy constructive basis even when it is a spontaneous result, produced unconsciously, I still don't care to be regarded as a constructor on account of the bit of juggling I can do with series, because that would be doing too little to deserve it. I think more has to be done to deserve such a title, and actually I think I am capable of fulfilling the considerable demands made on me by those entitled to do so. (Letter 143)

I append to Schoenberg's remarks some observations by a man who benefited greatly from his creative example, one of the wisest heads and finest composers among his pupils: Roberto Gerhard, in a passage [1] whose justice and elegance of expression it would be impertinent to paraphrase.

The 'method of composition with twelve tones related only to one another'—as Schoenberg called it—is just what it says it is: a method of composition. It cannot, therefore, be too strongly emphasized that it is entirely and exclusively the concern of the composer. It does not concern the listener at all. Above all, the listener must not believe that,

[1] From his article 'Tonality in Twelve-note Music' (*The Score*, May 1952).

if only he knew more about it theoretically, he might find 12-tone music less difficult. This is a hopeless delusion. He will find it easier to listen to only if he hears more of it, often enough. He must, of course, learn how to listen to it, but this will come only from listening itself; and he must remember that it is the *music*, and nothing but the music which matters. It must particularly be stressed that the listener is not supposed to detect the 'series' on which a given piece of 12-tone music is based, as if it were Ariadne's thread: or to follow the ways in which it is woven into the sound-fabric. That, incidentally, can only be discovered by analysis, and though listening and analysis have certainly something in common, they are basically antithetical mental operations.

To insist, however, that the 12-tone technique is no concern of the listener is not to say that he is not affected by it. . . . The fact that the listener may remain unaware of the specific effect it has on him does not in the least detract from the reality of that effect: just as there can be no doubt that an intelligent listener who is yet entirely ignorant of the principle of tonality may still entirely enjoy, and even form a valid aesthetic judgment of, a piece written, say, in C major.

For this is the real issue: the 12-note technique must be understood as a new principle of tonality.

Like a rondo-theme, the subject has surfaced once more. Tonality is—if the reader will pardon the expression—the key: tonality, at least, in the sense of Schoenberg's large definition quoted on p. 79, with its general connotation of comprehensible harmonic relationships and movement. He denied that he was making any break with previous music. In 1923, when we might expect him to have been fullest of his achievement, he wrote that in twelve-note music 'five tones have been drawn into composition in a way not called for before—*that is all*, and does not call for any new laws'; he had provided simply a 'more inclusive sound-material' which could be applied to the existing musical forms, but was convinced nothing essential had changed.

Gerhard, in the passage just cited, was speaking in the context of a remark in the 1922 edition of *Harmonielehre* about 'the tonality of a twelve-note series'. Certainly every note-row has its individual properties which profoundly influence the harmonic character of the final work—for instance, one may result in a preponderance of 'dissonant' sevenths and ninths, another in 'consonant' thirds and sixths. But there is another point. The twelve chromatic pitches are only equal in the abstract note-row, which is not so much 'atonal' as *pre*-tonal. Even if a composer was able, in an actual work, to maintain an ideal, undeviating revolution of the twelve at all times in melody and harmony (and as soon as more than one row-form is employed, that becomes virtually impossible), even then, a tonality-denying 'equality' of pitch would not result. Many other factors are in play: rhythm, register and phrasing, to name but three. Notes on strong beats will take precedence over those on weak ones; low notes will tend to act as roots, high ones as points of climax; the principal tones in melodic phrases will outrank those which are decorative; complex chords will suggest themselves as combinations of simpler harmonies. Ineluctably, hierarchies will be set up. However momentary, their effect is real, and with familiarity the listener's ear will interpret them in terms of a highly compressed, elusive, yet kaleidoscopic 'tonality' of quickly changing key-centres that embraces the simplest as well as the most complex relationships.

That was clearly what Schoenberg had in mind when he advanced, in contradiction to the term 'atonality', the idea of 'pantonality'—music which, far from lacking a key, includes all of them. The word never gained currency: perhaps fortunately, for it too is somewhat misleading. Just as the twelve notes never achieve their theoretical equality, neither do the key-areas. This is hardly surprising, for like many composers Schoenberg was highly sensitive to the different 'characters' of individual keys. The most obvious proof is his lifelong obsession with D minor, proclaimed in traditionally 'tonal' works both early and late (*Verklärte Nacht, Pelleas*, String Quartet No. 1, *Variations on a*

Recitative), which informs freely chromatic works (Five Orchestral Pieces) and twelve-note ones (String Quartet No. 4); more generally in his *œuvre* it is often revealed by an insistence on the pitch D at climactic or pivotal points.

The 'background' of traditional tonality seems to remain, therefore. Schoenberg provided significant confirmation of this when, for a talk given on Frankfurt Radio in 1931, he made a fresh harmonization of the Theme of the Orchestral Variations (our Ex. 12*b*) in a straightforward *F major*. A recording of this beautiful, faintly *Parsifal*-ish arrangement still exists.[1] Doubtless a theme can be harmonized in many ways; but to be faithful to its characteristics, all these versions must, presumably, have elements in common. Is the F major harmonization the tonal background or archetype which finds individual expression in Ex. 12*b*? The possibility gains force from a recent study [2] which finds that the harmonies of the 'real' version beginning with 12*b* can be analysed as components of two simultaneous keys—one of which is F. The other is B, harmonically speaking the negative pole to F and corresponding to the strong 'Neapolitan' element in Schoenberg's 1931 harmonization. This is not the only instance of two contending tonal centres a tritone apart in Schoenberg: the conflict between C and F sharp in the Piano Concerto has long been remarked on by certain writers, apparently without any inkling of general significance, and examples can be found elsewhere. Interestingly enough, this feature suggests parallels with those principles of 'axis' tonality that have been discovered in the music of Bartók.[3] And when a composer so infinitely far from Schoenberg as Edmund Rubbra can analyse the final bars of the *Phantasy*, Op. 47, as a 'striking

[1] Part of it was printed in *The Score*, July 1960, with the lecture text.

[2] 'Schoenberg's Atonality: Fused Bitonality?' by Kenneth L. Hicken (*Tempo* 109, June 1974).

[3] See Chapter I of *Béla Bartók: an Analysis of his Music* by Ernö Lendvai (London, 1971).

cadence in a clear G minor-major', ¹ it is high time for a detailed study of the tonal and harmonic aspects of Schoenberg's twelve-note music which lie deeper than 'the method', and their application on the smallest to largest scale.²

Schoenberg's insistence that he was employing a method, not a system, is significant. 'System' is closed, rigid, rule-bound, routine. 'Method' is a *modus operandi*, open-ended, flexible, apt to modification should circumstances demand. And so indeed it proved. It is nonsensical to regard the arrival at the twelve-note method as the consummation of Schoenberg's creative achievement. His musical style, far from crystallizing into a serial sameness, continued to develop for the remaining thirty years of his life. Almost every work shows a new approach, a new way of bending, ignoring, or turning to advantage the supposed 'rules' of the method. From the small-scale dance-forms of the Op. 25 Suite he progressed to the vast structure of *Moses und Aron*; from the fragmentation that was part of the Expressionist legacy he arrived at the richer, broader, less extravagant melodic style of the Violin Concerto and Fourth Quartet. Moreover, he felt able to return to tonal composition in the more traditional sense, with a parallel stream of works (starting with the Cello Concerto) that explore his beloved First Chamber Symphony style in the light of later experience.

The two streams mingle and enrich each other in a fascinating way—the 'tonal' *Kol Nidre* and *Variations on a Recitative* use elements of serial organization while the twelve-note *Ode to Napoleon* and Piano Concerto assimilate features of triadic

¹ In his revised edition of Casella's *The Evolution of Music* (J. & W. Chester, 1964), p. 74.

² Roger Sessions called for such a study in an article in *Tempo* over thirty years ago. So far there has been little response, apart from isolated instances such as O. W. Neighbour's 'A Talk on Schoenberg for Composers' Concourse' (*The Score*, June 1956), which confines itself to the first movement of the Fourth String Quartet.

tonality. In his final phase, with works like the String Trio, *A Survivor from Warsaw* and *De Profundis*, the serial stream seems to be diverted into darker regions again by an uprush from its Expressionist ancestry, but appearances are deceptive. In one of the most extreme of all Schoenberg's works, and one which was surely conceived as a musical testament—the String Trio—we encounter music of deep suffering and hysterical intensity, composed with a passionate spontaneity as great as that in *Erwartung*. Yet through the twelve-note technique Schoenberg is able to transmute this harrowing material into its opposite, into music of consolation and radiant tranquillity, such as we see in Ex. 13:

Ex.13

music whose internal organization is strictly serial, yet whose harmonies and onward flow (I hope the listener will agree) are by any definition profoundly and irreproachably 'tonal'. It is passages like this which make such distinctions finally irrelevant.

In this chapter [1] I have treated as fully as I dare the technical and stylistic issues raised by the music, so that in the following pages I may speak more simply and directly about the nature of the individual works. The last word, which also serves as an ideal introduction to Chapters 7 to 14, may safely be left to Schoenberg himself:

I am somewhat sad that people talk so much of atonality, of twelve-tone systems, of technical methods, when it comes to my music. All music, all human work has a skeleton, a circulatory and nervous system. I wish that my music should be considered as an honest and intelligent person who comes to us saying something he feels deeply and which is of significance to us all.

[1] It was written more than a year before I was able to study Charles Rosen's *Schoenberg* (London, 1976)—undoubtedly the most thoughtful study yet produced on the matters I have covered here. While I cannot accept all of Rosen's arguments concerning 'atonality' (as he chooses to call it) and the 12-note works (of which he gives a less sympathetic account than he seems to realize), his book provides many valuable insights, and I would recommend especially pp. 53–71 and 93–112 to the reader as a supplement, and contrast, to the present chapter.

7 Choral music

Schoenberg's output defies easy categorization. Throughout his career he sought to blend characteristics of various traditional forms into new ones—by adding a singer to a string quartet, combining the functions of orchestra and chamber ensemble, making speech aspire to the condition of song (and vice versa). Under the present heading I place all the music which employs a chorus, apart from the operas, *Die Jakobsleiter*, the *Modern Psalm* and the *Genesis* Prelude. The human voice—whether solo or in chorus, in speech, song or *Sprechstimme*—is vital to a large proportion of Schoenberg's music, and viewed as a whole the choral works form perhaps the most direct means of access to his central preoccupations, in ideas no less than in music.

Certainly there is no better place to begin than the *Gurrelieder*, Schoenberg's supreme contribution to musical late-Romanticism. Written when he was twenty-six, this gigantic work—part song-cycle, part oratorio, part melodrama, with strong operatic and symphonic elements—would have been an astonishing achievement at any age. For almost two hours, an enormous ensemble (five solo singers, speaker, three 4-part male choruses, 8-part mixed choir, an orchestra including 8 flutes, 5 oboes, 7 clarinets, 10 horns, 6 trumpets, bass trumpet, 6 trombones, 4 harps, and much percussion including heavy iron chains) is used to tell the story of Waldemar, twelfth-century King of Denmark, and his love for the beautiful Tove, whom he establishes in the castle of Gurre. His jealous queen has Tove murdered, and the grief-stricken Waldemar curses God—for which, after his own death,

95

he and his followers are condemned to rise from their graves and ride abroad every night.

So far, so romantic: the subject has all the favourite resonances of *Sturm und Drang*—the passionate, doomed love-affair, defiance of heaven, ghostly warriors, a wild hunt, the imagery of starlight, forests, graveyards and castles by the sea. Yet, though all these things are superbly rendered, in music that owes much to Wagner and especially *Tristan und Isolde*, this is no morbid exercise in romantic escapism. It is rather a kind of 'anti-*Tristan*'. Waldemar and Tove are indeed cast in Wagnerian mould, willing to renounce the world for their love, whose very intensity embodies a death-wish. But the world survives their deaths and Waldemar's spectral bravado; these dreams of ancient heroics fade into dreams indeed; life goes on. The *Gurrelieder* opens with a wonderfully delicate prelude evoking a sunset—an image which is often used to characterize the whole late-Romantic period; but it ends with a jubilant sun*rise*, on a note of hope and confidence in the future of life (and music). This is very far from the ambiguous 'love-death' of *Tristan*, and equally far from the conventional idea of 'decadent' late-Romanticism.

The *Gurrelieder* is already a mature work, and no one but Schoenberg could have written it. A cycle of poems might seem a convenient set of pegs on which to hang a large-scale musical canvas, but the music shows a high degree of internal logic from the outset. In the very first bars of the 'sunset' prelude, swaying, fluttering arpeggios on woodwind, harp and strings describe a triad of E flat with an added sixth. Then harmony becomes melody in a way characteristic of Schoenberg at all stages of his development: a calm, broad trumpet phrase turns the chord into a motif (Ex. 14*a*). It is not perhaps a vital structural point, but apt and prophetic, that when at the other end of the work the chorus greets the rising sun, the sun comes up (Ex. 14*b*) in C major on four trumpets, with the original descending motif *inverted* into a rising one:

Ex.14

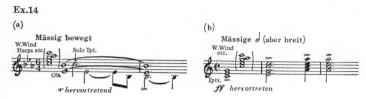

After the prelude, the love of Waldemar (tenor) and Tove (soprano) is presented lyrically as their voices alternate in a series of nine songs. The profusion of melodic riches is soon being deployed with something like symphonic logic—for instance, the urgent, agitated figure introducing the third song (Waldemar's hurried ride to Gurre) becomes the main waltz-theme of the fourth (Tove's triumphant welcome). The fifth, Waldemar's 'So tanzen die Engel', with its fine simple tune, has always been a favourite extract from the work; and Tove's reply (Ex. 15*a*) introduces what is to be the main love theme. A darker and just as persistent element, however, appears with Waldemar's next song, 'It is midnight, and unhallowed spirits rise from forgotten graves' (Ex. 15*b*)—a premonition of death. These two themes give some indication of the work's melodic variety, and Schoenberg's ability even at this stage to introduce highly chromatic material into a comparatively diatonic framework:

Ex.15

Tove's Isolde-like reply that they should welcome 'the mighty, the brave-smiling death' leads to the last and finest of the love-songs, Waldemar's calm, fulfilled 'Du wunderliche Tove'. Throughout these nine songs the emotional temperature (and the musical mastery) has steadily increased and motivic connections have been drawn ever tighter; now ensues a great orchestral interlude, a symphonic development of all the main motives containing some of the work's most glorious music and showing Schoenberg to be already the peer of Mahler and Strauss. But its end is sudden and brutal; lyric is abruptly forsaken for narrative in the famous 'Song of the Wood-dove'. Plangent orchestral bird-cries introduce a mezzo-soprano solo, telling of Tove's murder and the numbing grief that overcomes Waldemar. Part I of the *Gurre-lieder* ends in tragic gloom, with the suggestion of tolling bells.

The brief Part II opens with almost the same music. It is a single song: Waldemar's outcry against God, and his desire to become God's fool so he may mock His injustice. Part III, 'The Wild Hunt', then begins with the gloomy Ex. 15*b*. The graves open; Waldemar calls his vassals to join him in the grisly chase. Horns bellow in answer, and the sound of the hunt approaches—Schoenberg vividly suggests the chink of mail, the scrape of rusty weapons and the rattle of bones in scoring of uncanny precision. Watched by a terrified peasant (bass) the skeletal horde thunders by: Schoenberg gives them an almost entirely contrapuntal, often canonic chorus of barbaric force, supported by the full power of the gigantic orchestra.

Though Waldemar's longing for Tove remains unassuaged, there now arises a fool to mock *his* tyranny. The grotesquely tuneful, complaining 'Song of Klaus the Fool', denied the peace of an honest grave by Waldemar's obsession, is one of the work's high points, a bitter light relief that begins to put extreme romantic attitudes into clearer perspective. Waldemar is heard once more, still threatening to storm Heaven itself; but it is mere railing. In a remarkable chorus of despair and weariness, the vassals sink back to their graves with the coming of morning. Shimmering colours under long-held notes on four piccolos presage another 'Wild Hunt', that of the summer wind, which sweeps away the phantoms of the heroic past. It is set as a melodrama, with a speaker whose part, though assigned pitches, is intended to be less song-like than the *Sprechstimme* of *Pierrot Lunaire*.

We are well past the point where Schoenberg resumed the orchestration in 1911. Had he completed it in 1901, the *Gurrelieder* would still be a great work; but the experience of the ten-year interval makes it greater, and nowhere is that clearer than in this melodrama. Having lived through *Erwartung* and the Five Orchestral Pieces, he now insisted on sparer, clearer, chamber-musical textures, a web of shifting, iridescent colours, and the subtlest instrumental reinforcement of polyphony. So the dual nature of the *Gurrelieder* as a hinge-work between Romanticism and twentieth-century realism is made structurally explicit as it passes, in these final stages, from one sound-world to another. This second 'Hunt' has its own themes: the most important is a kind of smoothed-out version of Ex. 14*a*; but many other former motives, notably Ex. 15*a* and *b*, reappear in transfigured form. Contrapuntally it is the most complex section of the work, but its complexity communicates as the mysterious swirling brightness of an elemental force. The speaker describes the richness and variety of nature, set in motion by the summer wind, and calls upon all creatures to rejoice in life and sunlight. The music homes onto C major, and the full chorus enter in a triumphant Hymn to the Sun which, among other things, is a much-transformed recapitulation of the opening prelude. The work ends in a grandiose, unshakably affirmative C major. The expense and difficulty of production have always made performance of the *Gurrelieder* a rare event, but it has never failed to gain an enthusiastic reception. It is unquestionably one of Schoenberg's best-loved works.

A poem by the Swiss writer C. F. Meyer furnished the text for the chorus *Friede auf Erden* (Peace on Earth), Op. 13, which Schoenberg composed in early 1907—a poem which proclaims that the angels' message to the shepherds on the first Christmas Eve will surely become reality at last. 'An illusion for mixed choir', Schoenberg later called it—written at a time when he believed such harmony between human beings was possible. Though characteristically polyphonic in texture, harmony is certainly its most striking feature: tonal harmony (the piece is in D major) but marvellously fertile in exploiting distant key-relationships—notably in the long-drawn-out cadences to the refrain 'Friede, Friede auf der Erde!'. At one time this warm, amply proportioned, richly sonorous work was considered 'unsingable'; it is certainly not easy, and in 1911 Schoenberg provided an optional supporting accompaniment for small orchestra—but nowadays it is sung, as he intended—*a cappella*.

The choral writing in Schoenberg's opera *Die glückliche Hand* and in the unfinished oratorio *Die Jakobsleiter* (discussed in Chapter 14) leaves no doubt of his continuing mastery of the medium. It was not until the closing months of 1925, however, shortly before he departed to take up his professorship in Berlin, that he wrote two fascinating sets of choral pieces in the twelve-note method—the Four Pieces for mixed chorus, Op. 27, and the *Three Satires*, Op. 28.

The first two choruses of Op. 27 are to short poems by Schoenberg himself. 'Unentrinnbar' (Inescapable) celebrates people—like the 'Chosen One' in *Die Jakobsleiter*—who possess 'only the strength to conceive of their mission, and the character that will not let them refuse it'. In 'Du sollst nicht, du musst' (Not 'Thou Shalt'; you must), Schoenberg states what was to become the central theme of *Moses und Aron*:

> Thou shalt make for thyself no image!
> For an image restricts,
> confines, ties down
> what must stay unlimited and inconceivable.

Both these pieces are canons, the strictness of the polyphony mirroring the stern philosophy of the texts. The words of the other two pieces, in complete contrast, are poems from Hans Bethge's *Die chinesische Flöte*—a collection of translations from the Chinese which also supplied Mahler with the texts of *Das Lied von der Erde.* 'Mond und Menschen' (Moon and mankind) contrasts the calm splendour of the moon with the confusion, restlessness and inconsistency of human life. Schoenberg sets the poem in a kind of choral-prelude technique, each voice in turn taking a difference form of a twelve-note *cantus firmus* while the other voices weave imitative counterpoints about it.

Finally an uncomplicated lyric, 'Der Wunsch des Liebhabers' (The Lover's Wish): so far the choruses have been unaccompanied, but for this one Schoenberg introduces a 'Chinese'-sounding ensemble of mandolin, clarinet, violin and cello. The resultant little cantata is one of his most charming creations, executed with a beautifully deft, humorous touch. Inseparable from its effect is the fact that the music, though twelve-note, make a strongly 'tonal' impression, as witness the first choral entry:

The note-row, which consists of the five 'black' notes followed by the seven 'white' ones, enables the composer to produce such formations continually; and Schoenberg also isolates and repeats its sixth and seventh notes (E and B at the start of Ex. 16, then E♭ and G♯) so that their interval of the fifth (or fourth) gives a strong centre of tonal gravity. The ear, in fact, constantly expects the music to overbalance into traditional diatonicism; instead, it dances merrily into more and more unexpected regions—which it is nonsense to term 'atonality'. A striking feature of the piece is its rhythmic liveliness: there are three quite distinct rhythmic characters in the vocal lines of Ex. 16, and each is developed throughout. Meanwhile the 'Chinese' ensemble keeps up a tinkling background of repeated rhythmic figures, till the delightful little work melts away on liquidly burbling clarinet, softly tapping mandolin and chirruping string harmonics.

The *Satires* hold delights of a different order. Sentiments which, in a lesser composer, might have produced a mere occasional squib, were channelled by Schoenberg's passionate musicality into a curious but not inconsiderable work that crackles with a steady discharge of sardonic humour. Though the proximate cause of the *Satires*, as he explained in a pugnacious Preface, was the desire 'to give [younger contemporaries] a warning that it is not good to attack me', their lasting value is not a polemical one; it is, rather, the almost arrogant delight in music-making which they display. Schoenberg himself acknowledged this when he concluded his Preface with the (almost!) humble words:

I cannot judge whether it is nice of me (it will surely be no nicer than everything else about me) to make fun of much that is well-meant, in many respects talented, and in part deserving of respect, knowing as I do that it is certainly possible to make fun of everything. Much sadder things included. And much better fun! In any case, I am excused since, as always, I have only done it as well as I can. May others find themselves able to laugh at it all more than I can, since I know, too, how to take it seriously! Maybe I was trying to suggest that also?

The *Satires* are not parodies, except obliquely; they are strict twelve-note compositions whose mockery lies in their mastery as compared with the efforts of the 'mannerists'—the chasers after every different musical fashion—ridiculed by Schoenberg's texts. As in Op. 27 the first two pieces are unaccompanied canons. 'Am Scheideweg' (At the crossroads) depicts the poor would-be modernist who cannot make up his mind in which camp to place himself—'tonal' or 'atonal'. The twelve-note theme enacts the dilemma, opening boldly with a C major triad, but then wandering off into strange territory:

Ex.17

The text of the second piece, 'Vielseitigkeit' (Manysidedness), is rather transparently an attack on Stravinsky. 'Look who's beating the drum—it's little Modernsky! He's got a wig of genuine false hair! Makes him look like Papa Bach—he thinks!' The music, however, merely gently suggests that, if anyone deserves to be considered Bach's successor, it should be Schoenberg. It is truly 'many-sided', for it may be sung, by turning the page upside-down and beginning at the end, to produce exactly the same music! The difficulty of such an exercise is twofold: first to produce such an intricate, self-reflecting design, second to make true *music* of it—and Schoenberg succeeds on both counts.

There follows a 'kleine Kantate' for chorus with viola, cello and piano, entitled *Der Neue Klassizismus* (The New Classicism). Here Schoenberg's caustic wit boils over into a breathtaking display of sheer compositional virtuosity. His targets are those 'neo-classicists' who write in the new, chic style of vapidly simple tunes with meaningless dissonant harmonies. A brief instrumental introduction accordingly presents the note-row in the form of a descending scale of C major combined with a rising scale of D flat. (The overall tonal implication of the piece is a vastly expanded C major.) A tenor solo announces importantly, 'No more shall I be a Romantic . . . from tomorrow, I write only purest Classical', and the chorus sing the praises of this change 'from today to tomorrow' (*'von heute auf Morgen'*). Fully half the cantata is taken up with a diabolically ingenious fugue to the words of a gratifyingly flexible compositional creed:

> Classical perfection,
> Strict in each direction,
> It comes from where it may,
> Where that is, none can say,
> It goes where'er it will:
> That is the modern style.

Out of a final twelve-note cadence the voices blunder onto a triumphant unison C, decorated by the ensemble with all the other notes of the chromatic scale.

In late 1925 and early 1926 Schoenberg added to the *Satires* a 'tonal' Appendix (C major again), to show that he was just as capable of producing contrapuntal wizardries without the 'help' of a style that allowed dissonances and consonances an equal footing. There are three short, related mirror-canons for four voices ('An Aphorism and two Variations'); a jolly little mirror-canon for string quartet; and a more elaborate six-voice riddle canon entitled 'Legitimation als Canon' (The Canon as proof of identity)—this last is dedicated to George Bernard Shaw on his seventieth birthday. Musically these little compositions are comparable to the many other tonal canons, vocal and instrumental, which Schoenberg wrote as occasional pieces throughout his career (see Chapter 13).

In early 1929 he composed two choruses for male voices, 'Glück' (Happiness) and 'Verbundenheit' (Obligation), the second chorus of which was published by the German Workers' Chorus Association. About a year later he added four more, and the result constitutes his masterpiece in the field of unaccompanied choral music—the *Six Pieces for Men's Chorus*, Op. 35. The male chorus is a difficult medium whose textures can easily sound thick and clotted. Schoenberg avoids that danger by a perfect spacing of the individual vocal lines in a very wide range of up to three octaves, and by extremely varied melodic techniques—from the sweetest *cantabile* to the liveliest recitative-like declamation. Though the music is, as usual, predominantly contrapuntal, there is an emphasis on chordal harmony—especially harmony with a strong diatonic feeling. This is most obvious in 'Verbundenheit', which stands as No. 6 of the set: it is not a serial work at all, but beautifully inhabits a close-harmony world close to Schubert's male-voice quartets (cf. the opening, Ex. 18*a*). But it is almost as clear in the opening (Ex. 18*b*) of the chorus 'Hemmung' (Inhibition), which *is* a twelve-note work. And, though four of the *Six Pieces* are serial, and 'Glück' is highly chromatic, they contain many other examples of such strong key-feeling—which makes the cycle's culmination in the last calm D minor triad of 'Verbundenheit' both natural and satisfying.

The texts, Schoenberg's own, are among his best poems. Five deal tenderly or ironically with generalized aspects of human experience: the difficulty of giving voice to an idea ('Inhibition'); the recognition of natural law, and rebellion against it ('The Law'); awareness of kinship with the rest of humanity ('Means of Expression' and 'Obligation'); and how the nature of happiness lies precisely in its elusiveness ('Happiness'). It is fascinating to see how Schoenberg discovers lively musical forms for, and gives passionate expression to, subjects which could easily remain forbiddingly abstract. All these are basically four-voice choruses. The exception is chorus No. 5, 'Landsknechte' (Yeomanry). The most extended and elaborate setting, this is a real *tour-de-force*—a slow march in eight real parts, the voices providing their own rhythmic accompaniment

Ex.18

(a)

(b)

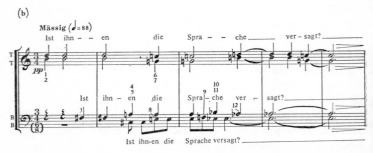

in a veritable fusillade of onomatopoeic drumming and trudging effects. The marching troopers of the title—exemplars of unthinking humanity—forage, pillage, rape, fight among themselves, and are finally slaughtered by an unseen enemy, never aware that there may be more to existence than to live for the present moment. This is, however, only the most striking number in what must be accounted one of Schoenberg's most richly varied and rewarding works. If 'Verbundenheit' is the most inviting approach to the *Six Pieces*, the other five, in time, yield equal delights.

His remaining choral works were written in America. *Kol Nidre*, Op. 39, for speaker, chorus and orchestra, was composed at the behest of a rabbi in Los Angeles, who also suggested the work's form. The speaker tells, and the orchestra illustrates, a legend from the Kabbala wherein God, having created light, crushed it into a myriad sparks that can only be seen by the faithful (including repentant sinners); then follows the singing of 'Kol Nidre', the chief liturgy for the release from obligations on the Jewish Day of Atonement. The text's original function had been to receive back into the community those Jews who in times of persecution had gone over to Christianity; so its personal significance for Schoenberg must have been considerable.

Although *Kol Nidre* is a tuneful 'tonal' work in G minor, the influence of serialism is stamped on all its musical processes. The traditional 'Kol Nidre' melody in liturgical use (of Spanish origin) was, Schoenberg considered, hardly a melody at all, but a collection of flourish-like motives resembling each other to various degrees. He therefore took certain of these and submitted them to what can only be described as serial treatment within a tonal framework. He preserved their melodic integrity, so that the music has at times a distinct 'Oriental', quasi-improvisatory character. But its construction is thoroughly disciplined: every bar, every idea is derived from the given melodic fragments, whether by mirror-forms or interpenetration of motives.

Kol Nidre is a colourful score: the dramatic introduction ncludes some imaginatively telling orchestration, notably the graphic description of the creation of light, with a bell-stroke, flickering trumpet, and whirring flexatone trill. The singing of the 'Kol Nidre' itself develops as a noble, purposeful march-movement with a fine swinging main tune, and recapitulates the music of the introduction in altered forms in a central section. The work dies away to a peaceful ending in a confident G major. This fine and easily assimilable music has remained almost totally unknown.

Similar in layout, but raised to the highest power of genius, is *A Survivor from Warsaw*, Op. 46, for narrator, men's chorus and orchestra—perhaps the most dramatic thing Schoenberg ever wrote, summing up one of the grimmest tragedies of the twentieth century in the space of six excoriating minutes. It is his personal tribute and memorial to the Jews who died under the Nazi persecution (and by extension to all victims of political tyranny), based on a story that had been reported to him by survivors from the Warsaw Ghetto. A group of prisoners are wakened before dawn and beaten. They are ordered to count their numbers out loud, so the sergeant may know how many are left to be herded into the gas-chambers; but in the middle of the counting they break spontaneously into the ancient Hebrew song of triumph, 'Shema Yisroel'—a last assertion of their human dignity against the exterminators.

The story called forth from Schoenberg music of the same blazing intensity as his recent String Trio. *A Survivor from Warsaw* is a twelve-note work, and perhaps the best of all introductions to the method—simply as an overwhelming demonstration of twelve-note music's fitness for communicating passionate human emotion. The explosive setting deepens and makes more immediate the impact of every simple, shocking spoken phrase, enhanced by a drastic economy and precision of musical gesture. In the very first bar, a shrieking twelve-note reveille for two trumpets (Ex. 19*a*) establishes the nightmarish, fear-ridden atmosphere of the death camps. This is sustained by the vivid, fragmented orchestration—all the characteristically 'Expressionist' details of string *col legno* and harmonics and flutter-tonguing brass reappear with unsurpassed rightness—while the narrator, the 'Survivor' from Warsaw, relates his memories of the strange episode, sometimes breaking into shrill German for the sergeant's voice, against a background of militaristic percussion. But not all the music is simply a brilliant evocation of terror. Towards the end, the broken, dejected rhythms of the 'counting out' gather speed in a tremendous *accelerando* 'like a stampede of wild horses'; at last the full orchestra enters, and the male chorus lift up their voices in the 'Shema Yisroel'—to a twelve-note melody (Ex. 19*b*) derived directly from the opening fanfare. The positive forces represented by this tragic affirmation are also serial music's province.

Ex.19

Two short unaccompanied choral pieces were Schoenberg's last completed compositions: *Dreimal Tausend Jahre* (Thrice a Thousand Years), Op. 50A for four-part choir, and *De Profundis*, Op. 50B for six-part singing and speaking chorus. The text of *Dreimal Tausend Jahre* is a brief lyric poem by Dagobert D. Runes entitled 'Gottes Wiederkehr' (God's Return), clearly inspired by the foundation of the state of Israel. The theme was much in Schoenberg's mind in April 1949, when he wrote the setting, for he was also sketching an unfinished work for chorus and orchestra to his own text, *Israel Exists Again.* Op. 50A is a twelve-note piece, but he at first placed it with the diatonic *Three Folksongs*, Op. 49 (see Chapter 13), and the original edition bore the opus number 49B. Its polyphonic construction has, in fact, much in common with the *Folksongs*, and we may surmise that subject-matter, rather than any artificial stylistic division, led him to alter it to Op. 50A: all three works in Op. 50 deal with specifically Jewish historical and religious issues.

'Gottes Wiederkehr' is the last phrase in the poem, and towards it the whole composition moves—the idea of the 'return' is continually embodied in the symmetry or near-symmetry of its individual lines (cf. for instance, Ex. 11*a* in Chapter 6). Other things 'return' too in this deceptively simple work—most of all a harmony that is 'tonal' in the broad sense to all but the tone-deaf.

In contrast, *De Profundis*—a Hebrew setting of Psalm 130 ('Out of the depths have I cried to thee, O Lord')—is turbulent and anguished. The idea of striving upwards towards God is a central theme in Schoenberg. That he should realize it powerfully in *De Profundis* is no surprise: but the texture of the realization is highly original. While a section of the chorus (or sometimes solo voices) sing the Hebrew text, the remaining sections—their rhythms notated exactly but the pitch hardly indicated—cry, whisper or shout the same phrases. The effect is intensely dramatic, like the confused response of a congregation, or giving the effect of a multitude of individual souls 'crying from the depths' by whatever means of expression each can command. The music is dodecaphonic, though again with significant relaxations of earlier serial rules. A comparatively rare example of true six-part singing, just before the end, shows Schoenberg's twelve-note harmony at its most refined, with (despite all the differences in style) an almost Bach-like strength.

8 Orchestra and chamber orchestra

Schoenberg's earliest orchestral efforts were not very ambitious —a serenade for small orchestra (1896; only one movement was finished) and a Gavotte and Musette for strings of 1897. A symphonic poem *Frühlings Tod* (The Death of Spring) was left unfinished in 1898 without having been worked into full score. However, by the time he essayed his first large-scale orchestral piece, the symphonic poem *Pelleas und Melisande* after Maeterlinck (1902–3), Schoenberg had scored a large part of the *Gurrelieder* and had, moreover, been engaged for some years on the chore of orchestrating operettas. The solid value of this drudgery should not be underestimated; it helped him become, very early, a master of the craft of instrumentation.

In *Pelleas* Schoenberg is already reaching out beyond the rich late-Romantic orchestral style of the *Gurrelieder*. It marks, in fact, a new stage in his development. As in *Verklärte Nacht*, he follows the action of his literary source quite closely; while at the same time he builds a self-sufficient musical structure in which the four movements of a symphony (in his favourite D minor) may be discerned. Throughout its course the main themes, associated with Mélisande, Golaud and Pelléas, are transformed in the manner of leitmotives. In this, as in other respects, Wagner is the work's main ancestor. Schoenberg goes far beyond Wagner, however, in the size of his orchestra (17 woodwind, 18 brass, 8 percussion, 2 harps and strings) and the constantly changing textures he draws from it. The score contains some quite new instrumental effects, notably the sinister trombone *glissandi* that illustrate the scene in the underground vaults.

Most remarkable of all, however, is the polyphonic density, which surpasses anything in Schoenberg's earlier work and shows his concern to communicate as much as possible in the shortest space, packing every bar with contrapuntal invention, imitative passages, or multiple combinations of themes. Ex. 20, near the beginning of the work, shows a beautiful and relatively straightforward instance: Melisande's mournful motif presented in canon on the woodwind, while the horns sound Golaud's more energetic theme for the first time.

There are also occasions when the sheer contrapuntal virtuosity appears self-defeating, the textures choked and the rhythms unclear. For all its riches, *Pelleas* is an uneven work, showing that Schoenberg had not yet fully mastered the new style he was trying to call into being. Too much of it can appear, on first hearing, to consist of hectic and unstable thrashing about.[1] Like

---

[1] Significantly, Schoenberg's version of the programme omits all mention of Golaud's father Arkel—the still centre of Maeterlinck's play and Debussy's opera.

other works of this period, it gets better as it progresses, even though the earlier stages contain some of the most prophetic music. Schoenberg himself summed it up fairly in a letter to Zemlinsky in 1918 when he admitted that it was far removed from perfection because too much of it was devoted to long-winded exposition. The later music (starting with the comparatively conventional 'Love Scene' which is nevertheless welcome for its direct melodic appeal) flows better, and the final Epilogue (the Death of Mélisande) is inspired music of undeniable power, sinking at last into grand Wagnerian gloom on muted brass. Despite one's reservations, the work deserves the toe-hold it has maintained in the orchestral repertoire since 1910.

The Chamber Symphony No. 1 in E major, Op. 9 (1906), stands in direct line of descent from *Pelleas*. Here, however, the forces have been reduced to a mere fifteen players (8 woodwind, 2 horns and string quintet), ensuring clarity of line; and the structural compression is far more successful. Half as long as *Pelleas* in performance time, the single movement has a taut, concise form which suggests the broad outlines of a sonata-design with episodes, but can also be analysed as five 'sub-movements' thus: (*i*) self-contained exposition functioning as first movement, (*ii*) scherzo, (*iii*) development of the substance of (*i*), (*iv*) slow movement, (*v*) finale which is both recapitulation and development of themes of (*i*) and (*iv*). Within these firm outlines two qualities characterize the piece—its spirited, optimistic vigour and its extraordinary contrapuntal elaboration. The second makes the first extremely necessary if the music is not to tie itself in polyphonic knots; but from the first statement of the horn theme (Ex. 5*a* in Chapter 6) which Schoenberg said was to express 'riotous rejoicing' and which presides over the proceedings at each turning-point in the structure, the music has an irresistible drive that carries all before it, however ambiguously chromatic the harmony. And ambiguous it often is, with the fourth-chords, whole-tone themes and other features apparent in Ex. 5. There is no lack of expansiveness or emotion in this material; but the clarity of the scoring also saves it from any risk of amorphousness.

In the early years of its existence, however, the technical demands raised by such scoring in a work of such dynamic virtuosity caused serious problems. In 1916, while working on Chamber Symphony No. 2, Schoenberg confided in a letter to Zemlinsky that he would score the new work for a normal small orchestra, and probably re-score its predecessor as well, as 'these solo strings against so many wind instruments are a mistake'. In fact, in 1922 and 1935 he *did* make versions of No. 1 for full orchestra—the latter an interesting transcription which deserves to be known, not least because it involves some actual reworking of the piece's substance. Nevertheless, the chamber version has held its own, and in the last decade or so has become one of Schoenberg's most frequently played works: aptly so, for it is a fine affirmative summing-up of his first period of development. Conductors are even learning to let the music breathe a little, forsaking the old vice (still perpetuated in some modern recordings) of playing the work as if it suffered from high blood pressure, rather than a simple access of high spirits.

Only three years separate the Chamber Symphony from the *Five Orchestral Pieces*, Op. 16; but stylistically the gap is a gigantic one. For all its forward-looking features the Chamber Symphony is essentially traditional in conception, conscious of an ancestry that includes the Brahms symphonies and the Beethoven quartets; in the *Orchestral Pieces* (whose very title asserts an 'unsymphonic' nature) we find the totally-chromatic language of 'Expressionism' in full flood, caught up in a sometimes exhilarating, sometimes frightening *now* of ever-expanding horizons. They have organic structures, recognizable themes, an overall key-centre, and harmonies that do, in their fashion, direct and punctuate the flow of events; but one hears them first, as did their earliest astounded audiences, in terms of frenzied activity

Schoenberg in early middle life

Schoenberg: a caricature by Hans Lindluff, 1913 (*Austrian National Library*)

Cartoon of Schoenberg and Zemlinsky by Emil Weiss, at the first performance of *Erwartung*, in Prague, 1924 (*Austrian National Library*)

Schoenberg at an art exhibition in New York, 1948, with three of his paintings: two self-portraits and 'Red Gaze' (*Universal Edition, London*)

Schoenberg with Roberto Gerhard and Webern in Barcelona, 1931 (*by courtesy of Mrs Roberto Gerhard*)

Schoenberg with his second wife, Gertrud, at St Pere da Riba, Spain, summer 1931 (*by courtesy of Mrs Roberto Gerhard*)

A page from the manuscript of *Seraphita*, first of the Four Orchestral Songs, Op. 22 (*Universal Edition, Vienna*)

Schoenberg in later years (*Universal Edition, London*)

Self-portrait from behind, April 1911 (*Universal Edition, London*)

and utter stasis, violent dissonance and weird tone-colours, incredibly complex polyphony and an outpouring of diverse ideas bewildering in its fervour—art used to intensify, not to render acceptable, the reality of the artist's innermost vision.

Schoenberg, at the suggestion of his publisher, eventually gave titles to the pieces, and a note about this in his diary for 1st January 1912 gives a revealing glimpse of his attitude to the work:

... I've found titles that are at least possible. On the whole, unsympathetic to the idea. For the wonderful thing about music is that one can say everything in it, so that he who knows understands everything; and yet one hasn't given away one's secrets—the things one doesn't admit even to oneself. But titles give you away! Besides—whatever was to be said has been said, by the music. Why, then, words as well? ... Now the titles I may provide give nothing away, because some of them are very obscure and others highly technical. To wit: I Premonitions (everybody has those). II The Past (everybody has that, too). III Chord-colours (technical). IV Peripeteia (general enough, I think). V The Obbligato (perhaps better the 'fully-developed' or the 'endless') Recitative. However, there should be a note that these titles were added for technical reasons of publication and not to give a 'poetic' content.[1]

'Poetic' or not, these titles do smooth the way in for many listeners. Pieces I and IV are in some respects similar: both are highly emotional and extremely concentrated, bursting forth with an explosive 'exposition' of multifarious motivic shapes and then launching into a fast-moving, wide-ranging development of them. In I this takes the form of a hectic accumulation of *ostinato*-patterns over a long-held pedal chord, dying away to an unquiet ticking before a brusque coda. In IV (for whose opening see Ex. 6) the tone is more overtly tragic, the development more fragmented; the *coup de grâce* comes in a curt, slashing cadence.

[1] Quoted in Rufer, *The Works of Arnold Schoenberg* (London, 1962), p. 34.

In strong contrast stand pieces II and III. II indeed admits that there *is* a 'past', with its firm anchorage to D minor and dreamily expressive opening tune (cf. Ex. 7)—as if Debussy's sad *Gigues* had been slowed down into near-immobility. The vestiges of a ternary form, the more decorative use of instrumental colour (in a tinkling celesta *ostinato*, for instance), the delicately canonic textures combine to make this the most easily assimilable of the set. III is the work's still central point—the stillness of the fixed stare that, held long enough, persuades a landscape to yield up all its secrets. There are no themes. The 'colours' of the title are seen in two instrumental combinations that spell out the same chord (Ex. 21a). Blending imperceptibly from one 'chord-colour' into the other, the harmonic content begins to change, subtly, gradually, note by note. The texture loosens: the orchestra becomes a shifting kaleidoscope in which points of colour change and mingle with ever-increasing frequency. A leaping figure (Ex. 21b) initiates movement, and for a moment the whole fabric comes alive in a shimmering turbulence of individual parts. Then it comes to rest again, returning

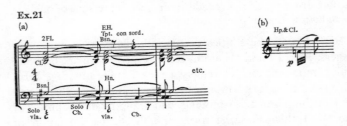

Ex. 21

to the opening chord and its colours. Actually, this magical little movement did *not* simply arise as a technical exercise: Schoenberg later admitted that in it he had tried to capture the impression of sunlight on the water of Lake Traunsee, as he had seen it once at dawn; he even pointed out a 'jumping fish' (our Ex. 21b). As for Piece V, its structure is the freest of all, one that seems to enact the very process of exploration. Its 'endless recitative' unfolds continuously as a single shapely wide-ranging melodic line, steadily growing without repetition of any of its various sections. With something of the character of an Austrian *ländler*, it winds its lyrical way through a labyrinth of surrounding polyphony in anything up to eight parts,[1] always changing colour as it passes from instrument to instrument, arching over the whole range of the orchestra, ever journeying onward.

Nearly twenty years elapsed before Schoenberg produced his next purely orchestral composition—and one of his very greatest. The *Variations for Orchestra* Op. 31, completed in 1928, may be regarded as the point at which the twelve-note method, growing and ripening in the smaller forms of Opp. 25–30, bursts into full flower. Expansive in duration (about twenty-three minutes), brilliant in orchestral resourcefulness, utterly personal in sound and character, it also stands firmly in the great orchestral-variation tradition of Brahms, Reger, Elgar and others.

There are twelve sections—Introduction, Theme, nine Variations proper, and Finale. The Introduction (briefly described on p. 85) foreshadows various significant melodic elements, not all immediately related to the Theme: one is the name B-A-C-H, spelled out mysteriously by a solo trombone as a kind of invocation. The Theme is then stated simply by cellos and violins. Ex 12*b* (p. 85) shows only its first few bars: it is twenty-four bars long in all, uses all four forms of the note-row (original, retrograde inversion, retrograde, inversion, in that order) and divides into two twelve-bar halves.

The ensuing Variations seldom obscure the Theme's identity. Schoenberg preserves its basic contours, its phrase-lengths, often its original pitches and rhythms, fairly strictly: the variation

---

[1] Here Schoenberg uses for the first time the *Hauptstimme* sign ⊢ to indicate to the conductor which is the principal voice. It became almost a standard feature of his later scores.

process is more often one of decoration, or of using the Theme as the binding thread in a polyphonic web as other motives are spun around it. A notable feature of the Variations is the way in which they alternate the full power of the orchestra with the intimate sonorities of a few solo instruments. They cover an enormous range of mood and character. Variation I (*Moderato*) is a nimble development of the Theme in the bass, in a fragmented, mosaic-like orchestral texture. II (*Adagio*) features solo wind instruments, violin and cello in a calm canonic conversation. III (*Mässig*) is brusque, the Theme blared out on horn and trumpet against a vigorous pattern of repeated semiquavers. Harp and mandoline maintain the pattern into Variation IV (*Walzertempo*), a stylized dance. Variation V (*Bewegt*) is the work's central climax, breaking up the Theme more forcefully than hitherto—a study in minor ninths, major sevenths and semitones, wherein the B-A-C-H motive makes a quite natural appearance. VI (*Andante*) is scored for similar forces to II, but its dance-like character parallels IV. VII (*Langsam*) constitutes the work's main slow section: a magical, dream-like episode in which the Theme appears in florid decoration, mainly on solo woodwind, lapped around by a gentle tracery of rocking figures on celesta, glockenspiel, harp, piccolo and solo strings. VIII (*Sehr rasch*) is impetuous but determined, with a continuous quaver pulse that is syncopated by unexpected shifts of accent; IX (*L'istesso Tempo*) continues the canonic exchanges in a lighter texture, with several momentary rallentandos which intimate that the Variations are about to make way for something else. The 'something else' proves to be the large-scale Finale—a synoptic epilogue which opens with a shimmering recall of the B-A-C-H motive and makes prominent use of it until the end. Two contrary impulses are at work as episode succeeds episode: that of lingering nostalgically in the sound-world of the gentler variations, and that of driving to a decisive conclusion. The tempo of these latter attempts steadily increases to *Presto*—at which point we hear a new version of the Theme in combination with B-A-C-H:

Ex. 22

but there is a last tender *adagio* moment for the cor anglais to recall the Theme's original form before the cheerful noise of the helter-skelter coda.

Schoenberg was interested in films—or at least their techniques and the musical possibilities they offered—throughout his life. One of the by-products of this interest was the short *Begleitungsmusik zu einer Lichtspielszene* (Accompaniment to a film-scene), Op. 34, for small orchestra, illustrating an *imaginary* sequence of emotions which might be depicted on film. Aptly for a period of the German cinema which saw the work of Fritz Lang and Robert Wiene, the sequence consists of 'Threatening Danger', 'Fear' and 'Catastrophe'. Schoenberg employs a free variation form, much simpler-textured than in the Orchestral Variations, and allows all the more 'atmospheric' elements of his orchestral style full rein. A piano in the orchestra lends a certain hard, brittle quality to the sonorities. It is a twelve-note work; but much is made of the traditionally 'tragic' interval of the minor third, and a C sharp minor tonality seems to lurk in the background, just out-of-shot of the mind's camera. *Begleitungsmusik* is a highly effective piece, which suggests that, given the chance, Schoenberg might have proved an excellent film composer. Certainly many lesser composers have drawn upon his characteristics for their own film scores.

The Suite in G major, for string orchestra, of 1934, is the first work Schoenberg completed after his arrival in America.

Between it and the *Begleitungsmusik* had come the two curious Concertos based on eighteenth-century models (discussed in Chapter 13), and it is a logical continuation of their concerns: a twentieth-century glance back at an older style, but this time employing original themes. Like Grieg's well-known (and not dissimilar) *Holberg Suite*, it uses old Baroque dance-forms (the movements are Overture, Adagio, Minuet, Gavotte and Gigue); and unlike his own Piano Suite, Op. 25, does so in an overtly tonal, non-serial context, though with personal adaptations of their harmonic style. The work was intended for the repertoire of American college orchestras, to prepare them for modern music and performance techniques without, in Schoenberg's wry words, 'giving them a premature dose of "Atonality Poison"'. Such has not, however, been its fate. It is certainly a tough work to play—but its difficulties are testing ones, and the quality of the music makes them well worth overcoming. For the listener, moreover, the Suite is most approachable; if the slow movement (the *Adagio*) is not one of Schoenberg's most memorable inventions, the other four more than make up for it with their colour, rhythmic vitality and splendid tunes.

The Violin Concerto, Op. 36, is a very different matter—but it too inherits certain characteristics from the peculiar 'recompositions' of eighteenth-century concerti. There, Schoenberg had first gained experience in building a whole work around the contrast of soloist and orchestra, in a fairly traditional style: he now carried it over into his first large-scale twelve-note concerto. He also took over from the earlier works the idea of making the soloist carry the main thread of the argument with a virtuosity that is enormously demanding precisely because it must encompass the music's main substance, not decoration. The violin part includes huge intervals, vast-spread chords, double-stopping in harmonics; the result is, technically, one of the most taxing works in the repertoire, yet one in which virtuoso display *per se* is almost entirely avoided.

Though one of the ripest examples of a perfect marriage between twelve-note technique and expressive content (see Ex. 10, in Chapter 6, for some of the main themes), the Concerto is cast in traditional mould. The first movement (*Poco Allegro*) has the proportions and thematic layout of a sonata form, which after the calm opening (Ex. 10*c*) soon assumes an impassioned and dramatic character. The orchestration is colourful and hard-edged, characterized by muted brass, percussion, much *pizzicato* and *col legno* string writing and flutter-tongue woodwind. The violin, always the focus of attention, moves through ever-changing rhythmic, melodic and textural liaisons with various groups of instruments, and has a staggeringly difficult unaccompanied cadenza before the coda, which returns to the mood of the opening. The *Andante Grazioso* second movement, with its sweetly singing main theme (Ex. 10*a*), has a ternary form that alternates two characters: an intense yet almost pastoral lyricism in the outer sections, and a livelier *scherzando* mood. The texture has a pellucid transparency, the orchestra reduced to a handful of solo instruments for most of the time. The *Allegro* finale is a species of sonata-rondo with the general character of a brilliant and purposeful march. Fairly early on occurs a brief, dramatically prepared 'Quasi Cadenza', but the movement culminates in a huge accompanied cadenza proper of immense difficulty, which begins with a version of the work's opening theme (Ex. 10*c*) and takes in during its course the slow movement theme 10*a* as well. At length the full power of the orchestra crashes in on a great wave of sound that combines the main themes of the first and last movements, while the violin sings out high above with thrilling effect (Ex. 23), after which the Concerto storms to a decisive conclusion.

In 1939, three years after completing the Concerto, Schoenberg managed finally to finish a work he had begun thirty-three years before—the Chamber Symphony No. 2 in E flat minor. Its history is a chequered one: begun in 1906, on the day that its

Ex.23

predecessor was completed, work on it seems to have faltered even before Schoenberg's marital crisis broke; yet we know he tried to continue with it in 1907, 1908, 1911 and 1916. On 12th December 1916 he had written to Zemlinsky:

I have decided to complete my 2nd Chamber Symphony . . . Two movements have been written, one is complete with the exception of the final bars and the other is half-finished. I shall merge these into *one* movement. This is the first part, because I plan a second part, but it is still possible that I shall abandon this plan. Consequently, I shall *not* compose the work for solo instruments but shall immediately write an entirely new score for (medium-size) orchestra . . . I hope to complete [the work] in a few days—if nothing gets in the way!

Something obviously did, for it remained a fragment, which for a time Schoenberg thought of using as introduction to a spoken text beginning 'To continue further along this road was impossible'.

Decades later, however, the conductor Fritz Stiedry commissioned a work for his Orchestra of the New Friends of Music in New York. At first Schoenberg made the interesting proposal that he do an orchestral transcription of his Wind Quintet or the Suite, Op. 29: but instead he decided to finish the Chamber Symphony. Trying, as he said, to discover after so long 'what did the author mean here?', he preserved the original formal outlines and material (which he still judged 'very good; expressive, characteristic, rich and interesting') as conceived by 1916, but reworked many passages in detail, re-orchestrated the first movement, composed a coda for it, and composed the remainder of the second movement. The completed piece, which he designated Op. 38, remained in two movements after some doubtful attempts at a third; but by ending the second with a coda that recalls, amplifies and deepens that of the first, he succeeded in producing a highly unified, self-sufficient design—one which, he soon began to feel, made further movements unnecessary.

Despite the lengthy gestation, there is nothing patchy or inconsistent about the Chamber Symphony No. 2. Though generally cast aside by those who like to view Schoenberg's output as a series of historical milestones, it is, to my mind, one of his finest achievements: a work of unusual beauty, compelling urgency and great melodic distinction. 'Chamber Symphony' is, of course, a misnomer: the orchestra is larger than for most Haydn or Mozart symphonies, and for all the delicacy of its instrumentation the piece has a truly symphonic largeness of line and gesture. The grave, melancholy flute melody with which the first movement opens is a case in point, and suggests that this Second Chamber Symphony may have been planned as a deliberate contrast of mood, pace and technique to the First:

Ex.24

The First is of course a splendid work, occupies a more crucial position in Schoenberg's development, and has been more generally admired on account of its individual harmonic language. But that of the Second is no less individual, and perhaps subtler—closer to the Second String Quartet; though the freedom with which Schoenberg combines distantly related harmonies in triadic form doubtless reflects experience gained in twelve-note music.

The slow first movement, characterized by flowing, expressive melodies such as Ex. 24, is a deeply felt elegy, with a somewhat nocturnal flavour that grows darker in the sudden shadows and tremulous half-lights of the coda. The large-scale second movement (*Con fuoco*) begins in a lighter, scherzo-like mood in G major, but soon blazes up in a torrential stream of continuous development that courses just as fiercely through the recapitulation and re-introduces themes from the first movement. Eventually darkness invades the music; the pace grinds to *molto adagio*, a solo horn sounds the opening phrase of Ex. 24 like a warning, and an extended epilogue—a dark, eloquent development and intensification of the coda of the first movement—begins.

Ex. 25

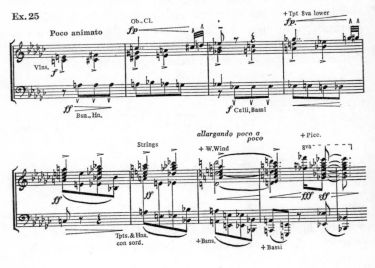

Mounting, through Ex. 25, to a climax of tragic fervour, the Symphony ends in the gloom of E flat minor. It is one of the very few Schoenberg works to have an explicitly tragic ending; but it is a tragedy with the inspiring effect of a Lear or Hamlet. Perhaps the long delay in the completion of the work was necessary for Schoenberg to tackle with sufficient objectivity the experience so powerfully embodied here.

In 1942 Schoenberg composed the magnificent Piano Concerto, Op. 42, premièred in 1944 by Eduard Steuermann under the baton of Leopold Stokowski. Like the *Ode to Napoleon*, Op. 41, this is a thoroughly twelve-note work which nevertheless has strong—one might almost say blatant—leanings towards traditional tonality. For all its serial ingenuity, it may be sensed as centring on the key of C (major/minor at the opening, clearly major at the end), but a C with a dark, disruptive F sharp region which exerts a strong influence on the course of events. There is a firm sense of harmonic movement—logical and inevitable, if not quite classical; moreover, the textures are more stable than in previous serial works, and Schoenberg allows much octave doubling in orchestra and piano. These factors plus some of the most whistleable tunes in twelve-note music (see Ex. 26) make the Piano Concerto one of the easiest of Schoenberg's major works to appreciate on a few hearings—its sound-world should affright no one who enjoys the concertos of, say, Bartók. In this work Schoenberg returns to the kind of portmanteau single-movement form he had used in early pieces such as the First Chamber Symphony—and the concerto is, in fact, symphonic in layout. It divides into four interlinked sub-movements, and the solo piano's role, for all its taxing qualities, is basically an extended *obbligato* one, *primus inter pares* with the orchestra.

Schoenberg provided the outline of a 'programme' for the Piano Concerto (see p. 217) which suggests it may be a kind of musical autobiography. Certainly the placid, graceful, *ländler-*

like theme which opens the work (Ex. 26*a*) has a distinctly Viennese flavour. The Concerto's first section is entirely built around this melody, which acts as *cantus* to various counterpoints of a similarly *gemütlich* cast. Suddenly the idyll is shattered by the irruption of a furious scherzo (*molto allegro*) which plunges the music into dark and desperate regions. This kind of musical psychological storm is not, of course, unusual in Schoenberg, but it has seldom if ever blown up from such a clear sky. As the tension heightens, the harmonic fabric begins to break into streams of ascending perfect fourths, bringing tonal movement to a standstill.

The ensuing third section, which functions as a slow movement, is a profound, reflective *Adagio*. New, long-spanned, tragically accented melodies intertwine with reminiscences of the scherzo; there is a short solo cadenza and an orchestral *tutti* of stark grandeur, ending in a minatory descent of perfect fourths in the brass. Another brief cadenza leads into the finale, *Giocoso,* in which peace and equilibrium are restored. Formally this section is a rondo, and its main theme (Ex. 26*b*) has a classic poise and wit. The struggles of the preceding sections are not forgotten—indeed, themes from the scherzo and adagio rear their heads again; but eventually the work's opening theme, Ex. 26*a*, returns, transformed into a defiant march, and a joyous *stretto* rushes the Concerto to a brusque but triumphant final cadence into C major, approached from F sharp (Ex. 26*c*—the final clinching chord telescopes the triad with its own leading-note). The sharp-eyed and -eared will notice that Ex. 26*c* is entirely built out of the opening phrases of Exx. 26*a* and *b*; and that these are, moreover, inversions of each other—which is just as things ought to be in twelve-note music!

There are no quibbles about 'tonality' in regard to the straightforward *Theme and Variations* in G minor, Op. 43. Composed in the summer of 1943, it was originally written for a forty-three piece wind band, with the 'pedagogic' purpose of

enriching the amateur bandsman's repertoire with something more substantial than the staple fare of arrangements; and Schoenberg also made a transcription for full orchestra. Neither version is much played—inexplicably, for the work's tunefulness and clear-cut traditional layout make it a most enjoyable introduction to Schoenberg in general. From many other composers it would be hailed as a major work. In Schoenberg's output its place is not particularly exalted, but he weighed up its merits pretty precisely in a letter to Fritz Reiner:

It is not one of my principal works . . . It is one of those works that one writes in order to enjoy one's own virtuosity and, in addition, to give a group of amateurs—in this case, wind bands—something better to play. I can assure you, and I think I can prove it—that as far as technique is concerned it is a masterpiece, and I believe it is also original, and I know it is also inspired. Not only because I cannot write even 10 bars without inspiration, but I really wrote the piece with great pleasure.[1]

Perhaps it is the obviousness of Schoenberg's pleasure that causes embarrassed commentators to look down their noses at the work. The unprejudiced listener is more likely to be captivated by its superb craftsmanship and sheer sense of fun. The awful solemnity of the Theme (Ex. 27*a*), whether intoned by a row of clarinets in the band version, or by solo trumpet in the orchestral one illustrated here, is beautifully undercut by the vigour and good humour of the following seven Variations and Finale. The work makes an interesting comparison with the Op. 31 Orchestral Variations—there are broad resemblances in structure, notably the expansive, multi-sectional finale, as well as many smaller similarities of technique. But whereas the earlier set more often treated its Theme in chorale-variation style, using it as a counterpoint to new subjects, in Op. 43 the main theme is always the focus of attention and we follow its metamorphosis and development in the time-honoured manner of Brahms's *Haydn Variations* or Elgar's *Enigma*. Variation 4, for instance, turns it into a waltz; in Variation 5 it becomes a sinuous cantilena which is also a canon by inversion (see Ex. 27*b*); and in Variation 6 a frisky fugue-subject.

The main subject carries its principal harmonies along with it throughout the work. As can be seen from its opening bars (Ex. 27*a*) these are unusually rich and sophisticated in their modulations; and at such moments as the climactic apotheosis of the Theme in the Finale, they undoubtedly help give the work its individual and oddly appealing flavour of rather schmaltzy grandeur.

[1] Quoted in Rufer, op. cit., p. 72.

Ex. 27

(a)

(b)

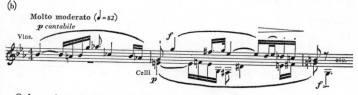

Schoenberg's final, least-known orchestral work was the result of the somewhat bizarre scheme of the Hollywood arranger, conductor and publisher Nat Shilkret to 'put the Bible on records' to musical accompaniment. This grandiose project got no further than the *Genesis Suite*—six movements for speaker, chorus and orchestra, contributed by six leading contemporary composers, financed and commissioned by Shilkret, who wrote a seventh movement himself. It was premièred in November 1945 and then quickly forgotten. Only two component numbers have maintained a precarious concert existence since then—Stravinsky's *Babel*, and the textless *Prelude*, Op. 44, which Schoenberg contributed to open the cycle.

Though short (some five minutes' duration) and difficult to mount, requiring a wordless chorus in addition to a large orchestra, the *Genesis Prelude* ranks high in Schoenberg's *œuvre* for its richness of thought and substance. Indeed it initiates the final period in his music that is typified by the high-pressure

expressiveness of the String Trio he was to write the following
year. Evidently he conceived of the Creation as the realization of
an already latent order in the universe. The opening section of
the *Prelude* is free in form, but the 'latent order' lies in its
twelve-note organization. The very beginning presents the note-
row in an ascending line, orchestrated over six octaves so that it
enacts a rise out of primeval murk (low tuba) into light (solo
violin) (Ex. 28a). Hesitant, rhythmically uncertain, various thematic shapes appear, seeming to press forward towards some more
definite form. And eventually the music emerges into a clearly
articulated structure—a fugue with a double subject (Ex. 28b).

Ex. 28

The bulk of the *Prelude* is occupied with the working-out of the
fugue in masterly counterpoint that embodies the full range of
traditional and twelve-note devices. Towards the end the
orchestra is joined by a wordless chorus, which in the final bars
soars up to a conclusion with a strongly tonal feeling—the
voices hold clear, triumphant octave Cs, dying away until only
a solo singer can be heard. Creation has been accomplished in a
mere five minutes: we have arrived at the voice of the individual
human being.

9   Chamber music

Schoenberg started learning the violin at the age of eight, and throughout his youth his most important experience of practical music-making was in playing chamber music with friends. It was hardly surprising, therefore, that his earliest compositional efforts were principally in this field; and he continued to devote a major part of his creative energies to the medium throughout his life.

During the 1890s the budding composer wrote several string quartets; only the last of these, the D major Quartet of 1897, has survived entire. A *Presto* in C major, of about 1894, may well be the rondo-finale of the quartet whose slow movement was played to Josef Labor. It is an ambitious, tuneful, eminently likeable piece, written with obvious zest and no very strong structural mastery; though even this early, Schoenberg is perfectly ready to turn his main tune upside down when he feels like it. A Scherzo and Trio in F, dated 1897, was almost certainly the original second movement of the D major Quartet, replaced by the present Intermezzo on Zemlinsky's advice.

The String Quartet in D major itself is not a negligible work, though the listener may at first distinguish the influence of the young composer's senior contemporaries more easily than the authentic voice of Schoenberg. Brahms—especially in the central movements, an Intermezzo and a Theme with Variations—was only to be expected. Dvořák and Smetana, unmistakable in the outer movements, are perhaps more surprising; but the Czech masters' quartets (even now much undervalued) were, unlike

Brahms's, among the most vital contributions to the genre in the later nineteenth century, and Schoenberg may well have found them the most fruitful contemporary examples from which to learn his trade. Certainly he is much indebted to them for the freshness and spontaneity of the tunes; and if the naïvety of the finale's main theme reminds us of Dvořák at his most rustic, it is none the worse for that. Apart from a few original touches (such as the muted *am steg* sonorities of the Intermezzo) and some prophetic turns of phrase and harmony, it is in the general melodic richness and contrapuntal dexterity that we sense the real Schoenberg. We may endorse the contemporary opinion at its first performance: this is a beautiful and promising work by a remarkably talented young man—nothing less, nothing more.

Two years later, with *Verklärte Nacht*, the promise is being amply fulfilled. On one level this single-movement string sextet is a symphonic poem after a sentimental but quite atmospheric poem from Richard Dehmel's 'Weib und Welt'. Two lovers wander among the trees on a cold moonlit night. She confesses she is pregnant, not by him, but by an earlier lover whom she took because—until now—she had believed that having a child would bring meaning, if not happiness, to her life. He, inspired to calm confidence by the beauty of the moonlit world, assures her that the love they have now found together will unite them and make the child their own; they embrace, and walk on 'through the high, bright night'. The layout of Dehmel's poem —in five sections, the woman's outburst and the man's reply framed by passages illustrating their walk in the moonlight— gives the basic form of Schoenberg's sextet, and every phrase is most sensitively illustrated in the music, from the dragging steps at the opening to the wonderfully radiant evocation of the 'transfigured night' at the close.

Yet on another level the music makes so much sense in its own terms that one hardly feels the programme to be a vital element in its structural logic, however it may have affected the initial inspiration. Maybe Schoenberg felt that the programme helped an audience to grasp a work of such ambitious scope: a half-hour symphonic movement for string instruments alone, highly emotional in expression, structurally elusive in its constant development of ever-metamorphosing thematic shapes, and above all *polyphonic* in a degree to which his hearers were quite unused.

Schoenberg's success in fulfilling this large design indicates how rapid had been his progress towards musical mastery in a mere two years. Several outside influences are still prominent —Wagner certainly, Brahms certainly, Hugo Wolf probably, Richard Strauss perhaps—but the work is thoroughly Schoen-bergian; the counterpoint has his characteristic boldness and clarity however great its elaboration, and the melodies have his distinctive plasticity. The handling of tonality over a large span is already masterly. The work's key-centre is D, minor in the first half, major in the second. But it is often quitted for remote areas; and decisive returns to D, often suggested, are almost as often suspensefully delayed. This makes the almost sententiously firm D major of the opening of the fourth section (the Man's reply) especially striking, and creates the work's main structural divi-sion, initiating a 'second movement' complementary to the first. The nocturnal loveliness of the D major ending, too, is all the more satisfying for being so long and so artfully postponed. Equally impressive, on a smaller scale, is the moment-to-moment ebb and flow of harmonic tensions from straightforward diatonicism to an already intense chromaticism, so that these opposing elements are kept in a living (because precarious) balance, melting into one another without incongruity. Ex. 29 is a good illustration—the relaxation from the very last climax (*Verklärte Nacht* does indeed, in Egon Wellesz's phrase, suffer from 'an excess of climax', but with music of such youthful ardour it is an easily-forgivable fault) towards the start of the tranquil coda.

Ex.29

The chord at (x), incidentally, is the 'single uncatalogued dissonance' for which the work was rejected in 1899. But once it reached performance *Verklärte Nacht* was not long in being accepted into the repertoire, and it remains to this day the most popular example—and no ignoble one either, if hardly typical—of Schoenberg's work. It is, however, most often heard in either of the later versions he made for full string orchestra, where the greater richness of tone is certainly an advantage, though not a decisive one, over the string sextet original.

Schoenberg's 'official' String Quartet No. 1, Op. 7 in D minor, dates from five years later. It sets out to be a masterpiece from the first bar, with a grimly determined, heaven-storming opening theme:

Ex. 30

It very nearly succeeds—certainly much of it is greater music than any he had written before. In this crucial work of his first period, he tackled the problem of writing a piece on the largest scale that dispensed with the prop of a text (as in the *Gurrelieder*) or implied literary programme (as in *Pelleas und Melisande*). In so doing, he was undoubtedly inspired not only by the large-scale forms of Wagner (who, with Brahms, profoundly influences the Quartet's language) but by those of Beethoven—not just the Beethoven of the late quartets, but of the *Eroica* symphony, a work Schoenberg acknowledged as his conscious model. The result is forty-five minutes' 'pure' music of the most highly wrought and concentrated kind—probably the largest continuous movement for string quartet that had ever been written. It is a single gigantic sonata-form, which (like *Pelleas*) expands to accommodate the semblance of a four-movement structure. A scherzo interposes between the two halves of the development section, and a 'slow movement' before the recapitulation—which, in turn, is cast in the form of a rondo with a slow epilogue-like coda, and in true Schoenbergian style continues the developmental process (of the scherzo and slow movement themes as well as the others).

That is the large-scale design. On the smaller scale the music is incredibly intricate. It has often been said, with justice, that almost every note is thematic: there is no filling-in anywhere, and the texture is usually highly contrapuntal, each instrument having something important to say—often something different from what the others are saying at the same time. The work is very rich in melody and the expressive contrasts necessary to sustain such a large conception—indeed, it packs in the widest range of style and mood that Schoenberg had so far attempted. Many aspects of it are forward-looking. The freedom of the polyphony, especially in the vast initial exposition and development, combines in places with the chromatic characteristics of certain themes to produce abrasive, linearly-determined harmonies that are already close to the world of the total-chromatic works. Schoenberg also introduces a whole range of string sounds which, though they had been used in orchestral contexts, were still new to chamber music—widespread use of harmonics, *col legno* tapping of the strings with the wood of the bow, *sul ponticello tremolandi*, contrasts between muted and unmuted playing.

It goes without saying that it is a very difficult work to play; and, in all but the best performances, an exhausting one to listen to. The explosive passion and intellectual force, daunting enough in themselves, are allied in the earlier parts of the Quartet to a certain hectoring earnestness which can seem intimidating. Schoenberg himself commented near the end of his life that he had, perhaps, demanded too much of the listener's stamina.

Nevertheless, the work presents a challenge to performers—to articulate its massive structures while bringing out the interplay of its many moods—which assures it a special place in the repertoire. For there is no lack of contrast, and many welcome moments of comparative relaxation and direct melodic appeal. One might instance how, in the first development section, a kind of hurdy-gurdy rhythm invades the music, and we hear what might almost be a snatch of some tearful Viennese street-ballad:

Ex. 31

Or there is the forthright, vaunting theme of the scherzo; or, most celebrated of all, the lovely E major viola melody from the slow movement:

Ex. 32

The latter half of the work is perhaps more approachable than the opening sections: the rate of development is not so feverish, and the harmony appears to have had the corners rubbed off it in the previous struggles—it is more familiarly tonal. This is most true of the warm, long-drawn-out epilogue in D major, where all the work's conflicts attain a resolution of untroubled calm; and where Schoenberg, with his four string instruments, closes in a romantic lushness that rivals Richard Strauss.

A few weeks after completing the Quartet, in October 1905, Schoenberg began, but did not finish, another chamber work after a Dehmel poem: *Ein Stelldichein* (A trysting-place) for oboe, clarinet, violin, cello and piano. Even more than 'Verklärte Nacht' the poem is a presentation of a guilty psychological state, similar to that of the protagonist of Schoenberg's *Erwartung*; and the music is striking enough for us to regret its non-completion. A serene, nocturnal prelude in a much-expanded E flat exists in fair copy; and a continuation—some three minutes of a turbulent *allegro* in E flat minor—survives in a sketchbook and can be played. Its hectic contrapuntal vigour is comparable to the opening moments of the First String Quartet, with some whole-tone inflections that anticipate the First Chamber Symphony.

For dramatic convenience I have briefly described the String Quartet No. 2, Op. 10, at the beginning of Chapter 1. Here I would only point to some structural features. Compared to the form of the First Quartet the Second seems highly conservative.

This reflects an obvious desire on Schoenberg's part to make its expressive idea—so intimately bound up with its exploration of new harmonic resources—as comprehensible as possible. Gone is the vast, taxing, forty-minute movement. Instead, we find the familiar four separate movements of a classical quartet, taking some twenty-eight minutes to perform; the counterpoint as masterly as ever, but not quite so involved; the textures transparent, the points of structural division obvious, the development and derivation of the themes made clear. The first movement is a concise sonata form (hardly longer to play than the First Quartet's exposition) with the order of its main themes altered in the recapitulation. The second falls clearly into the pattern of scherzo (with three contrasting themes) and trio, with 'Ach, du lieber Augustin' carrying familiarity to the point of grotesque in the transition back to the scherzo.

With the third movement we find what seems an enormous innovation—the addition of a soprano singer. But the song, 'Litany', is cast as a tightly organized set of variations, so tight that every single figure relates to the main theme, while that theme itself is built of four already-familiar figures, three from the first movement, the other from the scherzo. And at least one reason for the sung text, surely, is that it may act as an explanation, make quite explicit the kind of emotional experience implied by the music. Likewise the finale, 'Entrückung', is not just a song-setting, but a musical enactment provided with a verbal correlative. Even here, after the free-chromatic introduction evoking the 'air from other planets', Schoenberg gives the movement the layout and proportions of a sonata-form, and adds a peaceful, transfigured instrumental epilogue that puts us back on purely musical ground and closes the tonal circle in a quiet but fulfilled F sharp major. This reversion to comparatively simple, traditional structures created an important precedent: when Schoenberg came to write twelve-note works he first of all preferred to cast them, too, in classical moulds—not just because he loved the forms, but because they were positive aids to comprehensibility, and helped him to stress the continuity of tradition in his music.

I suggested in Chapter 1 that if the Second Quartet is the preface to the great upheaval of 1908–9, *Pierrot Lunaire*, Op. 21 is its ironic epilogue. 'Light, ironic, satirical' was the tone in which *Pierrot* was conceived, according to Schoenberg himself; and even if that tone is not maintained throughout, it is better to keep it in mind than to wax over-serious about this strangest and most notorious of his compositions. Elements of the Expressionist nightmare do indeed gain entrance, but the deliberate mannerism of the music's highly sculptured forms helps distance and undercut them (as does the simple, rigid structure of Guiraud's texts). The self-absorbed artist is satirized in the guise of Pierrot, the *Commedia dell'Arte* clown grown morbid aesthete, while Schoenberg's choice of ensemble invokes fleeting resemblances to a kind of surrealist cabaret act. There are five players handling eight instruments (flute and piccolo; clarinet and bass clarinet; violin and viola; cello; piano) and each of the twenty-one numbers uses a different combination of them—the full eight appear only in the very last. While the instrumentalists convey the musical substance, the poems—and much of the work's disturbing effect—are delivered by a female reciter employing the device known as *Sprechstimme* ('speech-song').

Towards the end of the nineteenth century several composers had sought to control the interaction of a speaking voice with a musical accompaniment, not only rhythmically but in terms of pitch—as Schoenberg himself did in the monodrama of the *Gurrelieder*. In *Pierrot*, however, he went further, writing a melodic line for vocal declamation in which the speaking voice must momentarily touch the indicated pitch, then rise or fall away from it in a *glissando*—it should resemble neither song nor a sing-song manner of speaking. The precise interpretation of Schoenberg's instructions has often been found difficult: they imply *relative* pitch, a free voice-line, yet he notates *exact* pitches, and at certain points exact pitches are indeed necessary for motivic interplay with the ensemble. Nevertheless, many artists have attempted the work with a fair degree of success—there is no sign of this problem driving it out of the repertoire, where it remains more firmly entrenched than most other Schoenberg works.

Pierrot is divided into three parts of seven numbers each. Part I is nearest to the 'light, ironical, satirical' ideal: a series of character portraits and nocturnes in which—as throughout the cycle—the moon is a silent, omnipresent influence. In Part II the nightmare takes over, with the vision of giant moths, blotting out the sun with their wings, and proceeds to explore images of violence, guilt and retribution. In Part III it gradually ebbs away again, and a nostalgia enters verses and music: Pierrot travels home to Bergamo, and the poet, liberated, awakes to 'the ancient scent of far-off days'. The various numbers sum up in microcosm the experience of the earlier total-chromatic works. The fixed form of Guiraud's thirteen-line rondels (in which lines 1 and 2 recur as 7 and 8, and 1 again as 13) bestows brevity, and often induces elements of musical recapitulation as well. But the forms are free for the most part—No. 13, 'Enthauptung' (Beheading) is, indeed, an example of a freely evolving form like Op. 11 No. 3 or Op. 16 No. 5; the strict organization of the passacaglia 'Nacht' (No. 8) or the contrapuntal miracle 'Der Mondfleck' (No. 18), though indicative of future developments, is the exception rather than the rule. The cycle presents, rather, a series of fantastic or lyrical musical images—the sweet and skittish violin solo of 'Columbine' (No. 2); the pale, stylized waltz of 'Valse de Chopin' (No. 5); 'Der kranke Mond' (The Sick Moon), in which the reciter is accompanied only by a mournful solo flute (No. 7); the extreme emotionality of 'Die Kreuze' (The Crosses, No. 14); 'Serenade' (No. 19) with its superb and virtuosic cello solo (see Ex. 33);

Ex.33

the gentle barcarolle of 'Heimfahrt' (Homeward Journey), and the infinitely tender awakening, with its hint of tonality regained, of 'O alter Duft'.

The *Serenade*, Op. 24 is, as its title suggests, one of Schoenberg's most relaxed and ingratiating scores. It was begun in 1920, but the bulk of the music dates from 1923. It thus spans the final stages of the period of searching that led to the adoption of the twelve-note method, and the music's warmth and gaiety surely bear witness to a certain relief and return of confidence as the way ahead began to seem clear and certain. The work is in seven characterful movements, of which several use various kinds of serial technique, for the most part unobtrusively. The ensemble consists of seven instruments—clarinet, bass clarinet, mandolin, guitar and string trio—with the addition of a bass or baritone soloist in the fourth movement. The sound-world recalls not only the more clownish moments of *Pierrot Lunaire*, but also the near-contemporary chamber works of other composers—notably Stravinsky's *Ragtime* and *The Soldier's Tale*—and some commentators have claimed to detect a jazz influence; but to this hearer at least, the confection is entirely and engagingly Austrian.

The first movement is a jaunty march in a telescoped sonata-form, the lead most often being taken by the clarinets while mandoline, guitar and strings add pattering or *pizzicato* rhythmic figures that seem to tumble over each other with enthusiasm. There follows a gracefully poised minuet and less well-mannered trio with a viola solo whose acerbities recall the 'Serenade' movement of *Pierrot Lunaire*. The third movement is a set of five variations and coda on a ruminative theme (of eleven bars length, using eleven tones of the chromatic scale arranged in a fourteen-note series) announced by unaccompanied clarinet in its lowest register. Though the variations preserve the proportions of the parent theme, they are notable for their rhythmic flexibility and textural inventiveness.

The only strictly twelve-note movement is the fourth, a vehement setting of Petrarch's Sonnet No. 217 ('If I could take revenge on her'). The method is somewhat primitively applied, as the voice part consists of thirteen rotations of the original untransposed row, while the ensemble derives accompanimental figures more freely from the same source. It requires extremely sensitive singing to avoid the impression that it inhabits a lower level of inspiration than the other movements. The work's most expansive section follows—the delightful 'Dance-Scene', whose design is enlarged (as in some other movements) by the use of formal repeats. Two principal dance-characters are alternated—a lively, capricious waltz and a delicately soulful Austrian *ländler*, complete with Mahlerian cuckoo-calls in the tune:

Ex. 34

The sixth movement is a Song without Words, a hushed twenty-six bar miniature of rapt beauty, through whose muted textures a wide-spanned melody gracefully arches its way. Then the seventh movement, a potpourri using the first movement's march as a basis and 'recessional', passes themes from the other movements in affectionate review (with the *ländler* Ex. 34 much in evidence) and brings the work to an end in high good humour.

If the *Serenade* is one of Schoenberg's most likeable works, his next chamber composition, the Wind Quintet (1923–4), is one of the most forbidding. It is the first really large-scale twelve-note work, and the first piece since the Second Quartet in which he felt himself able to return fully to the classical forms of the eighteenth- and nineteenth-century masters which meant so much to him. He celebrates the return with an extended display of compositional virtuosity which to many listeners makes the Quintet one of his most 'abstract' pieces. It is not really so, but it *does* pose difficulties. Wind Quintets tend, on the whole, to be shorter than chamber works for strings, for simple reasons of breath-control and audience stamina. Schoenberg's is over forty minutes long, in four big movements, and is extremely difficult to play. It follows that really well-rehearsed, affectionate, ingratiating performances are rare—and anything below a very high standard of playing tends to become an assault on the ear.

Moreover, this is one of the few cases where the harmonic aspect of the music seems to be almost entirely subordinated to the thematic, polyphonic employment of the twelve-note method. I say 'seems' because it would in fact be very difficult to prove, and the work does actually suggest an overall key-centre —a good one for wind instruments, E flat. But in the nature of things a quintet of flute, oboe, clarinet, horn and bassoon does not blend with anything like the smoothness of a string quartet: the ear is bound to pick out the individual lines in any chord, as much as the homogenous entity. The music, then, is as intensely contrapuntal as most other Schoenberg, but the medium magnifies our awareness of the fact while diminishing our perception of the harmonic sense which holds the intertwining lines in balance. In addition, to an extent rare in Schoenberg, the music does not often present explicit melodies; rather, various kinds of polyphonic texture.

It is, in sum, a fascinating work (and in the rare first-rate performance a most enjoyable one), full of contrasts of colour and mood, but one feels he had not yet assimilated the twelve-note method into his natural style as perfectly as he may have believed. The first movement (*Schwungvoll*) has the proportions of a broad, reflective, sonata-form. The second is a good-natured, rather heavy-footed scherzo with a livelier trio, and the calm slow movement (*Etwas langsam*) is in ternary song-form. The most immediately appealing movement is undoubtedly the rondo-finale, not least because its perky main theme (announced at the outset by clarinet) gives a more clearly melodic and rhythmic basis to the music and is easily recognizable at each return. At the very end of the work, too, Schoenberg suddenly relaxes the apparent harmonic saturation: he liquidates the twelve-note row into the chains of ascending and descending fourths of which he was so fond, and achieves thereby a beautifully terse, biting final cadence into E flat (Ex. 35).

The Suite for seven instruments, Op. 29, raises some of the problems demonstrated by the Wind Quintet in an even more acute form. It is one of Schoenberg's wittiest and warmest-

Ex.35

hearted works: but an inadequate performance infallibly turns it into an arid, sour-toned endurance test. Partly it is a question of the ensemble. The combination of E-flat clarinet, B-flat clarinet, bass clarinet, piano and string trio can easily be a hard, unblending one. The technical difficulties are as uncompromising as ever, and there is an added stylistic problem. The work is dominated by dance-rhythms of various kinds, but Schoenberg tends to play the music off *against* these rhythms by highly sophisticated shifts of accent, cross-rhythms, sprung rhythms, syncopation and off-beat entries. When the players are able to sense and convey this tension and interplay between the apparent and actual pulse, it adds tremendous rhythmic life to the music. But if they are just occupied in counting the beats (which fly by very quickly!) and in playing their own notes, then scramble and confusion ensue.

The work, composed between 1924 and 1926, was a kind of wedding present for Schoenberg's second wife, Gertrud. He originally planned a seven-movement, *Serenade*-like piece, including a waltz and a foxtrot; but in the event the Suite comprised four large-scale, highly developed movements of a pronounced dance-character. As in the Quintet, a key-centre of E flat is discernible; the construction of the twelve-note row enabled him to begin and end each movement with figures including the notes G and E flat (S) for 'Gertrud Schoenberg'. The 'classical' sounds of thirds and sixths are derived directly from the row's salient intervallic properties. The row had more valuable constructional characteristics, however: it is here that Schoenberg's practice of combining different, related row-forms really begins in earnest.

The first movement, 'Ouverture', is a bright and vigorous piece: it resembles a sonata-form with a big ternary exposition, but the 'drunken waltz' (see Ex. 11*b* in Chapter 6) takes the place of the development proper and returns after the recapitulation (which has been thoroughly developmental) in the coda. The next movement, 'Tanzschritte' (Dance-steps) is a fiery, rather sardonic character-piece, resembling if anything a highly stylized polka. The pace is fast and furious for the most part, but the coda is quieter, more reflective. The third movement, a Theme with Variations, is usually treated as a 'curiosity' of twelve-note music, instead of the straightforward piece of splendid music-making it is. The theme is a perfectly tonal one in E major: a Schoenbergian adaptation of a tune well known in Germany as 'Ännchen von Tharau'—no folksong, as is sometimes stated, but the work of the composer Friedrich Silcher (1789–1860). Schoenberg presents it on bass clarinet, which picks out the requisite notes from the piano's chattering twelve-note accompaniment. The four variations never stray far from the source-melody, but are strongly contrasted: and the third, with its dreamy high clarinet line, crystalline piano figuration, violin harmonics and *col legno* pattering from the other strings, is music of ethereal beauty. The finale is a Gigue with elements of a fugue and the proportions of a sonata-form. Here Schoenberg' rhythmic dislocations are at their most developed, and the move ment is either invigorating or messy depending on the performance. There is a beautifully delicate reminiscence of the above-mentioned third variation (with elements of the first movement intermingled) before the agile coda, which concludes with a reference to the Suite's very opening.

Schoenberg's next work, the Third String Quartet, Op. 30 (1927), is one of the most poised and serene he ever wrote, 'classical' in spirit as well as in form. If less colourful and dramatic than the other quartets, the Third gains a special place in the listener's affections through its positive, optimistic character, its lucidity of thought, its unfailing melodiousness and lyric grace. And again a 'tonal centre'—of C—is discernible. It is much less simple a work than it first seems, but its emotional complexities are hinted at, not directly stated.

There are four movements. Schoenberg regarded the first (*Moderato*) as unorthodox in layout, though there are few obstacles to regarding it as a beautifully proportioned sonata form. Doubtless the composer was thinking of the running quaver motion, presented at the very outset in an eight-note *ostinato* pattern in second violin and viola, which—though it assumes many guises—courses through almost every bar of the movement, and against which the graceful, long-breathed melodies we think of as first and second subjects are continually played off. In fact, it is exactly this quaver motion which gives the movement its 'classical' sense of athletic, uninterrupted flow, and welds it into a satisfying whole.

The *Adagio* second movement is a blend of rondo and variations. Two calmly expressive themes alternate, but are much transformed at each appearance. The second has a characteristic *staccato* accompaniment, which as the movement proceeds brings to mind a suggestion of distant marching. The third movement is labelled an Intermezzo, but is a straightforward scherzo and trio, the scherzo's elegant opening theme preserving something of the character of a minuet. The finale is a spirited sonata-rondo, with the same sense of 'classical' momentum as the first movement: a vigorous main theme alternates with a smoothly lyrical cantilena in which the cello is prominent in its high register, and a more rhythmic episode that may recall the march-like music of the *Adagio*. In the coda, Schoenberg dissolves this brilliant and charming Quartet into a final, ambling *ostinato*.

The Third Quartet was commissioned by the great American patroness of chamber music, Elizabeth Sprague Coolidge (who also provided the proximate cause of some of the finest works of Bartók, Frank Bridge, Hindemith, Prokofiev, Stravinsky and Webern, among others). In 1936, when Schoenberg was living in the U.S.A., she repeated her commission. The result was the String Quartet No. 4, Op. 37—a work of rare mastery, rich in substance and magnificent in its craftsmanship. Again we find the traditional four-movement layout, but the scale is larger than in the Third Quartet. The range of expression, too, is much wider—this is a dramatic work, full of contrasts of character and pace, often tough and hard-bitten in sound, but holding its component parts in a dynamic equilibrium that prepares the way for a sanely optimistic finale without unnecessary heroics. In character it most resembles the Violin Concerto on which Schoenberg was engaged at the same period. To largeness of gesture is allied more far-reaching use of string harmonics, *col legno* playing and other effects, which had been almost entirely eschewed in No. 3.

The first movement (*Allegro molto, energico*) can be likened to a sonata-form, though Schoenberg again disdained the identification. Certainly there are two contrasting thematic groups, but in retrospect the movement seems dominated by the downright utterance of the theme announced at the very outset (Ex. 36*a*). This powers the argument with passionate force, and the whole movement has an irresistible momentum which is, nevertheless, very different from the easy onward-spinning motion of the Third Quartet. The music is much more strenuous and volatile, as would befit a work in Schoenberg's favourite D minor—and indeed D seems to be the suggested key-centre, in Ex. 36a as in many other passages.

The second movement (*Comodo*) is an intermezzo—a large-scale, dance-like piece in 3/4 with a somewhat faster trio in 2/2. Lighter moods predominate here, but they are subtle, not superficial ones. The outer sections might be a minuet or *ländler*, but their soft-stepping rhythms convey no hint of nostalgia—rather a tense, alert vitality to which the use of harmonics and *sul ponticello* playing adds a touch of the light fantastic. The *Largo* slow movement begins with a tragic, declamatory theme for all four instruments in unison (Ex. 36b—it uses a transposition of the original row as found in Ex. 36a): its improvisatory, chant-like nature might just possibly be the sublimation of some memory of Hebrew cantillation.

Ex.36

(a)

This introduces a bipartite movement in whose first half the first violin more than once attempts a florid, impassioned cadenza in the spirit of Ex. 36*b*. That theme returns, inverted, to announce the second half, which begins with a thoughtful fugato and gradually binds rebellious elements into a threnodic but calmer unity.

The finale (*Allegro*) contrasts two principal ideas, characterized by their respective markings *amabile* and *agitato*. Both are march-like, and for all its resemblances to sonata-rondo the movement might best be described as an extended march (a feature of several Schoenberg works of the period, cf. the Violin Concerto, *Kol Nidre* and the Piano Concerto). Passing through many vicissitudes in a particularly eventful and wide-ranging development, the movement strives for and eventually attains a mood of quiet confidence which the gentle *calando* coda confirms.

The *Ode to Napoleon Buonaparte*, Op. 41 of 1942, is a setting for string quartet, piano and reciter of a poem by Lord Byron whose 171 lines are a *tour-de-force* of unbridled sarcasm, kindled by disgust at Napoleon's capitulation in 1814. The parallel with Hitler in 1942 (still very much in command in Germany) was hardly exact, but doubtless Schoenberg saw in Byron's text an opportunity to express his own loathing of contemporary totalitarian dictatorship; that he set the last stanza (which Byron excised from his final version of the poem) with its reference to Washington, 'the Cincinnatus of the West', perhaps indicates his faith in eventual victory, and pays a compliment to the country that had now been his home for eight years.

By nature Schoenberg was superbly equipped to compose music for this outpouring of passionate scorn. He gives the reciter the freer and simpler form of heightened declamation he favoured in his last works, in which pitches are only approximately indicated by reference to a central stave-line, but the rhythms are exactly notated, the general shape of phrases delineated, and more minute vocal inflections suggested by sharps and flats. The form of the work is free, though several principal motives recur and are developed—the welter of images borne along on the flood of Byron's tirade is reflected at every stage in the twists and turns of Schoenberg's coruscating stream of musical thought. The range of instrumental colour is very wide, and includes some highly memorable effects—for instance, the words 'but who would soar the solar height, to set in such an endless night?' are illustrated by an eerie, downward-swooping *glissando* in harmonics, played *sul ponticello, col legno* on viola and cello.

The *Ode* is a twelve-note work, but the most traditionally 'tonal' in sound that Schoenberg ever wrote. Its note-row allowed the formation of plentiful triadic chords: moreover, he here relaxed his customary vigilance against octave doublings, and began to re-order the notes of the row's two hexachords with unprecedented licence, concentrating more on its characteristic interval structure than on an unalterable succession of tones. The result is often close to the harmonic world of the 'late tonal' works such as *Kol Nidre*, and the *Ode* at several points suggests—and finally cadences triumphantly into—the key of E flat major. Its use is perhaps ironic—recalling the key of the *Eroica*, which Beethoven originally dedicated to Napoleon; and unmistakably ironic is the music for the line 'the earthquake voice of victory', where Schoenberg quotes the opening motive of Beethoven's Fifth Symphony!

In August 1946 Schoenberg suffered the near-fatal heart-attack mentioned in Chapter 4—and shortly afterwards, in a great burst of creative energy, wrote what many consider one of his greatest works, the String Trio, Op. 45. Thomas Mann records a conversation about it with the composer in October of that year:

He told me about the new trio he had just completed, and about the experiences he had secretly woven into the composition—experiences of which the work was a kind of fruit. He had, he said, represented his illness and medical treatment in the music, including even the male nurses and all the other oddities of American hospitals. The work was extremely difficult to play, he said, in fact almost impossible, or at best only for three players of virtuoso rank; but, on the other hand, the music was very rewarding because of its extraordinary tonal effects.[1]

It would be misguided, even so, to regard the Trio as too exclusively a 'fruit' of Schoenberg's 'temporary death' (he had, in fact, begun sketching it two months before the attack)—to regard it as pathological programme music or a musical medical report. Indeed, although Schoenberg later told Adolph Weiss that he had even depicted the entry of the hypodermic needle, the present writer sees no point in hunting out such details. The music is simply not comprehensible in those terms. It is enough to know that it reflects an experience of extreme physical and mental disorientation—and reflects it brilliantly, in violent dissonance and rhythmic disruption, the most intensive use Schoenberg ever made of 'extraordinary tonal effects' with string instruments, and above all, the fragmentation of melodic material. The freedom of form and expression is of an order Schoenberg had scarcely approached since *Erwartung*.

To seek to encompass such a desperate experience and give it artistic form is not necessarily morbid; first and foremost, it is the most convincing demonstration of being alive, of not having succumbed to disaster. Even so, the Trio would be a lesser work than it is were that *all* it contained. Rather, the physical catastrophe appears to have impelled Schoenberg to produce a creative statement that would sum up, in the most concentrated form, the essential aspects of his art. It is, therefore, not only the most adventurous piece he ever wrote, stylistically, structurally and in its application of the twelve-note method. It also enshrines the deepest contrasts. For every nightmarish passage of hammered chords, clicking *col legno* bowing or glassy harmonics, there is one of profound peace or reflective tenderness—and it is

[1] *The Genesis of a Novel* (London, 1961, translated by Richard and Clara Winston), p. 172.

these elements, eventually, which are left unchallenged at the end. Though the 'revolutionary' aspects of the Trio have claimed most of the attention of commentators, it is the work's expressive *totality* that is the most impressive thing about it. The point can hardly be better illustrated than by quoting the opening two bars, and the beginning of the second main section (Exx. 37*a* and *b* respectively):

Ex. 37

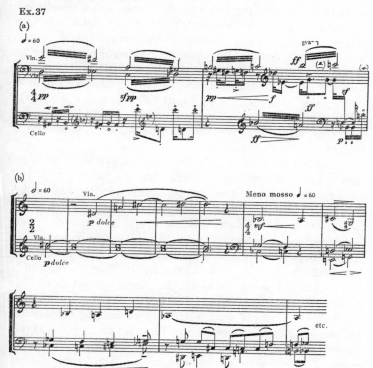

The Trio returns to the single-movement form of Schoenberg's early works, but in a new way. The structure has five

spans, three 'Parts' divided by two 'Episodes'. Part 1 and the
First Episode together comprise what may loosely be termed the
exposition. But we cannot think in terms of first and second
subjects: motives there are in plenty, but they are short, and
uncompromisingly juxtaposed—it is their manner of presentation, most of all, which characterizes these first two sections.
Part 1, with Ex. 37a, plunges us into a fantastic world in which
we seem to have lost our bearings completely. Trills, *tremolandi*,
harmonics, rhythmic figures, snatches of melody, motivic blocks
—graphic images and outbursts of frightening intensity—are
flung, apparently at random, upon the listener. We seem to be at
the centre of a psychological storm. But when Episode I begins
we are confronted with something familiar, even comforting—a
serene rising phrase on the violin, in a clear A major (Ex. 37b).
The Episode then continues with more calm, pacifying material
—though it is some time before an extended melodic statement
appears.

Part 2 and the Second Episode can be viewed as a 'development'. Part 2 attempts to continue the tranquil moods of the
First Episode, and for the most part succeeds. Ex. 13, in Chapter
6, is a good example of the warmth and gentleness of much of the
music: its sound-world seems almost to approach that of the late
Beethoven quartets—and, considering the circumstances of its
composition, it is not wholly fanciful to see in passages such as
Ex. 13 a Schoenbergian equivalent of the 'Heiliger Dankgesang'.
In the Second Episode, however, the frenzied, disruptive music
regains the upper hand, and explodes with new force at the outset of Part 3. This final section begins as a drastically compressed
recapitulation of Part 1 and the First Episode: Exx. 37a and b both
return verbatim, other bars are much altered, others simply disappear—Schoenberg concentrates on the most striking images of
the earlier music. But a final fury of the 'psychological storm'
gives way to one of Schoenberg's most consolatory codas. A
lyrical melody that first emerged in Part 2 is heard *cantabile* in the

violin's highest register, shining through a halo of harmonics from viola and cello, before the work floats light as thistledown to a quiet, undemonstrative close of profound calm; the Expressionist nightmare has finally been transcended.

Schoenberg's last instrumental work, the *Phantasy*, Op. 47, 'for violin with piano accompaniment' followed three years later in 1949. The phrasing of the title is significant: the violin is the dominating instrument throughout, and Schoenberg actually composed the whole violin line before writing a note for the piano. There could be few clearer illustrations of the primacy of *melody* in his music, and the *Phantasy* is one of his most uninhibited demonstrations of melodic prowess. Ex. 38*b* below, for instance, is merely the opening of a beautifully sly waltz-tune. The String Trio's traits of galvanic energy and extreme expressive diversity are maintained, while Schoenberg's concern to compress several movements into one attains its ultimate refinement. There are five distinct sections, and the work lasts about eight minutes.

Ex.38

The first section, an impassioned, declamatory *Grave*, is given a much-curtailed recapitulation in the last. The three central episodes each have their distinctive characters: a sweeter *Lento* melody, a dance-like *Grazioso* and a tough, vitally rhythmic *Scherzando*. Commentators seem agreed that there are no connections, apart from rather technical serial ones, between these three and the outer sections; but the ear is likely to perceive some nonetheless. Take the violin's opening pronouncement (Ex. 38*a*), which returns to close the first section. Compare the start of the *Grazioso* (Ex. 38*b*): certainly the mood is different, intervallic correspondence is not exact—but the similarity of shape and gesture are sufficient to establish an audible relationship. Likewise the slightly later chorale-like melody (Ex. 38*c*), beginning with the same attention-claiming repeated-note figure as *a* and *b*, is not just an inversion of Ex. 38*a*'s intervallic content, but also a perfectly audible broadening-out of the first section's second main theme (Ex. 38*d*). Moreover, much of the *Scherzando* section could be regarded as a playful elaboration of that repeated-note figure with which *a*, and the work, begins: a feature which reaches its apotheosis in a fusillade of repeated Ds in the final section. These audible similarities help clarify the work's unity for the listener. Perhaps it was this very freedom, this lack of formal constraint on his invention, that Schoenberg was indicating when he called this mercurial work *Phantasy*.

Schoenberg was no pianist, and showed no especial interest in the piano in his first mature works except as accompaniment to the voice. His earliest pianistic attempts have little distinction—witness the gauche, sub-Mendelssohnian, but withal rather like-able *Lied ohne Worte* of about 1890. A set of Three Piano Pieces of 1894 are not unskilful (if still not very pianistic) essays in an effusive late-Romantic style, leaning especially on Brahms's late Capricci and Intermezzi—at that time the latest thing in piano music. Though somewhat heavy-handed, they are musically in no way contemptible—least of all the third, a *Presto* in A minor. Some tuneful, rather Schubertian four-hand pieces of 1896 bene-fit from their distinctly modest formal ambitions. At this stage of his development, clearly, Schoenberg was more at ease in writing for voices or strings.

Yet the first true totally-chromatic work was the epoch-making *Three Piano Pieces* Op. 11, of 1909. It may be that entry into this new musical region, as well as the experience gained in the accompaniments of *Das Buch der hängenden Gärten*, had liberated Schoenberg from any inhibitions about the instrument: for the new harmonic vocabulary dictated an entirely new kind of pianism, in which he need fear no competitors, and could have no peers.

Yet inevitably, in a composer so creatively concerned with tradition, the 'newness' is only relative. Through the keyboard layout and emotional content of Op. 11 we still discern the influence of late Brahms. The deep basses, massive chords, syncopations and cross-rhythms—these are all Brahmsian features, but employed within a totally-chromatic context their effect is quite different. It is a totally thematic context too, so that Brahms's usually detailed motivic working is extended by Schoenberg to virtually every figure.

Beyond the broad stylistic similarities these are three very different compositions. They all, none the less, convey a sense of a frontier having been irrevocably crossed, and a definite choice of roads now lying open. Nos. 1 and 2 take paths which never entirely lose sight of the frontier: some at least of their powerful elegiac effect derives from the extent to which they are still haunted by tonal functions. In No. 2 this produces an extreme tension—we feel the opening F-D pedal in the bass ought to define a key-centre, while the melodic line does its best to reject the implication:

Ex. 39

Instead the dragging 'pedal', recurring again and again, becomes a motive in its own right, an obsessive, sinister force binding to earth the music's flights of passion; and back to which it must sink, exhausted, after a tremulous, fluttering $f\!f$ climax in high register. No. 1 is more tranquil, more self-determining in its total thematicism—tonality here is at most a distant memory of *Tristan*. The third piece, by contrast, troubles nothing about what music once was, but lunges out boldly into new regions. This is the earliest (and one of the most radical) of Schoenberg's attempts to discover a new formal imperative that could direct the new language of total chromaticism. While the other pieces display more traditional elements of development and recapitulation, Op. 11 No. 3 is cast as a continuously—apparently intuitively—unfolding sequence of diverse, self-contained ideas. None of them is repeated, each functions as a little 'development section' on its own, and progress to the next seems principally the result of accumulated momentum: a momentum created by the rate of discharge of musical thought. Schoenberg imposes a unity, a linear sequence, upon a string of tenuously related events almost by sheer will-power—from the explosive chords of the opening to the cryptic diminuendo with which the piece ends. Only in *Erwartung* was he to succeed in something comparable on the largest scale, for the self-contained 'non-tonal' fragment has a fatal tendency to act as an expressive end in itself.

The problem is seen most clearly in the *Six Little Piano Pieces*, Op. 19, of 1911, which are the briefest of miniatures. No. 1, the longest, occupies only eighteen bars, the shortest (Nos. 2 and 3) nine each. They illustrate the stubborn self-sufficiency of the material with which Schoenberg was trying to work in his larger compositions; the pregnancy of each phrase, the hyper-emotional concern with the passing moment that is such a feature of musical 'Expressionism'. This was what Webern turned into such a virtue in his own music. But Schoenberg's struggle, at this period, was almost always to wrest larger forms from the intense fragments, and for him such a lapse into epigram is rare. After hearing these pieces we may detect the note of personal experience in the famous preface he wrote for the 1924 publication of Webern's *Bagatelles* for string quartet. 'Think what self-denial is necessary', he says there, 'to cut a long story so short . . . to convey a novel in a single gesture, or happiness by one catch of the breath.'

However, the language of Op. 19 is not Webernian. Rather these pieces present an extreme distillation of the expressive essence that informs Op. 11, isolating single elements in simpler, more delicate textures, pinning them down like a butterfly to a board. Perhaps the most moving of the six is the last, with its two tolling bell-like chords that sound throughout the piece. Schoenberg wrote it after accompanying Mahler's coffin to the graveside. This, too, speaks volumes in a 'catch of the breath'—a sigh (*ein Hauch*):

Ex.40

The *Five Piano Pieces*, Op. 23 and the *Suite for Piano*, Op. 25 were composed concurrently between 1920 and 1923, at the crucial period of Schoenberg's creative life when he was moving at last into 'composition with twelve notes related only to each other'. The fifth piece of Op. 23, a Waltz, was the first twelve-note composition to be published (in November 1923); but the Prelude of Op. 25, not published till June 1925, was the first twelve-note piece Schoenberg actually composed (in July 1921) —the one of which he spoke to Josef Rufer in Traunkirchen. Whereas the twelve-note Waltz exists in Op. 23 alongside music in less rigorous style, the *Suite* was the first entire work to be derived from one note-row.

In fact, all the other Op. 23 pieces exhibit serial procedures, since each is founded on a little row or rows containing a varying number of notes (the maximum number, in the second piece, is ten). Naturally enough this interesting evolutionary stage in Schoenberg's language has, like the non-serial movements of the

Op. 24 *Serenade*, tended to bulk larger in importance for most commentators than the expressive content of the pieces themselves.

The piano style of Op. 23 is now far removed from the Brahmsian archetype. The textures are translucent, and Schoenberg uses the whole range of the keyboard with a delicacy that suggests a kind of 'Expressionist Impressionism'. Though complex in structure, conveying a succession of fleeting moods with great subtlety, these pieces are more objective than the intense Opp. 11 and 19—each has a touch of the light-fantastic about it. The first (*Sehr langsam*), with its calm, flowing onward movement, is a three-part invention, spinning its chromatic counterpoint with Bach-like tranquillity. The second (*Sehr rasch*) is a small-scale sonata-form exposition and development; but the listener is more likely to hear it first of all as a succession of vigorous upward-rushing figures, rising to a brief climax and ending with a slow coda that reverses the direction and sinks down once more into the depths.

No. 3 (*Langsam*) is the longest, the most extensively developed, and the most lyrical of the *Five Pieces*. It could almost be a nocturne, with its shimmering trills and gleams of luminous piano colour. In this piece Schoenberg's keyboard writing attains a crystal clarity that even Ravel might have admired:

Ex.41

The fourth piece (*Schwungvoll*) is the scherzo of the set, in which no less than five note-cells are pulled about in a concentrated and capricious development. It rises to an impassioned central climax, from which the music relaxes progressively to a surprisingly tender close.

The last piece, the famous twelve-note Waltz, is hardly a waltz for dancing to, but rather a highly stylized fantasy in waltz-time, not without a hint of affectionate parody. It comes to a gently poetic end, evanescing in a repeated trill that suggests curtains stirred in the draughts of a deserted ballroom.

The dance-models for the various movements of the Op. 25 *Suite* are much more obvious, both in rhythm and formal layout. Indeed on first acquaintance it seems odd to find this 'revolutionary' twelve-note music comfortably accommodated in ancient ternary structures, complete with formal repeat sections. From 'Expressionist Impressionism' we appear to have moved into 'Serial Neoclassicism'. But that is not the real state of affairs: the work is not 'Neo-' anything. Unlike the venture into total chromaticism, in which every further step he took was fraught with imponderable dangers, the discovery of the twelve-note method provided Schoenberg with a law by which his music could live—and, as Goethe once remarked, it is only in laws that we find true freedom. It is more likely that, just as he confined himself throughout the *Suite* to only four forms of the note-row, at first he needed the strict design of the old forms simply to 'put a brake' on his fertility of invention while he worked out the implications of the new style.

Perhaps this is why, for all its significant position in musical history, the *Suite* is not a particularly heavyweight work. The central Intermezzo inhabits again the subtle world of the Op. 23 pieces. For the rest, it is a sardonic divertimento 'im Alten/Neuen Stil', a witty recreation of the Bachian keyboard suite in twentieth-century guise (the twelve-note row actually includes the B-A-C-H motive). The Präludium, with its repeated notes and semiquaver flourishes, poses as an updated Baroque toccata; and the gawky Gavotte, tripping Musette (using a tritone instead of a perfect fifth as a drone bass), the periwigged Minuet with its sternly professorial canonic Trio, and the wildly abandoned Gigue all display Schoenberg's musical humour at its best. The element of parody is obvious enough in some of his late tonal works: the respect in which the twelve-note ones are held ought not to prevent us from acknowledging it in some of them as well.

Yet perhaps Schoenberg's ripest music for solo piano has tended to be eclipsed by the historical importance of Op. 25. His last two piano pieces, written in 1928 and 1931 and published as Op. 33A and 33B respectively, are not epoch-making. But each is a grand synthesis of the best aspects of the preceding piano works. Each might stand as a concert item on its own, for they are broadly similar in layout—each has two principal subjects which are extensively developed in true Schoenbergian manner, but kept distinct and recognizable throughout. As a pair, the pieces make a fine twentieth-century counterpart to Brahms's Two Rhapsodies, Op. 79.

Their language, though twelve-note, has something of the late-Romantic warmth and tonal suggestiveness of Op. 11—but viewed with the 'objectivity' of the Op. 23 pieces and the *Suite*, and expressed in piano writing that matches theirs in gracefulness, though it has a richer, mellower texture. Thus Op. 33A and B emerge as at once the subtlest and most relaxed of Schoenberg's piano pieces. Here the composer has no need of strict dance-forms to discipline his inventiveness—nor indeed of any narrow view of twelve-note 'orthodoxy': in Op. 33, as in the other works of his Berlin years, it is rapidly becoming clear that serialism is precisely what Schoenberg makes of it. Opus 33A, for instance, announces its row not as a melodic idea but as a lush succession of four-note chords, which are only given melodic identity towards the end of the piece. Opus 33B, after an ambling opening that states *its* row in the clearest possible terms, passes on to an amiable idea in which, because of plentiful note-repetition, key-feeling is very strong:

Ex.42

pp molto staccato

This kind of passage points forward to the more euphonious harmonic world of some of Schoenberg's later compositions, which is only one reason why the two pieces of Op. 33 are among his most representative works, and a good introduction to his many-sided art.

Much fine piano music still lay ahead—in the *Ode to Napoleon* and the Piano Concerto—but no more solo pieces. Instead, and rather ironically, Schoenberg's largest keyboard composition was for the organ, an instrument with which he had only limited sympathy. As early as 1907 he had criticized the Romantic-style organ of the day for its tendency to obscure the different voices in contrapuntal music and its inability to make any but the roughest alteration in dynamics. The same viewpoint underlies his orchestral arrangements of Bach organ works. Later he envisaged the appearance of a much more adaptable machine, somewhat on the lines of the present-day electronic synthesizer. Nevertheless, a commission from the publisher of a series of contemporary organ works led Schoenberg, in 1941, to essay two pieces whose musical content far outweighs their occasional conflicts with the limitations of their specified medium.

The first, an Organ Sonata, was never finished. But its largest fragment—a substantial portion of a *Moderato* first movement—has been played and published, and other hands have attempted its completion. A rhythmically lively, quite light-textured piece, with some virtuoso writing that anticipates the style of the Piano Concerto, it shows a marked preoccupation, harmonically and melodically, with chains of perfect fourths *à la* Chamber Symphony No. 1. There is also a short fragment of another movement (an *Allegretto* with a delightfully waltz-like main theme) and brief sketches for at least two more. However, for reasons which remain obscure, Schoenberg abandoned the Sonata and fulfilled the commission instead with the *Variations on a Recitative*, Op. 40—a massive work comprising a theme, ten variations, an unbarred 'cadenza' and a freely fugal finale, which stands in the great tradition of such works as Brahms's *Variations and Fugue on a Theme of Handel*.

Whereas the unfinished Sonata is a twelve-note work, the *Variations* inhabits a highly chromatic D minor. This does not mean the latter is the less 'dissonant' work: if anything, the reverse is the case. The harmonic world is much the same; the theme of the *Variations* (which includes all twelve notes) shares some features with the Sonata's note-row, and there is again a marked predilection for chains of fourths in melody and har-mony. The rate of modulation is quite as high as in most twelve-note works, and in fact Schoenberg employs quasi-serial organization of pitch in this faintly more traditional tonal context. The real difference is that the 'tonal' work is much denser in texture, darker and more violent in character, than the twelve-note one.

The opening of the so-called 'Recitative'—a complex, rather declamatory theme comprising seven short independently variable phrases—closely recalls the sinister motif (also in D minor) of Waldemar's midnight song ('unhallowed spirits rise from forgotten graves') in the *Gurrelieder* (see Ex. 15*b*, p. 97). Not only the 'Recitative', but also two subsidiary motifs intro-duced in the first variation, are exhaustively developed through-out the work in some of the most elaborate contrapuntal complexes (in up to seven voices) found in Schoenberg's entire output. Despite the greatly diversified character of the variations, the prevailing mood is grim and uneasy. When the music finally clinches its arguments on a thunderous triad of D major, triumph is implicit, but it has been very hard won, and has swayed in the balance till that very last chord. The *Variations on a Recitative* is utterly characteristic Schoenberg, and one of his most searching works; but as one of the most difficult pieces in the organ repertoire it is, unhappily, seldom performed. Perhaps, in truth, it demands more of the instrument than it can deliver, and only an orchestral version could really bring out its full qualities.

11　The songs

Schoenberg composed one immortal song-cycle, but we do not usually rank him among the great *Lieder*-composers. His songs with piano are less consistently masterly than his works in other fields: *Das Buch der hängenden Gärten* and a few other items apart, his finest *Lieder* are found among the *Gurrelieder* and in the Op. 22 Orchestral Songs. And song-writing was not, in Schoenberg's case, a continuing passion: in the last half of his life, he seemed virtually to have 'outgrown' the medium, with the result that the really mature songs are comparatively few. But neither are his songs negligible. At least they throw interesting sidelights on his literary taste, and the best of them deserve a high place in the repertoire of any singer who favours the works of Strauss, Wolf and Mahler.

The three early groups of songs, Opp. 1-3, were composed between 1898 and 1903, though Schoenberg wrote or began many others during the same period which remain unpublished. The three published sets are certainly richer in substance than most songs of the period, for there is never any suggestion of mere repetition in material or figuration. They illustrate Schoenberg's rapidly developing mastery of chromatic harmony, if not quite with the intensity he was achieving in other fields; and though the tonality of several songs ranges far in a short musical space, most of them begin and end firmly on tonic triads. The piano writing is assured and reasonably idiomatic, though less adventurous or intrinsically interesting than his contemporary treatment of the orchestra or chamber ensemble—but he is clearly well adapted to the genre, well able to undertake songs of widely differing characters.

The Two Songs for baritone, Op. 1, are an ambitious effort, undertaken perhaps a little too soon. The poems by Karl von Levetzow glorify the rejected lover whose sufferings ennoble him and place him apart from other men—an early form of a characteristic Schoenbergian theme. They are large-scale songs, quasi-symphonic in organization, sharing some of their material. The piano writing is rather heavy and very Brahmsian, but the melodic ideas are fresh, with plenty of contrapuntal interest, and in the first song, 'Dank' (Thanks), there are already some glimmers of the real Schoenberg. The overall effect is however still rather immature: the songs do not contrast well, neither is varied enough in character for its length, and both climax in rather thinly rhetorical *tremolando* effects for the piano.

The Four Songs Op. 2 are much shorter and more effective, almost mood-pictures. The voice-part gains independence from the piano, and from now on is always the principal line. 'Erhebung' (Exaltation) is a simple love-poem, quite conventionally but attractively set; 'Jesus bettelt' (Jesus begs) is less simple, being a love-song to Mary Magdalene, which Schoenberg sets in a somewhat tortuously chromatic idiom which successfully disguises the main key for extended periods, but has a Wagnerian rather than Schoenbergian tinge. Both poems are by Richard Dehmel, whose verse was soon to inspire his first instrumental masterpiece; and so is 'Erwartung' (Expectation). In this beautiful song a lover waits in the moonlight for an assignation by 'the sea-green pond near the red villa'. Schoenberg illuminates the scene with a motive that might have come from, and certainly points the way towards, *Verklärte Nacht* (Ex. 43).

The fourth song, 'Waldsonne' (Forest Sun), to a poem that celebrates the preciousness of summer memories, is a lovely piece, with a delightfully infectious lilt and simple tunefulness characteristic of Schoenberg's earliest period.

Ex.43

Sehr Langsam

Aus dem meer – grü-nen Tei – che   ne-bender ro-tenVil-la

(Piano)

The Six Songs Op. 3 mark a further advance, and on the whole are more dramatic in character than Op. 2. The first, 'How Georg von Frundsberg sang of himself', is the monologue of a proud, upright, godfearing knight whose services were ignored at court. Schoenberg must have found the character sympathetic, for he later planned a choral work about him; here he sets the poem (from *Des Knaben Wunderhorn*) to appropriately sturdy, deeply-felt music. 'Die Aufgeregten' (The flustered ones) is more tongue-in-cheek: a mock-pathetic prelude and postlude enclose a tragedy under the magnifying glass, the 'passion and savage grief' of butterflies, bees and flowers in the wild May breeze. The most dramatic and maybe the most remarkable of the set is another Dehmel setting, 'Warnung' (Warning). The speaker has had his dog killed because it growled at the woman he loves ('I hate everybody who makes trouble'); last night he saw her with someone else; tonight, she had better be alone— 'You: remember my dog!' The swift-moving piano conveys the repressed fury, and the frequent stress on 'Du' (normally the familiar, affectionate form of 'you') is sinisterly effective. The three remaining songs are simpler. 'Hochzeitslied' (Wedding Song) is a strophic song with a fine swinging tune and chordal accompaniment, no less effective for its directness. 'Geübtes Herz' (The experienced heart) is a beautiful love-song of a different kind—the subtle shading of the piano part is appropriate to the 'practised' heart of the speaker, so much more valuable for having loved so often already. The set concludes with 'Freihold' (Independence), to a poem celebrating the Romantic archetype of the man alone, secure in the force of his will, like a milestone resisting wind, rain and lightning. Schoenberg's setting, despite a certain four-squareness, endears by reason of its youthful teeth-gritting passion and the gusto of its bold refrain.

With the Eight Songs Op. 6 (1903–5) we arrive at the period of Schoenberg's early maturity. Stylistically they illustrate his development as far as the First String Quartet; their especially thorough motivic working is the furthest extension along the lines explored by Schumann, Brahms and Wolf. Almost every song is built on one or two figures of a few notes each, which Schoenberg develops continually, whether by transposition, augmentation, diminution, or in retrograde or inverted forms, in a way that clearly anticipates his later serial practices. But the songs are most important as music in their own right, consistently surpassing the best things in the earlier groups. 'Traumleben' (Dream-life) is a rapt, ecstatic love-song whose mood presages that of the finale of the Second Quartet. The vocal line's intensity is heightened by the use of wide-leaping intervals, particularly major sevenths and minor ninths, that foreshadow the characteristic expressive phraseology of the freely chromatic and serial works. But the work towards which Schoenberg is most clearly moving, both in this song and in the tremulous half-lights of the next, 'Alles' (Everything)—another Dehmel setting—is *Das Buch der hängenden Gärten*. 'Mädchenlied', a girl's song to her bold lover, is suitably breathless and impulsive, while 'Verlassen' (Forsaken) graphically portrays a forsaken lover walking the empty streets in the grip of black despair. The song is founded almost entirely on a sullen, dragging chromatic figure of four notes rising by successive semitones. A very similar figure is crucial to the next song, 'Ghazel'—an imitation of the Persian *ghazal* form by the Swiss poet Gottfried Keller—but here the expressive effect is entirely different. It is one of

Schoenberg's most glowing songs, harmonically simpler than most of the set though no less intricate in motivic work; its serene melodiousness accords well with the poet's assurance that human love is as much part of the natural order as the arrangement of petals on a rose.

Fine songs though these five are, they are if anything surpassed by the last three. In 'Am Wegrand' (By the Wayside), to a poem by the Scoto-German writer John Henry Mackay, a man stands on the sidelines of life, watching the passing human throng, staring in vain for the one person who will give meaning to his existence. The strong, swift-moving, self-contained piano part has a powerful impetus that suggests the heedless bustle of the roadway, and the tragedy of the speaker's unwilling alienation from it. The teasing, delicate wit of 'Lockung' (Enticement) is a complete contrast: this is a cajoling seduction with a deliciously light, playfully capricious piano part. Harmonically it is the most advanced and free-floating of the set, and I am inclined to rate it the most perfect; but it is run very close by the final song, 'Der Wanderer'. Nietzsche's text is a kind of parable of how the *Sturm und Drang* of early Romanticism decays into late-Romantic sentimentalism. It describes that archetypal Romantic figure, the lone wanderer, striding resolutely through the night. But he is halted by the song of a nightingale; and though the bird patiently explains that the song was not for his ears and has nothing to do with the beauty of the night, he is unable to continue on his way. Schoenberg's setting characterizes every phrase with uncanny aptness, yet with an ironic objectivity and strict musical logic that exorcise the late-Romantic malaise just as surely as had the *Gurrelieder*.

The Six Songs for voice and orchestra, Op. 8, contain some fine inspirations, but taken as a whole the set (most of which preceded Op. 6) is something of a disappointment: the music, while not exactly 'regressive', lacks the character and precision we might expect. The orchestration, too, though efficient enough, sounds rather clotted when compared with even the early parts of the *Gurrelieder*. 'Natur', to a poem by Heinrich Hart, is an impressive, noble-sounding, well-proportioned song, but also the most frankly Wagnerian of the set, so steeped in *Tristan* as to present almost no recognizable Schoenbergian personality. By contrast, 'Das Wappenschild' (The Coat of Arms), whose text comes from *Des Knaben Wunderhorn*, is the most forward-looking, with its wildly galloping rhythms, hectic yet tight-woven counterpoint, tonal instability, and its quite un-Debussyian use of the whole-tone scale, which anticipates important features of the First Chamber Symphony.

The briefest number, 'Sehnsucht' (Longing), another *Wunderhorn* setting, brings to mind Mahler's song-cycle from that source in its *ländler*-like character, the deceptive simplicity of the vocal line, and the wry delicacy of the orchestration. The remainder of the set is occupied by three Petrarch settings. 'Nie ward' ich, Herrin, müd' (Never, mistress, did I tire), with its bombastic orchestral postlude, is probably the least interesting; 'Voll jener Süsse' (Full of that sweetness) is better, but the high point of Op. 8 is undoubtedly the third Petrarch setting, 'Wenn Vöglein klagen' (When little birds weep). As in 'Sehnsucht', the orchestration is free from the prevailing thickness of the rest of the set; the flute's melancholy bird-cry persists throughout the song with plangent effect; and there is an ecstatic climax, worthy of the composer of the *Gurrelieder*, at the words 'Do not mourn for me—I have died to enjoy eternal presence'. The song ends with an orchestral postlude of great beauty, the equal of any in the better-known orchestral songs of Richard Strauss.

'Der verlorene Haufen' (The Suicide Squad) was written in early 1907, as an entry for a competition for the best new ballad for voice and piano. It was unsuccessful, but Schoenberg added to it 'Jane Grey'—to a version of the ballad by Heinrich Ammann—and they were published together in 1920 as Two

Ballads, Op. 12. In keeping with the balladic tradition they are expansive songs with clearly defined refrains and immediate melodic appeal, but they sacrifice nothing in richness of musical thought. 'Jane Grey' is a very great song, worthy to stand with the ballads of Schubert and Löwe. Every detail in the tale of the execution of Queen Jane and her husband is caught in a spirit of tragic nobility, no less effective for being understated, until the music flowers into a great lament at the words 'Many maidens have died young from the highlands to the sea, but none was more lovely and innocent than Dudley's wife, Jane Grey':

Ex.44

After this, pathetic, fluttering figures in the piano's highest register evoke the chill wind blowing across the young queen's grave. 'Der verlorene Haufen' (poem by Viktor Klemperer) is not quite so fine, and performed after 'Jane Grey' is likely to sound rather hectoring, portraying as it does the bravado of soldiers drinking a last toast before going into a battle they know they will not survive. But it is an exciting song that swings along with tremendous impetus: in character and harmonic language it recalls 'Das Wappenschild' from Op. 8, but is undoubtedly a superior work.

The Two Songs Op. 14 (1907–8) are immediately contemporary with the Second String Quartet—and like that work they form a bridge to Schoenberg's so-called 'atonal' period. They are his last songs to employ key-signatures; and though both achieve their intensity through a continuous apparent suspension of tonality, with harmony built on fourths rather than thirds, they still float in the orbit of definite key-centres. 'Ich darf nicht dankend' (I must not thank you) seems to antedate the third and fourth movements of the quartet and must thus be Schoenberg's first setting of Stefan George; it is an impressive song, concise and restrained yet with an oddly haunted atmosphere that conveys much which is not directly expressed. The other song of Op. 14—'In diesen Wintertagen' (In these winter days) is one of the most beautiful in Schoenberg's entire output. The poem, by Georg Henckel, tells how love and friendship can light up the winter of the soul; and the setting has a quiet rapture and serenity that etch a passage like the opening ('In these winter days, when light veils itself') unforgettably on the mind.

Ex.45

During much of 1908 and the beginning of 1909 Schoenberg composed his most important set of songs, the cycle *Das Buch der hängenden Gärten*, Op. 15—fifteen lyrics from Stefan George's collection 'The Book of the Hanging Gardens'. George was a poet of sensitivity and aristocratic poise, able to condense much powerful yet clearly apprehended emotion in a few beautifully proportioned lines. The poems of the 'Hanging Gardens' (of which Schoenberg set about half) are all miniatures, elliptically relating the progress of an intense, ultimately doomed love-affair. There is a beautiful, aristocratic woman; a man (the narrator) abashed, awkward, impulsive, who loves and loses her; and as background and objective correlative, a landscape garden, formally laid out but essentially wild—at first a paradise, later alien and uninvolved.

In a famous, but ambiguous, note for the first performance, Schoenberg said that in *Das Buch der hängenden Gärten* he had for the first time succeeded in 'approaching an ideal of expression and form' which had been before him for many years. Expression and form—that is, matching words and music, just as George matched feeling and words, in an indissoluble organic unity; *not* 'atonality', though that is what many commentators have taken Schoenberg's words to mean. The treatment of tonality is merely an adjunct to the larger 'ideal', and is as varied as the expression demands. Though the songs lack key-signature, their language is no more dissonant than in Op. 14; they employ the same already familiar Schoenbergian harmonies built on fourths, but chains of thirds and triads are still an essential ingredient, imparting a strong tonal feeling in many places with clear harmonic logic. And, though most of the songs eschew a conclusive cadence, many of them clearly have a main key—no less an authority than Webern pointed out the G major nature of No. II; No. VIII has a strong pull to F minor; the D major of No. X is almost too obvious. In others (notably No. III) the 'tonal' feeling is strong without the main key ever revealing itself. In yet others certain fixed pitches function as centres of harmonic gravity, to which everything else has reference (cf. the repeated F sharps of No. XI, or the F of No. XIII); and some songs may be interpreted in more ways than one—for instance No. V, which leans towards G major, but also uses the tritone axis of the pitches A and E flat as 'reference' points of the kind already described.

The whole harmonic situation is thus not one of 'atonality'

but of tonal *ambiguity* that reflects the spiritual labyrinth through which George's narrator wanders. The poetic images of the Hanging Gardens reflect interior emotional states; and so Schoenberg's music, too, is interior—not scene-painting, but the matching in music of fleeting yet complex moods. The vocal line, more supple and recitative-like than in any previous songs, is extraordinarily wide-ranging. Since much of it is low-lying, the cycle is customarily sung by a mezzo-soprano; but Schoenberg really has in mind a high soprano, whose low register, precisely because it lacks the mezzo's strength, can better achieve the quiet, almost whispered quality the music requires.

From the bald, unaccompanied, tonally equivocal, rhythmically ambiguous bass line with which the cycle opens, the songs traverse an amazing diversity of piano colour and texture. They can be very still or very swift-moving (though only one, the climactic No. VIII, is really fast in tempo); the accompaniment of No. V is almost entirely chordal, while others (for example No. III) are predominantly contrapuntal; the accompaniment of No. VII is for right hand only; No. VIII is wild and stormy; No. XIV, the penultimate song, the shortest (a mere 11 bars) and the most delicate. By contrast, the final song, No. XV, is the longest and most varied within itself: perhaps, too, the greatest. The love-affair is over; and the narrator stumbles through the garden, distraught, on an oppressively hot night, his way impeded by the foliage, which is no longer that of Eden but something malevolent, while withered leaves hiss, driven before the wind. The song begins with a desolate melodic line, shown in Ex. 46a, whose main figure (x) derives from No. XI (the cycle is full of subtle interconnections of this kind). Both this line and its accompanying chords are subjected to continual development in every conceivable way. Some of it is very complex; the actual climax (on the final line 'The night is overcast and sultry') is simpler in texture—but even so it can stand (Ex. 46b) as an epitome of the whole cycle, with its organic development of earlier material, low-lying vocal line, definite but ambiguous tonal progression, and subtle emotional world.

Ex.46

About the time he was composing *Das Buch der hängenden Gärten*, Schoenberg also wrote an isolated setting of a poem said

Schoenberg

to be by Rilke,[1] 'Am Strande' (On the Beach), which remained
unpublished till recent years. It is nevertheless one of his
greatest songs, adapting the language developed in Op. 15 to
quite different ends, and looking forward to the spirit of the Four
Orchestral Songs Op. 22. The poem begins:

> The high tide is past.
> It still roars in the distance.
> Wild water. And above
> Star after star.

—and the suppressed violence of the extraordinary piano part,
impelled by strange surging figures in the left hand, conjures up
at once the menace of a distant, turbulent sea.

Schoenberg's marked lack of interest in the song-medium after
his achievement in Op. 15 is curious, and has never been wholly
convincingly explained. Perhaps he simply felt the need of a
more flexible medium than voice and piano alone could provide.
At any rate his next and perhaps most extraordinary song was
Herzgewächse (Foliage of the heart), Op. 20, for high soprano,
celesta, harp and harmonium, written in 1911. Webern called this
little Maeterlinck setting 'the summit of music', and it is chiefly
famous for its immense difficulty, containing as it does one of the
highest notes (a sustained F *in alt. pppp*) in the vocal repertoire.
The sense of strain which the approach to this peak tends to
engender in performance seems to run counter to the emotional
progression towards spiritual fulfilment—not dissimilar to the
finale of the Second Quartet—which the piece describes. The
poem speaks of 'formless sorrows' sinking to rest and prayer
finally rising; so the soloist begins in her lowest register, among
fragmentary flutterings and murmurs from the accompanying
instruments, and soars progressively higher and higher until the
voice floats far above a glinting 'foliage' of continually changing,
merging and intertwining instrumental patterns. The final

[1] It has not so far been traced elsewhere.

arching phrase, for all its difficulty, is when confidently sung a thing of breathtaking beauty:

Ex.47

Perhaps the greatest of all Schoenberg's song-collections, apart from Op. 15, is the Four Songs for voice and orchestra Op. 22—which, written slowly over the period 1913–16, was the only new work he brought to completion in the ten-year gap between *Pierrot* and the earliest serial pieces. It is one of his most beautiful and fascinating, but—for several reasons—one of his least known. One reason is that the only published score is a 'simplified study-and-conducting score', an innovatory idea of Schoenberg's in which the music is rationalized into just a few staves, with complete instrumental indications, as if it were a particularly detailed short score: it is difficult to read for conducting purposes, and Schoenberg never used it in such an extreme form again. Also, apart from the usual technical difficulties, the instrumentation itself poses problems. Each song inhabits a different and wholly unique sound-world: only the last requires something like a standard orchestra. The first demands 6 clarinets, a trumpet, 3 trombones, tuba, percussion and 45 strings (without violas); the other two call for independently constituted chamber orchestras of 16 and 24 solo instruments respectively (which add to the requirements 5 members each of the flute and oboe families, and 3 bass-clarinets). But none of this is mere extravagance—each has a precise role to play. In the first and longest song, for instance—'Seraphita', to a poem by Ernest Dowson—the long, ecstatic opening melody for 6 clarinets in unison, and later developments in which the clarinets fan out into six-part chords, invest the music with a quite new, dream-like sonority.

The name 'Seraphita', of course, relates to Schoenberg's religious preoccupations and his interest in Swedenborg, as well as his plan to compose an opera or oratorio on Balzac's novel of the same name,[1] and all four song-texts betray a supra-denominational exploration of aspects of religious experience. Indeed, one wonders if Op. 22 does not represent a series of studies for the long-planned Choral Symphony.[2] The other three poems are by Rilke: 'Alle, welche dich suchen' (All who seek Thee) already states the central concern of *Moses und Aron*—whereas others want to bind God with images, the poet wants simply to 'know you / in the way the Earth knows you'. 'Mach mich zum Wächter deiner Weiten' is a prayer ('Let me be the watchman of your distances'); while the last song, 'Vorgefühl' (Premonition), speaks of someone about to risk all in some desperate and overwhelming spiritual experience. In style the songs are elusive, motivically dense and tightly threaded, rhythmically free and floating, subtler and more iridescent in colour than almost any other Schoenberg score, and generous in tonal reference. The vocal writing makes customarily formidable demands, but the broken recitative-like phrases of *Erwartung* or the *Sprechstimme* of *Pierrot* are not among them. The voice-parts are conceived in true song-style, with long arching phrases that demand superb breath-control as well as a huge vocal range. And, despite the dramatic moments in 'Seraphita' and 'Vorgefühl', the set as a whole is memorable for some of Schoenberg's most sustainedly lyrical writing. For all the difference in expression, these songs haunt the memory in the way that some of Busoni's late works do.

[1] A fragment of an opening for this work dates from late December 1912; the basic impulse seems, however, to have been diverted thereafter first into the Choral Symphony and then *Die Jakobsleiter*.

[2] It is worth noting that, presumably about the same period as Op. 22, Schoenberg made sketches for five different Psalm-settings for solo voice and similarly heterogenous orchestral combinations (none was ever completed).

Only one small set of songs followed, almost twenty years later: the Three Songs for low voice and piano, to poems by the contemporary German poet Jakob Haringer, are the last work of the Berlin period, dating from 1933. Even so, they were not published till after Schoenberg's death, with the misleadingly high opus number 48. In the upheaval of his enforced emigration he had forgotten about the songs, and only discovered them among his papers many years later.

They are twelve-note works, but to the unbiased ear they rank among his most attractive songs. The piano textures are translucent; the vocal lines are if anything more singable than in some earlier sets; and the three distinct moods complement each other admirably. 'Sommermüd' (Summer weariness) is the most lyrical, to a wise, quiet text about counting one's blessings in adversity, for 'many others have had to die without a star'. 'Tot' (Dead—here really in the sense of 'emotionally dead') darkly mirrors a bitter epitaph-like text: 'What does it matter! It's all the same: he had the luck, I didn't.' Lastly, the delightful 'Mädchenlied' shows Schoenberg exercising a vein of contemporary humour akin to that of *Von heute auf Morgen*. It's the song of an office-girl afflicted with her own 'Sommermüd'—a nameless boredom of the spirit that makes her contemplate jumping in the river or taking the veil ('It's all the same to me' —in some ways, this poem parodies the other two). The voice-part is beautifully self-pitying in its tearful phrases, while the piano offers a lively, chattering accompaniment.

These rewarding little songs are hardly ever performed—but the same might be said of almost all Schoenberg's output in this field. Yet his songs, if not a central pillar of his achievement, have much to offer singer, accompanist and listener alike; and the continued absence from recital programmes of such jewels as 'Lockung', 'Der Wanderer', 'Jane Grey', 'Am Strande' and and 'In diesen Wintertagen' is a matter for regret.

12 Three stage works

Schoenberg's three completed operatic works display three different approaches to the problems of writing for the theatre. Two attempt to create new forms: they are major products of his 'Expressionist' upheaval, the one a freely associative, painful exploration of an individual subconscious mind, the other a highly symbolic representation of the creative artist's existential predicament. The third, a large-scale twelve-note work from his Berlin years, reverts to more traditional theatrical conventions as a 'domestic comedy' opera. His unfinished *Moses und Aron* (discussed in Chapter 14) is also fairly traditional in structure, but in it he can be said to have created a new genre, or re-created a very old one: that of sacred opera.

Something has already been said about the nature and significance of the monodrama *Erwartung* (Expectation), Op. 17. It was the furthest point Schoenberg reached in the great creative exploration of 1909—not a point of no return, but one from which the recovery of a sure, negotiable path would be a long and arduous journey. Written at fantastic speed, it was his most intense and sustained foray into the perilous forest of the subconscious mind: that forest which he insisted should be realistically represented on stage, and through which the single character, an unnamed Woman, must make her apprehensive, somnambulistic way, seeking what she most fears. Marie Pappenheim's libretto makes the Woman (soprano) reveal herself involuntarily in an interior monologue, which is partly an imagined dialogue with the absent lover for whom she is searching as the work opens. Past and present merge into one another as fright, longing, jealousy and exaltation, sense impressions and memory associations, pass through her stream of consciousness. The broken, discontinuous sentences might have been wrung from a patient under psychoanalysis.

Three short scenes trace the Woman's progress through the forest. In the first, she is still on its outskirts, about to take the path that leads into its depths and, she hopes, to her lover. She is clearly in a febrile, overwrought emotional state. In the second scene, she is in the middle of the forest, imagining she hears things or is being attacked. There is no sign of her lover. Startled by a bird, she runs and stumbles against a tree-trunk, which at first she mistakes for a body. Scene III is set in a clearing: the Woman is even more distraught, but she soon plunges back into the forest, calling on her lover to help her. The remainder of the work is occupied by the long fourth scene. The Woman is weary, her dress torn, her hair awry, her face and hands cut and bleeding. In the distance a dark, shuttered house is visible. Again she stumbles—and this time the obstacle *is* a body, which she soon identifies, with mounting horror, as the still-bloody corpse of her lover. The shock is a further blow to her doubtful sanity. She embarks on a long 'dialogue' with the dead, imploring him to come back to her, recalling their life together. Suspicious of another woman (perhaps the occupant of the mysterious house?), she throws a tantrum of jealousy and kicks the corpse. Has he really been murdered by the 'other woman'? Or has the Woman on stage done the deed herself, and returned to the scene in demented anguish? The latter implication seems more likely, though in the monodrama's sleepwalker's world an answer is neither forthcoming nor especially important. At the end, the events are already slipping from the Woman's mind: dawn begins to glimmer and, imagining she sees her lover far off, she wanders away saying, 'I was seeking . . .'. Her 'expectation' remains unsatisfied; her quest goes on.

Schoenberg once said that *Erwartung* was a slow-motion representation of a single second of maximum spiritual stress, and termed it an 'anxiety-dream'. The phrase should warn us against too literal an interpretation of the lurid details. The 'action' is a purely psychological one, a product of the Woman's fevered imagination. No subject was more perfectly suited to the loosened formal framework and swift juxtaposition of disparate elements in his 'totally-chromatic' style; and it is generally agreed that in this Representation of (mental) Chaos that style found its most impressive outlet. Note—a representation is not a transcription. The music itself is not chaotic. Its combination of extreme structural freedom with a willed unity of atmosphere, of a myriad intensely imagined details with a powerful sense of continuity and inevitability, could only have been achieved under iron control.

As I remarked in Chapter 6, the continuity is not demonstrable in analytical terms: it can only be grasped in performance (and a good performance is a shattering experience). Schoenberg uses a large orchestra, but there are few big climaxes—rather he draws upon it for an unprecedented range of sonorities: virtually every instrument is a soloist, and the tone-colours change from bar to bar with amazing speed and fluency. So do the pace and density of texture. The woman's halting phrases call forth an instrumental response of fantastically evocative precision: the sudden rushes and equally sudden hesitations are mirrored in the sequence of agitated and static elements and a remarkable rhythmic freedom which, graphically conveying every small-scale nervous movement, never allows a single tempo or pulse to dominate. The result is an absence of familiar musical time-sense; a realm without fixed boundaries, in which the unconscious mind roams at will.

Example 48 shows a fairly typical passage from the First Scene. Here we see the snatches of melody, on horn, cellos and flute; the continually changing colours; a static element (the

Ex.48

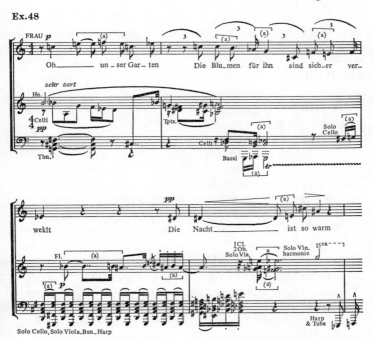

ostinato in the third bar) and the vocal line, seeking to merge elements of recitative and song in a way that owes much to the experience of *Das Buch der hängenden Gärten*. We can also see some binding elements. *Erwartung* is often called 'athematic'—another nonsense word, as practically every figure in the score is 'thematic' in the sense that it plays a part in maintaining the work's imaginative continuity. It is true, however, that substantial themes neither recur nor are developed—there is always new material, seemingly conjured up by an inexhaustible process of free association. Yet there has to be something to associate. Some small-scale entities—similar melodic shapes, rhythmically plastic motives, common note-formations, especially at the beginnings of phrases—do run through the monodrama. Their development is not systematic, but they help to create the sense of the work being a single musical organism. They work deeper than thematicism, at an almost subliminal level. (In these terms it might be said, for instance, that Ex. 48 is to a large extent constructed out of the semitone oscillation I have marked *a*.)

Nor is *Erwartung* devoid of calmer moments, though they are invariably short-lived. An expressive horn solo, shortly before the Woman recognizes the dead man as her lover, is one of the places where the legacy of late-Romantic music can still be clearly felt. Another tremulously beautiful passage occurs towards the end in the delicate evocation of the coming of dawn. The music, for a moment, feels as if it may be moving towards the kind of emotional transfiguration common to many Schoenberg works. But then the Woman hails the imagined apparition of her lover in a climax of grinding dissonance, and in two last ghostly bars of contrary chromatic scales the music dissolves, shivering, into nothingness. The nightmare—for us, at least—is over. *Erwartung*, unique in its structure as in the intensity of its emotional involvement, must be ranked among Schoenberg's greatest achievements—which is not to say that time is ever likely to render it less disquieting as a musical experience.

Though shorter than *Erwartung*, Schoenberg's next stage work, the 'Drama with Music', *Die glückliche Hand*,[1] Op. 18, evolved slowly, over the years 1910–13. The libretto, in which characters and action are treated symbolically, is Schoenberg's own, and its construction shows the influence of Strindberg's later plays and the early Expressionist dramas of Kokoschka. Certain details of the action—such as the hero's deeds of creation

---

[1] The title—literally 'The lucky hand'—is almost untranslatable: it refers ironically to the protagonist's creative gifts, which bring him suffering as well as exaltation. Schoenberg once rendered it as 'The Hand of Fate'; Hans Keller has suggested 'The Knack'; another approximation might be 'The Midas Touch'.

at the anvil—are of course reminiscent of Wagner. Much more important still is the example of Kandinsky, whose attempted synthesis of music, movement and coloured lighting in his stage work *Der gelbe Klang* seems to have fascinated Schoenberg.

As in *Erwartung*, the action is concentrated in a single figure, in this case an unnamed Man: apart from a chorus, the other characters are mimed. The Man is a success as a creative artist, but a failure at establishing lasting relationships with other people. We need not seek any elaborate parallel with the crisis in Schoenberg's marriage; it is enough to admit the probability of a generalized autobiographical element in the action.

The five scenes are symmetrically arranged, the first and last acting as a frame that distances us from the main action. The first is a static tableau: the Man is seen prostrate beneath a huge 'mythical beast', a sort of bat-like hyena, with its teeth sunk in his neck—presumably an exteriorization of his own self-lacerating ego. The faces of six men and six women are seen: they perform the same commenting function as the chorus in a Greek tragedy. In a remarkable vocal texture that combines song with *Sprechstimme*, they ask how long he must go on tormenting himself, seeking earthly happiness when he should have faith in a truth that is more than earthly (a partial adumbration of the main theme of *Moses und Aron*). Then the beast vanishes, the Man rises, and in bright sunshine the second scene begins. The Man is approached by a beautiful young woman; but she soon abandons him in favour of an elegant and prosperous 'gentleman'; returns for forgiveness; and betrays the Man a second time. The central scene displays the hero's artistic prowess. He enters a metal-working shop in a mountain ravine, and to the consternation and jealousy of the other artisans (who probably symbolize Schoenberg's rivals and critics) forges a magnificent diadem at a single hammer-blow. A searing orchestral crescendo leads to the fourth scene: the Man tries to win back his beloved, who has been seduced by the 'gentleman', but she eludes him and, to halt his pursuit, pushes a huge boulder down on top of him. The boulder changes into the 'mythical beast', and the opera ends with the same tableau as before—the man prostrate, the chorus singing, 'Did you have to experience again what you have so often experienced? . . . You poor man!'

Thus baldly stated, the action is as unattractive as most symbolical drama. But, in fact, it is inextricably dependent on the music. In *Die glückliche Hand*, Schoenberg was seeking a new form of *Gesamtkunstwerk*—one in which every element could be combined in a completely unified but specifically 'musical' conception. To this end, he not only wrote his own text: he specified the movements of the characters, the costumes, scenery and lighting in unusual detail, as integral parts of the composition. His opinion (clearly influenced by the theories of Kandinsky) was that it was possible to arrange all these elements to produce an effect akin to the music itself. The clearest demonstration of this is in the use of lighting. In the big crescendo, representing the internal storm of the Man's emotions, that links the third and fourth scenes, Schoenberg specifies a 'crescendo' of light from pitch black, through brown, green, blue-grey, violet, red and orange, to bright yellow. Simultaneously the orchestra increases in volume from *ppp* to *fff*, and each progressive modification of shade is complemented by the entry of a new instrumental colour.

The music of *Die glückliche Hand* is perhaps at the most basic level more immediately attractive than *Erwartung*. The scoring, while no less brilliant, is iridescent in contrast to the glooms and lightnings of the earlier work; and much of the material has clearer associations with traditional tonality. It is just as compressed, but the more obviously patterned structure can be grasped on a few hearings; moreover the tempo remains constant over longer periods and rhythmically the music is more clear-cut. There are actual recurrences and developments of themes, and leitmotives to characterize the main characters. Those of the Man and his faithless, unattainable sweetheart are shown as Ex. 49*a* and *b*—note that they are often associated, too, with specific tone-colours, respectively the cellos and a solo violin. Though development of these motives is often wide-ranging, they remain identifiable, as for instance in Ex. 49*c*, the waltz-tune to which the woman enters in Scene 4 after her seduction by the Man's rival.

Ex.49

The quasi-fugal music of the workshop-scene, too, shows a retreat from the dangerous freedom of *Erwartung*. Despite these easily assimilable features, the difficulties and expense of properly staging this twenty-minute opera have rendered *Die glückliche Hand* one of Schoenberg's least performed major compositions. It and *Erwartung* are the supreme examples of what is meant by the term 'Expressionistic' music. Schoenberg in fact disliked the word, preferring the phrase 'the art of representing inner occurrences'—but, as he remarked wryly in a lecture in 1928, he didn't like to say so too loudly for fear of being condemned as a Romantic.

It was in 1928 that he essayed his third stage work; and like most of his twelve-note compositions this one represented a return to at least superficially more orthodox forms. *Von heute auf Morgen* ('From today to tomorrow', or 'From one day to the next') was intended, according to a letter Schoenberg wrote while at work on it, as

a cheerful to gay, even sometimes (I hope at least) comic, opera; not grotesque, not offensive, not political, not religious. The music is as bad as mine always is: that is, appropriate to my intellectual and artistic condition. But it is also appropriate to the subject and therefore continually produces self-contained forms that are interrupted and linked by distinct (but naturally 'non-tonal') recitatives that do not set up to be melodic. There are several ensembles: duets and quartets. (Letter 107)

The libretto of this one-act domestic comedy of marital strife was by 'Max Blonda'—a pseudonym for Gertrud Schoenberg, working in close collaboration with her husband.

In the *Satires*, Op. 28, Schoenberg had attacked the irresponsibility of modish modernity in art; *Von heute auf Morgen* deflates similar attitudes in life. There is a single scene, set in a modern living-room in the small hours, and only four singing characters: an 'ordinary' husband and wife (baritone and soprano), and two 'modern, sophisticated' people—the wife's friend (soprano) and 'the celebrated Tenor', a minor Richard Tauber figure.

The couple have met the latter two at a party. On their return home the husband is afflicted with hankering for a different life, one in which he could pay court to the friend, the witty, modern, casual woman of the world who seems such a contrast to his plain, unexciting wife. The wife bears these unflattering comparisons until her patience is exhausted. She suddenly turns the tables on her spouse by transforming herself into precisely the kind of desirable woman he has been talking about. She appears in an eye-catching negligee, pretends she has spent all their money on new clothes, flirts with the famous Tenor over the phone, declares her intention of leaving at once to start looking for lovers (since that is the modern fashion), forces him to have a farewell dance with her and to help her pack, leaving him to look after their small, bewildered child. The discomfited husband is so taken aback and out of his depth that he is only too glad when, as day breaks, his wife ceases her 'dangerous game' and resumes her normal, placid identity. The friend and the Tenor, having spent the night in a nearby bar, come in and try to tempt husband and wife into casual affairs: but without success. The latter recommend to them the virtues of a stable marriage; the advocates of superficiality in relationships leave, shaking their heads over these 'faded stage-characters'; as the curtain comes down the child asks, over the breakfast-table, 'Mummy, what are *modern* people?'

A twelve-note opera is a familiar enough idea: but a twelve-note *comic* opera? *Von heute auf Morgen* has seldom been staged, so its success is difficult to judge. At the purely musical level there are no belly-laughs: but it is a very rich score, full of real musical substance yet written with a beautifully deft, light touch. The humour is one of tone—benevolently satirical, with some sharp parodic touches that range from Wagner through Puccini to jazz. In this work Schoenberg augments his orchestra with soprano, alto, tenor and bass saxophones—they are of course the principal means of reference to jazz, as in the syncopated accompaniment to the wife's aria at the beginning of her 'character-transformation'.

Ex.50

An ensemble of harp, piano, celesta, mandolin, guitar and banjo is also an integral part of the fabric, adding a sharp, 'modern' tang to the sound. Still, the work presents all the difficulties that might be expected of a major Schoenberg score (almost an hour's continuous music) and needs very careful handling to come alive dramatically. It is full, too, of customary contrapuntal subtleties: the husband and wife quarrel in a canon by inversion, while the big ensemble for all four characters is a succession of double canons. In a good performance, however, it is by no means a tough score for the listener: it abounds with tonal references, and as a fine illustration of how Schoenberg could be light over serious things, it deserves to be better known. For ultimately it is a celebration of faithfulness in human relationships: of a stable marriage and family life which has meaning, rather than a brittle round of flirtation which has none. Moreover the whole score (composed with obvious enjoyment in a mere two months) was invaluable preparation, at a lower level of intensity, for Schoenberg's finest stage-work, *Moses und Aron*.

13   Miscellany

The various pieces described in this chapter are a heterogeneous collection that receive scant notice from most commentators. In general they are regarded as mere footnotes to Schoenberg's main creative work; but in fact they all have intrinsic interest, and help round out the picture of their composer, especially in his lighter moods.

The *Brettl-lieder*, the eight cabaret songs which helped him secure his post at the Berlin Buntes Theater in 1901, certainly fall into this category. 'Nachtwandler' (Night Wanderer) is for voice, piccolo, trumpet, snare-drum and piano: a bizarre little piece in march-tempo, to a poem by Gustav Falke, its instrumentation probably suggested by the village band that the narrator leads through the moonlit streets. The remaining songs are all for voice and piano. Though of uneven quality they are tuneful and direct in appeal (apart perhaps from the rather dull setting of Wedekind's 'Galathea'). Most display a very Viennese vein of humour, by turns pawky and ironic. Perhaps the best—because most inventive—are two delightful settings of poems by Hugo Salus, both composed on the same day in April 1901. 'The Modest Lover' (who wins his mistress's favour by a somewhat unceremonious treatment of her favourite cat) has an irresistible lilt, and 'simple Song' (about the perils that befall a king who goes for a walk like an ordinary man) is fascinating in its characterization and plodding cross-rhythms.

This seems the only appropriate place to mention the *Alla Marcia* in E flat, a tiny march which has been performed recently as a piano piece, though the manuscript is clearly a short score. All the evidence—especially the harmony—suggests that it is roughly contemporary with the original version of the Second Chamber Symphony and the Second Quartet. With a duration of less than a minute it is merely a chip from the work-bench, but a chip of very high-grade timber.

The Three Little Pieces for chamber orchestra, which likewise remained unknown during Schoenberg's lifetime, are equally diminutive. They were written in February 1910, and their expressionistic brevity surpasses even the *Six Little Piano Pieces* Op. 19. They are scored for single woodwind, horn and string quintet, with a celesta and harmonium in the third. The first is twelve bars long, the second merely eight. The third builds up a ghostly, pattering *ostinato* and then breaks off, again at the eighth bar, apparently unfinished—though there is no effect of incompleteness. Like the other two, it is a tight, glinting, self-sufficient aphoristic statement of mood, an odour from the forest of *Erwartung*.

Der eiserne Brigade ('The Iron Brigade')—a spoof march for piano quintet, written for a 'merry evening' in camp during Schoenberg's military service—is of less interest, but real entertainment value. It contains several good musical jokes, and what appear to be popular regimental melodies are worked into the texture. The ridiculously tuneful Trio opens with a fanfare on the piano, which is later turned into a bugle-call against a 'dramatic' string *tremolo* background. For all this it must be one of the least militaristic marches ever written—if the Good Soldier Schweik had been a composer, he might have produced something like this.

Schoenberg wrote some little pieces of chamber music for himself and his family to play together, usually at Christmas time. The most notable is the exquisite *Weihnachtsmusik* (Christmas music) of 1921, for two violins, cello, harmonium and piano—a five-minute fantasia on two well-known Christmas carols, in an unsullied C major, written with the apparent simplicity of the art that conceals art. The main tune is 'Es ist ein' Ros' entsprungen', to which 'Stille Nacht, heilige Nacht' appears as a counterpoint in the delicate flow of string polyphony, while the piano, with carilloning chords, adds a tranquil commentary. Comparatively speaking *Weihnachtsmusik* is a very minor work, but it is an extremely beautiful one, and deserves to be better known.

Schoenberg's most numerous 'occasional' works were canons, vocal or instrumental. Like Bach or Brahms before him, he wrote many of these throughout his career; sometimes simply, one suspects, to keep his hand in with a little 'tonal' composition in the old style, sometimes as riddles or as greetings or presents for friends, often fitted with whimsical texts of his own devising. Those in the 'Appendix' to the *Satires* Op. 28 are typical of the genre. Towards the end of his life Schoenberg began to collect together all those others he thought worthy of publication; and in 1963 his pupil Josef Rufer edited a volume of thirty of them. They vary greatly in quality, from mere workshop ingenuity to miniature compositions of genuine artistic value. Of the latter kind, the following deserve mention: two beautiful four-voice canons (1905) on proverbs by Goethe; a riddle-canon in four keys with a free fifth voice, in celebration of the jubilee of the Concertgebouw of Amsterdam (1928); the two splendid three-voice *Canons for Carl Engel* on his sixtieth birthday (1943) with their fine related tunes and use of double and quadruple augmentation; the elaborately structured, highly chromatic instrumental *Canon for Thomas Mann* (1945); and the last canon Schoenberg completed, in 1949—a four-voice one in a clear C major with a definat text: 'Centre of gravity of its own solar system, circled by shining satellites, thus your life appears to the admirer.'

The art of transcription, of arranging a work in one medium for another, was close to Schoenberg's heart. His own career as an arranger began with hack-work at the turn of the century, but he came to find it a useful form of compositional relaxation, and it appealed strongly both to his pedagogic and interpretative instincts. Some of his own works came in for this treatment—for instance, he arranged *Verklärte Nacht* and the Second Quartet for string orchestra, the First Chamber Symphony for full orchestra, the Second Chamber Symphony for two pianos—but the bulk of his transcriptions were of other composers' works. Appendix B lists all those he is known to have made, but is probably not exhaustive; he may have had a hand in many more that appeared under his pupils' names on the programmes of the *Verein fur Privataufführungen* (whose constitution specifically encouraged the transcription of orchestral works for chamber ensembles). Schoenberg's arrangements demonstrate the catholicity of his taste. For instance, there is the transcription for chamber ensemble of Busoni's *Berceuse Elégiaque*, with its sensitive use of harmonium and piano; three Johann Strauss waltzes, one the famous *Kaiserwalzer* arranged for the same ensemble as *Pierrot Lunaire*; and a delicious version of Luigi Denza's 'Funiculi, funiculá' for clarinet, string trio, guitar and mandolin. In a somewhat different category, for they are really original compositions, come his arrangements of fifteenth- and sixteenth-century German folksongs, of which there are three sets. The first is a group of three for a cappella mixed choir, arranged in early 1929. Four folksong-settings for voice and piano soon followed; and as late as 1948 Schoenberg made a fresh set of arrangements for mixed choir, to which he gave the opus number 49. All three song-melodies had appeared in the second 1929 group, and one, 'Es gingen zwei Gespielen gut', must have been a special favourite as it had been used in the first set as well.

Pride of place, however, must go to Schoenberg's orchestrations of Bach and Brahms. In 1922 he arranged two Bach chorale preludes—*Komm, Gott, Schöpfer, Heiliger Geist* and *Schmücke dich, o liebe Seele*—for large orchestra; and in 1928 did the same with the E flat Prelude and Fugue (the famous 'St. Anne') which stand at the beginning and end of the Third Part of Bach's *Clavierübung*. He regarded them as popularization— and they have upset purists and delighted ordinary listeners wherever they have been played. *Schmücke dich* is a simple, beautiful setting; the chorale melody is assigned to a solo cello and the string writing is of luminous transparency. However, both here and in the more lively *Komm, Gott,* Schoenberg is at pains to add to Bach's basic text all the particulars in which the Baroque organ was deficient: detailed phrasing and articulation, differentiation of accents and octave registers, contrasts of dynamics and, of course, contrasts of colour. There is some minimal, but appropriate, fleshing-out of the musical fabric. All these characteristics reappear with increased significance in the big Prelude and Fugue. To bind the two movements into a unity of substance as well as of key, Schoenberg embedded some surreptitious anticipations of the Fugue subject in the Prelude. The gamut of colour—including harp, celesta and glockenspiel, six clarinets of various sizes, and a very agile bass tuba—is brilliantly kaleidoscopic. The instrumentation has a serious purpose, however: it emphasizes structural divisions (the three sections of the Fugue, for instance, begin respectively on woodwind, strings and brass) and, above all, brings out the individual contrapuntal lines. It might be argued, with a certain degree of justice, that Bach did not write these pieces for a medium that allowed such clear definition, and therefore part of their true nature may lie in the very *concealment* of their contrapuntal ingenuity. But Bach's lines are strong enough to survive Schoenberg's own characteristic concern for maximum clarity; and the objection in no way invalidates Schoenberg's creative interpretation of Bach (any more than it does Stokowski's, say, or Elgar's), nor the fine additions to the orchestral repertoire which are the result. Bach himself, the greatest transcriber of them all, would surely have winked approval.

Yet in some ways even more impressive is the superb arrangement for full orchestra which Schoenberg made in 1937 of Brahms's Piano Quartet No. 1 in G minor, Op. 25. All his love of Brahms—in whose music he had been steeped for half a century—comes out in this sustained act of creative homage. He called it, jokingly, 'Brahms's Fifth Symphony'. It is not that: chamber music depends on a greater intimacy of expression and shorter-range effects than orchestral music, and it is one of the qualities of Schoenberg's transcription that much of the intimacy is preserved. But it is a masterpiece of orchestral writing, ready-made for popularity, if only it were played sometimes. Brahms's original is left almost unaltered—Schoenberg occasionally doubles melodic lines in thirds and slightly refashions the piano cadenza of the last movement (here given mainly to clarinets) but that is all. He is unfailingly resourceful in re-creating the piano figuration in meaningful orchestral terms. The whole *sound* of the work is, at least in the first three movements, uncannily Brahmsian. The sharp-eared will however notice that the brass writing is more chromatic than was Brahms's wont, and the percussion section that emerges in the third movement is a good deal larger than anything to be found in the *Academic Festival Overture*. The best surprises are reserved for the finale. This 'Rondo alla Zingarese', in the original, is one of the fieriest and most uninhibited of Brahms's 'gypsy' pieces. Schoenberg, tongue firmly in his cheek, goes one better in abandon with his battery of xylophone and glockenspiel and his trombone glissandi. Yet a trio of solo strings is allowed a tender reminiscence of Brahms's own instrumentation just before the breathtaking, helter-skelter coda.

It might seem, at first sight, a small step from these orchestrations to two of the most neglected—and most curious—of Schoenberg's larger works: the Cello Concerto 'after' Monn (1932) and the String Quartet Concerto 'after' Handel (1933). If the Bach orchestrations give purists pain, these are enough to induce heart-failure. They do, indeed, represent an extension of

Schoenberg's arranging activities, but a very long extension indeed: no mere transcriptions but drastic recompositions, new pieces founded on another composer's work in much the same way as Stravinsky's *Pulcinella* is founded on tunes by Pergolesi. In each case the mixture is about twenty-five per cent 'adopted' material and seventy-five per cent 'original' Schoenberg. Quite apart from their own qualities (and they make highly enjoyable listening) they hold a significant position in Schoenberg's *œuvre*: they formed a bridge to his wholly original 'late tonal' works, and provided experience in *concertante* writing that was to benefit him in the Violin Concerto (begun in 1935).

The Cello Concerto is founded on a harpsichord concerto in D minor by one of the 'fathers of the symphony', the eighteenth-century Viennese composer Georg Matthias Monn.[1] Schoenberg wrote it for Pablo Casals, who never played it in public, though he is known to have done so in private. Perhaps the dedicatee's known tastes influenced Schoenberg's choice of material; but he plainly wrote the whole work with considerable relish. Each movement starts with a free arrangement of the exposition of Monn's original, but the continuation is wholly Schoenberg's own, in a harmonic style that reaches as far as, and sometimes further than, that of Brahms. A large orchestra is used with wit and vivacity—this is a work of bright colours, with trumpets, oboes, harp and celesta much to the fore. The solo part, with its rapid bowed passages, double and triple stopping and frequent harmonics, is virtuosic in the extreme, but always cellistic. The first movement (one of the toughest in cello literature) concentrates on a merry theme which to British ears sounds suspiciously like 'Rule Britannia!'. Schoenberg turns Monn's bland little slow movement into a mock-sinister funeral march, while the finale, a lilting minuet, contains a *pizzicato* episode, no doubt in homage

---

[1] This Schoenberg Cello Concerto should not be confused with Monn's own Cello Concerto in G minor, which Schoenberg edited in 1912 for the *Denkmaler der Tonkünst in Österreich*.

to Casals, in which the soloist imitates the sound of a Spanish guitar.

Clearly Schoenberg must have enjoyed himself, for he soon embarked on another work in this vein—the Concerto for String Quartet and Orchestra, founded on Handel's Concerto Grosso in B flat, Op. 6 No 7. This time he had the Kolisch Quartet in mind, and the solo parts are accordingly diabolically difficult. Writing the piece seems to have sustained him through his exile in France after leaving Germany—and its unquenchable gaiety is a sign of his resilience of spirit. Op. 6 No. 7 is the only Concerto Grosso of Handel's Op. 6 that does *not* have a string concertino, and this very fact may have guided Schoenberg's choice of it. He employs a rather larger orchestra than in the Cello Concerto (the combination of harp and piano features prominently as a 'continuo' at various points) and extends the range of harmonic 'updating'—the whole work is a treasure-trove of harmonic practice from the early eighteenth to early twentieth centuries. His overall strategy, however, differs from the previous concerto. The first movement is a free arrangement of Handel's original, adding much but following its course and observing its proportions quite closely—except for the insertion of a fearsome 'cadenza' for string quartet. The lovely slow movement, for muted quartet and small orchestra, is an almost exact, reverential transcription of Handel's. But in the third and fourth movements, little remains of Handel but the basic tunes—instead we have a lilting, wickedly chromatic *Allegretto grazioso* which in itself is an entire compendium of ways of writing for string quartet for those who like to live dangerously; and finally an outrageous Hornpipe—slower, weightier, more symphonic, but just as uproariously alive as Handel's own—which rises to several big climaxes yet fades away at the end on the sound of the quartet's *tremolandi* and the romantic tones of cellos and horns.

The almost total neglect of these brilliant concertos is unjust, and to audiences' loss. It cannot be denied that their humour—and their virtuosity—contain a certain element of the perverse, and their significance for the onward sweep of musical history is negligible. But the tunefulness, high spirits, magnificent craftsmanship and sheer delight in music-making which they display should be enough to ensure them popularity, and they are a better approach than many to the understanding of Schoenberg's more difficult works.

14   Unfinished torsos

Schoenberg was a religious man by temperament as well as conviction—for, though his forms of belief altered through the years, the innate religious *impulse* seems never to have deserted him, and it affected his whole spiritual and intellectual life. Not only was it a prime source of strength (above all in the lonely years of exploration between 1908 and the evolution of the twelve-note method) to feel some higher justification for his perseverance on his dark and dangerous path. We may also opine that for Schoenberg, with his implacable fighter's ego, to believe in and relate to some power higher than and outside himself was a necessity that helped preserve his psychological balance. It is hardly surprising, therefore, that he saw prayer—the process of relating to the spiritual source—as the fundamental act in religious experience. Prayer is central to the three works that remain to be discussed—the oratorio *Die Jakobsleiter*, the opera *Moses und Aron* and the *Modern Psalms*. They are his three major artistic statements of religious belief; but all three, significantly, are in some sense unfinished. Yet they are performable, and the first two must be reckoned among his most important creations.

Die Jakobsleiter (Jacob's Ladder) would, had it been completed, have lasted well over two hours in performance—yet even that huge stretch of music was originally conceived as just the *fourth movement* of the vast religious Choral Symphony on which Schoenberg worked at intervals in the years just preceding the First World War. Eventually he decided to make the oratorio an independent composition, drafted his own text in

1915, and began composing with his usual speed in the summer of 1917. He had composed more than half-an-hour's music in short score before his second call-up into the Austrian army—a disastrous hiatus after which, despite attempts up to 1922, he found it impossible to continue the work. It was not just that the tide of inspiration had ebbed: he had progressed stylistically in a direction to which the relatively free language of *Die Jakobs-leiter* was fundamentally unsuited. He often spoke of wanting to complete it, and made some important revisions in 1944, but it advanced no further in his lifetime.

Some years after Schoenberg's death his pupil Winfried Zillig, at the behest of Schoenberg's widow, collated the existing material and made a performing version. This involved no extra composition on his part: Schoenberg's short-score is continuous, and Zillig's task was essentially to translate it into full score, following Schoenberg's own, sometimes very full, instrumental indications and orchestrating in appropriate style where such instructions were lacking. When the actual musical texture was incomplete he left it so, believing the music strong enough to stand unsupported. He used the fairly standard symphony orchestra which Schoenberg stipulated in 1944—rather than his original 1917 conception, which would have called for an orchestra of 250 (with 10 piccolos, 18 clarinets and so on), a chorus of 750 plus unseen choirs above and below the stage, as well as four offstage orchestras.

In the form we now have it, *Die Jakobsleiter* is a setting of the first (and shorter) part of Schoenberg's two-part libretto, up to and including the symphonic interlude which was to have divided the two parts, and now functions adequately as a coda. An urgent, thrusting orchestral prologue (see Ex. 9 in Chapter 6) introduces a vision of a multitude of souls, struggling onward in some limbo between death and reincarnation, urged forward by the archangel Gabriel (bass, partly sung, partly in *Sprechstimme*) who acts as guide and counsellor. His opening injunction,

'Whether to right or left, forward or backward, uphill or down-hill—you must go on, without asking what lies before you', very much mirrors Schoenberg's predicament at the time of writing these words, and takes us to the heart of the drama. An extra-ordinary choral passage ensues, in which various groups of souls—the Dissatisfied, the Doubters, the Rejoicers, the Indifferent, the Resigned—respond to the call in their own way. The choral texture, which mingles song and *Sprechstimme*, is a bold development of a style Schoenberg had first used in *Die glückliche Hand*, and is often divided into as many as twelve parts.

Gabriel summons forward various individual souls who feel that in their life on earth they were able to draw near God. They stand as different types of humanity. Each makes his profession: first a self-satisfied aesthete, who is roundly rebuked by Gabriel for having no vision; then 'A Protestor', in revolt against both the God of the instincts and the God of organized religion—an attitude which Gabriel condemns as wholly negative; then 'One Wrestling', whose continual struggles with doubt, Gabriel tells him, bring him nearer salvation. 'The Chosen One', the type of the true, inspired artist, now comes forward: he finds himself rejected and humiliated by his fellow men because of the origin-ality of his vision, yet he feels his own humanity and kinship with them, inescapably: 'They are the theme, I the variation.' Next a Monk speaks: he fears to continue in his vocation, for he knows his own weaknesses, and knows he cannot avoid sinning. Gabriel comforts him—he will indeed sin, but sins are punish-ments that cleanse—now he must go forth and be a prophet and martyr.

In this series of dialogues, the real breadth of language in *Die Jakobsleiter* becomes plain. Despite the proto-serial derivation of material from Ex. 9's opening *ostinato*, each soloist is charac-terized with almost operatic intensity in music of a different kind, so that the oratorio comes to seem like a compendium of Schoenberg's stylistic discoveries. For instance, the music of the aesthete ('One of the Called') is almost traditionally tonal, the most frankly Wagnerian Schoenberg had written for years. The general musical idiom, however, as typified by that for 'One Wrestling' (see Ex. 51: the text is translated as the epigraph to Chapter 5), relates perhaps most closely to the Op. 22 Orchestral Songs, not only in harmony and the extremely wide range of instrumental colour, but also in the sweep of the vocal lines.

Ex. 51

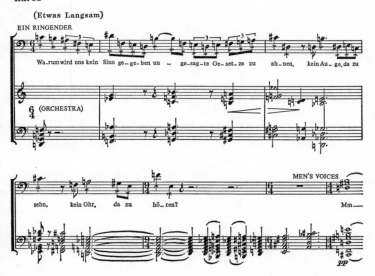

Into this purgatorial judgement-scene now breaks a woman's voice: the soul of 'One Dying'. Her monologue begins as rapid *Sprechstimme*, then gradually becomes more melodic as life ebbs away, until, at the point of death, she breaks into true song, an ecstatic wordless vocalise that follows the last words 'the supremely happy dream comes true: To fly! Onward! To the goal!' (the sentiment is very reminiscent of 'Entrückung' from the Second Quartet). As the rapturous song soars up to the dizzy heights of an F *in alt*, the 'Great Symphonic Interlude' begins: quiet, floating music of great beauty and rhythmic freedom, in which the orchestra is joined, not by off-stage orchestras as Schoenberg originally envisaged, but by pre-recorded instrumental groups whose music is broadcast into the hall on loudspeakers. A final reminiscence of the singing soul, duetting with solo violin and distant choir, ends the fragment in far-off, interstellar regions.

Fragment though it is, this is certainly an impressive creation. The music has enormous dramatic force, which seems to communicate much more immediately at each performance than is the case with many Schoenberg works. This almost in spite of the text, which is no literary miracle—wordy and intimidatingly abstract in style, its philosophic content an original but bleak compilation from Blake, Swedenborg, Strindberg, Schopenhauer, anthroposophy and Hindu mysticism. The character of the 'Chosen One' has long been recognized as a Schoenbergian self-portrait, and read in cold print his speeches sound insufferably arrogant. But, in fact, all the characters are partly projections of Schoenberg himself, an examination of his weaknesses and the various stages of his life as a representative human being: and their words are only meant to come alive in a musical setting. To a great extent they do, and with splendid vividness. Nevertheless, *Die Jakobsleiter* remains a torso: the overall form is unbalanced—after the magnificent choral opening the chorus has relatively little to do, while the five main dialogues with Gabriel, successfully characterized though they are, make the body of the work undeniably episodic.

We lack the second, and what should have been the greater, half—in which it is reasonable to suppose that much material that remains undeveloped in the existing portion would have found its fulfilment. The text for that half is complete, and was in fact published over fifty years ago. In it, the souls who spoke in Part I are being prepared for reincarnation, to return to earth to

begin their struggles anew. 'The Chosen One' is again prominent in the proceedings. Gabriel has a long final speech in
glorification of prayer as the chief means of reconciliation to a
God who knows man's inadequacy. Then the voices of all
creatures were to be heard in a great chorus of praise—musically
intended as an enlargement and intensification of the 'symphonic
interlude'. Schoenberg noted down his mental impression of it
thus: 'The choir and the soloists join in: at first mainly on the
platform, then more and more far off—offstage choirs located
next to the offstage orchestras—so that, at the close, music is
streaming into the great hall from all sides.'

But this mighty ending was never composed; and we may
wonder whether Schoenberg really thought himself capable of
it. In fact, the incompleteness of *Die Jakobsleiter* seems especially
fitting in view of its stylistic diversity and proto-serial working.
The 'Jacob's Ladder' is a bridge to the twelve-note method, and
thus remains more important as a process of becoming than as
something wholly achieved.

Schoenberg's second main religious statement in music, and
the most important product of his full maturity, is the opera
Moses und Aron, written between 1930 and 1932 to a libretto
drafted in 1928. It might be viewed as a sequel to *Die Jakobsleiter*, in that it portrays the difficulties experienced by a 'chosen
one' in accomplishing his prophetic mission. It also relates
closely to *Der biblische Weg* (The Biblical Way), the play on
which Schoenberg worked in 1926–7. There the protagonist,
Max Aruns, seeks to found a new Jewish homeland in twentieth-
century Africa but is defeated because his own human weakness
cannot sustain his vision. In *Moses und Aron* Schoenberg goes
back to the original search for the Promised Land and presents
the contending impulses in the two opposing brothers, the
prophet and the preacher. Unlike *Die Jakobsleiter*, however,
the work is to all intents and purposes complete, even though
the music for the short third act was never composed. And the

result is unique in the annals of opera—a 'philosophical' work about the incommunicability of the nature of God, which is yet vividly dramatic in its impact and contains some of Schoenberg's finest and most immediately communicating music.

In the first scene of Act I the Voice of God (six solo singers, reinforced by speaking chorus) calls to Moses from the Burning Bush. His first words of reply, in the halting *Sprechstimme* that characterizes all his utterances, sums up his whole problem: 'Only one, infinite, thou omnipresent one, unperceived and inconceivable God!'

Ex.52

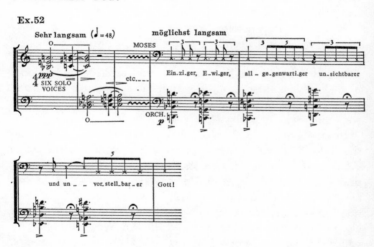

The Voice appoints Moses to be God's prophet, although he protests that no one will believe him, for he lacks the ability to express what he knows. He is told that his brother will speak for him and that Israel is God's chosen people. In Scene 2, Aaron and Moses meet in the wasteland, and their respective characters are made clear. Aaron (an agile, lyrical high tenor) is silver-tongued, quick to grasp the externals of Moses' conception and able to interpret it in more easily presentable terms—he thinks through images and words, and of a God who punishes and rewards. Moses, the deep thinker, is so concerned to speak the exact truth, rather than an easy approximation, that he can hardly speak at all: his dogged *Sprechstimme*, reiterating the reality of the omnipresent God whom no image can properly represent, makes an uncouth contrast to Aaron's florid arioso, but an effective one, cutting through the fine-sounding phrases with greater clarity than any singing line.

Moses and Aaron go together to the Israelites, who in Scene 3 are shown divided and demoralized under the Egyptian oppression, yet eager for a new god to lead them from slavery. Apart from the two brothers, the people *en masse* are the opera's other main character: fickle, unstable, slow of understanding, yet with the potential to develop into a great nation. In Scene 4 Moses tries to deliver his message to them, but his simple proclamation that one mighty, invisible, unimaginable God requires their devotion meets with hostility and derision. Moses despairs—but Aaron seizes the initiative and performs three miracles, changing Moses' rod into a serpent, curing Moses' leprous arm, changing Nile water into blood. Faced with these demonstrations of divine power, though still untouched by the central idea, the mob's attitude alters completely; they put themselves under Moses' and Aaron's guidance and, singing a hymn of fervent nationalism ('Almighty, thou art stronger than Egyptian gods are, Thou wilt strike down Pharaoh and all his servants'), make ready to march out of Egypt.

Act II (after an interlude, a whispered canonic chorus 'Where is Moses?') takes place before the Mountain of Revelation. Moses has been away praying on the mountain for forty days and the people have grown restive, afraid and violent. They think Moses' God must have killed him, and want their old gods back. Aaron, to escape their wrath, gives in, and stills their fears by presenting them with a new god—the image of the golden calf. 'Revere yourselves in this gold symbol!' he says. Now follows the work's most notorious—and exciting—scene, the 'Dances round the golden calf'. The preliminary rejoicing and merrymaking soon degenerate into all the vilenesses of which man is capable when freed from the claims of the divine idea. Human sacrifice, fighting, murder of dissidents, suicide, rape and total destruction ensue. Moses returns, bearing the Tables of the Law, just as the people are groggily recovering from their communal hangover. He makes the golden calf vanish with a word and rounds angrily on Aaron. The final scene presents their argument. Aaron defends himself skilfully: he acceded to the people's demands out of love for them; if Moses refuses to compromise, the people are never going to understand even a fraction of the truth. The Tables of Law—they, too, are an image, a simplification of the idea. In despair, Moses breaks the tablets, and is chided by Aaron for faint-heartedness. A pillar of fire springs up; the Israelites, seduced back to God by yet another image, march on into the wilderness, singing their hymn, while Moses sinks down, in defeat: 'Unimaginable God, inexpressible thought of many meanings! So I am defeated! So everything I thought was madness and cannot and must not be spoken. Oh word, oh word that I lack!' The only hint of consolation is in the violins' long, poignant, independent monody, one of Schoenberg's most magnificent melodic creations, which has all the expressive power that Moses is denied, and seems to say all he would want to say (Ex. 53).

Act III was never composed, apart from a few sketches. The text, however, is complete: it consists of a single scene, another debate between the brothers. This time Moses has regained the ascendancy: Aaron, in chains, is castigated for having 'betrayed God to the gods, the idea to images, this chosen folk to others, the extraordinary to the commonplace'. Aaron is set free, but, since he is only able to live in the images he creates, he falls dead. Moses tells the people that they will remain in the wilderness, for only there can they attain union with God.

Ex.53

On the whole, one does not regret that this Act was never set to music: unlike the rest of the libretto, it seems to lack dramatic conviction. There is no explanation of how Moses has gained the upper hand, nor why his arguments should triumph now when they failed before. It reads just a little like the wish-fulfilment of a man who really knew that Aaron, whether right or wrong, inevitably gets the better of the arguments in this life. And indeed as Schoenberg depicts him in music Aaron, for all his pliancy and shallowness, is not an unimpressive character: he has quick wit, acts with decision, and is an artist with words. The opera, in truth, is as much about the artist as the religious man— the struggle, and the paradox, involved in trying to give outward expression to any inner vision. Schoenberg had to have something of Aaron in his own makeup to attempt the opera— for is not *Moses und Aron* itself an 'image' such as Moses would condemn—an 'image' which by its very existence betrays the idea it tries to convey? If so, its incompleteness saves it: for the final revelation of Moses' triumph and unity with God is left unexpressed, and the torso that we have portrays the essence of the graspable, believable, human situation.

Subconsciously, Schoenberg must have realized this, for the two acts of *Moses und Aron* form a complete musical and dramatic unity. They also comprise one of his greatest achievements. Leitmotives are few: instead Schoenberg weaves a continuously fluctuating texture of remarkable orchestral brilliance, in which spoken recitative, arioso, ensembles and large-scale choral passages succeed one another with unerring dramatic flair. In two hours' music only a single note-row is employed, and the work emerges as a grand summing-up of all the different expressive possibilities of twelve-note music. One thinks of the unearthly stillness of the scene before the Burning Bush, followed by the suave, elegant yet insubstantial dance-like music for flute, violins and harp that characterizes Aaron on his first appearance. Then there is the polyphonic energy of the big choruses, which convey joy, fear, mockery or triumph in counterpoint of a rhythmic fluidity and grandeur that go far beyond anything Schoenberg had previously achieved in this field. Or there is the mysterious, questioning, half-whispered, half-sung chorus in double canon that forms the interlude between the two acts; the intensity of the debate between Moses and Aaron, and the tragic eloquence of the ending.

But perhaps most compelling of all is the great central scene of Act II, the 'Dances round the Golden Calf', in which the orchestra takes the leading role. For sustained rhythmic force and dynamic, barbaric energy it stands alone in Schoenberg's *œuvre*: a five-movement dance-symphony, or a 130-bar complex of themes with four large-scale variations, of nearly half an hour's length. This music is full of vivid strokes: the ponderous fanfares that begin it, the militaristic march of the Ephraimites, the dance of the butchers, into which Schoenberg introduces the open-air sound of violins fiddling on open strings as background to a leaping, mercurial theme:

Ex.54

Moreover, there is the at first innocent, slightly befogged waltz that accompanies the orgy of drunkenness; and the violent disintegration and frenzied rhythms that accompany the scenes of mass destruction and suicide. In its sheer ferocity and propulsive power this whole vast sequence seems to me to stand in the annals of twentieth-century music on a par with *Le Sacre du Printemps*. Indeed it perhaps deserves to be ranked higher than Stravinsky's piece, for it is not so hermetic: it is placed in a dramatic context where its violence can be seen as only part of the story—but a vital part, disregarded at peril—of the nature of mankind. For it is at the human level, as a tragedy of any real seeker after truth, that *Moses und Aron* evokes a response from those who may not share its religious convictions.

In the last year of his life, Schoenberg again returned to the problem of presenting a comprehensive religious statement in music, with his series of *Modern Psalms*—or, as he described them in a letter to his boyhood friend Oskar Adler, 'Psalms, Prayers and other Conversations with and about God . . . our contemporaries' religious problems'. He originally entitled the first of these prose texts in German (some of which are only unpolished drafts) 'Der 151. Psalm', indicating that he thought of himself as adding to the biblical series of 150 psalms in a contemporary context. He wrote fifteen of them, and began a sixteenth only ten days before his death.[1] Presumably they were all intended for musical setting, but he only essayed the composition of the first, and did not complete it.

The extant psalm-texts show a great range of subject-matter. If they have a common theme, it seems to be the question, 'What attitude should a Jew, or any religious man, adopt towards moral and spiritual matters in the modern world?' One psalm examines the role of prayer in the machine age; another celebrates the Jews as the 'Chosen People' and defends them from charges of arrogance; another is an attack on atheism engendered by a blind belief in the power of science; another approves the moral force of the Ten Commandments. The most substantial text, virtually a short essay, is an examination of the character of Jesus—Schoenberg concludes that in minimizing his importance Jewish history has made a grave error. Yet others treat of sexual love, the innocence of children, the atomic bomb, and prayer as an expression of humility. The fragment of the

---

[1] We should perhaps also include the English text for *Israel Exists Again*, written one year previously in 1949. All that Schoenberg completed of this work for chorus and orchestra was a promising looking 55-bar fragment, chiefly a declamatory prelude with a prominent piano part.

sixteenth psalm condemns 'National inbreeding, national incest' as 'just as dangerous to the race as that of the family and the tribe'.

To this miscellaneous collection the first psalm stands as prologue and invocation—a prayer to God from one who asks if God attaches any significance to whether he prays or not. The words strongly recall Moses before the Burning Bush: 'I am . . . speaking of the only, eternal, omnipotent, omniscient and unimaginable, of whom I neither can, nor should, create an image.' Schoenberg began to set this text to music, as his *Modern Psalm*, Op. 50c, late in 1950, scoring it for speaker, chorus and small orchestra. The setting remained a fragment of some five minutes' length, which probably represents about three-quarters of the whole. Stylistically the music is a fine example of Schoenberg's last period, having something of the dramatic agitation of *De Profundis* but also the underlying calm apparent in the String Trio and *Dreimal Tausend Jahre*. The reciter announces the words of the psalm against an orchestral background of notable translucency, and the chorus develop the words into musical ideas, usually in euphonious canon. But the final section of the text, which speaks of prayer as itself a rapture 'greater than any fulfilment', leading, finally, to union with God, was not set—the fragment breaks off in mid-sentence, with the sopranos singing 'And nevertheless I pray . . .' (see Ex. 55, p. 229. Here, again, the incompleteness is somehow artistically satisfying, its open-endedness expressing the yearning, rather than the achievement. Perhaps Schoenberg sensed this, for in the last months of his life he made no attempt to return to the unfinished score. Like *Die Jakobsleiter* and *Moses und Aron*, the *Modern Psalm* stands as a noble monument to Schoenberg's religious longings, rather than an unanswerable statement of faith.

15 . . . and idea

Now do you grant the power which
Idea has over both word and image?

(Moses in *Moses und Aron*, Act 2)

In the preceding chapters I have treated it as axiomatic that
Schoenberg's music possesses a significance beyond the sum of its
note-rows and counterpoints; that it is no abstract number-
game but—in Schoenberg's own phrase—the presentation of an
idea. But what idea? Insofar as music has a dialectical or philosophical content beyond its architectural forms, what does
Schoenberg's music *say* to us?

By its very nature, this content is not easily verbalized.
Schoenberg rather presents us—through music's progress in
time, and through its continual variations and developments,
with a recurring pattern of experience. He did, however, once
give a verbal clue to that pattern. The American jazz and
classical pianist Oscar Levant considered performing Schoenberg's Piano Concerto. To help Levant approach the work, the
composer noted down 'a few explanatory phrases' to characterize the work's four sections:

Life was so easy
Suddenly hatred broke out
A grave situation was created
But life goes on.

At the simplest level, that is a fair summary of the Concerto's

emotional progression. The same 'programme' might apply
with little modification to several classical and romantic pieces.
But the listener who explores Schoenberg's output in any
kind of breadth or depth soon becomes aware that a very
large proportion of his works, from all periods of his career,
seem to embody different forms of the same experiential
pattern.

We encountered one form of it at the very beginning of this
book, in String Quartet No. 2; and we may adduce further,
varied examples. The *Gurrelieder*, in its comparatively simple
late-Romantic manner, charts the decline of a *Tristan*-esque love
affair into the spiritual abysses of death, blasphemy and ghost-
life; but the phantasms are eventually dispelled by the summer
breezes, and the final melodrama and chorus exhort us to greet
the daylight and reawakening life. *Pierrot Lunaire* indulges in
risky sport with ludicrous images of decay and grotesquerie
until real violence and madness invade the music; but at length
they recede, the air clears, and at the end we stand once more in
daylight and breathe 'the ancient scent of far-off days'. In *A
Survivor from Warsaw* violence and madness are confronted in
an actual contemporary situation, in the ultimate nihilism of
which twentieth-century man has proved capable—but that
nihilism is denied its final victory because the victims elect to
stand and sing together, affirming their humanity and subverting
the hell's logic of the gas-chamber.

The lineaments of the pattern grow clearer. It is no crudely
optimistic one. The music explores extremes of emotional
experience, in the cause not of sensationalism but of self-
knowledge: to help us see clearly. And when clarification comes
its effect, however high the price, tends naturally to be affirmative. This is plainly the case in the earlier works, where 'clarification' is associated with orthodox tonal resolution, as in the grand
C major conclusion of the *Gurrelieder*, the shimmering D major
of the sextet's 'Transfigured Night', or the warm, tranquil D

major epilogue that fulfils all the chromatic strivings of the First String Quartet. Later the affirmation takes other forms, though often—as in the *Ode to Napoleon*, the Piano Concerto, the *Genesis* Prelude and the String Trio—these include at least an implicit acknowledgment of tonal roots.

In fact, had there been less discussion over the past fifty years of the syntactical construction of Schoenberg's music, and more of what it says, people might more readily have noticed what an essentially positive composer he is. There is no trace in his music of the post-Wagnerian 'death wish' that infected so many of his contemporaries, and can even be traced in the music of younger men like Berg. He explored horror and disorientation because he believed they could not be effectively rejected and transcended until they had been fully known. 'Clarification' abounds, on every level, whether as form emerging out of amorphousness (*Genesis* Prelude) or the strengthening of marital ties by putting mutual affection to the test (*Von heute auf Morgen*). Far from encouraging morbidity, hardly any Schoenberg work has a tragic or truly depressing ending. Even *Erwartung* and *Die glückliche Hand*: the predicaments of their respective protagonists are hopeless indeed, but we do not identify with them— instead the action, like a case-history, works through and makes those predicaments understandable, and in so doing clarifies something in ourselves. *Moses und Aron* ends at a tragic juncture, but that was not Schoenberg's ultimate intention. Perhaps only the Second Chamber Symphony ends in utter darkness, and even here we know that he considered adding a more affirmative third movement. But as it stands, the effect on the listener is hardly depressing—rather cathartic.

Certainly many works do not, and ought not to be made to, fit this pattern of clarification through extreme emotional, spiritual or psychological experience. But several embody individual stages in the process, depending when they were written; and as a result we begin to see that the pattern must be in some senses an autobiographical one. The music of Schoenberg's earliest period—not only the most ebullient pieces such as the D major Quartet and the First Chamber Symphony—has something of the 'life was so easy' feeling about it; this is, at least, the work of an extraordinarily gifted young man confidently extending a tradition of which he feels a part and rather relishing his forward position in it. Then 'hatred breaks out': the personal and spiritual crises of the years 1908–9 release disruptive forces which can only be caught and held in the first totally-chromatic works—traditional musical architecture and large-scale forms become, for a time, impossible, with consequent personal disorientation. The 'serious situation' thus created necessitates years of painful searching for a way forward; and when 'life goes on', it does so by clarifying the chromatic content of the disruptive elements through the twelve-note method. The 'classical' twelve-note works—such as the Wind Quintet, Orchestral Variations, and Third and Fourth quartets —represent clarification achieved. But at a price: the traumatic events of previous years are implicit in them, as witness the Op. 29 Suite, whose genuine gaiety of spirit dances on a razor's edge between order and disorder. In Schoenberg's last fifteen years, the whole pattern seems to be repeated. Perhaps under the influence of events in Europe, the dark forces erupt again—strangely enough in *tonal* or near-tonal works, the Second Chamber Symphony, *Variations on a Recitative* and *Ode to Napoleon*. But now he has better weapons with which to meet the crisis. Three very different twelve-note works—the Piano Concerto, String Trio and *A Survivor from Warsaw*, seem to be his most concise and positive embodiments of the whole process. Yet in his last music the struggle for some ultimate resolution is still going on.

For Schoenberg, that 'ultimate resolution' had to be religious. To the religious temperament, Unity with God is the supreme clarification, and in this world can only be secured by prayer. Its realization is implicit in three works. The Second Quartet, here as in other respects a document of cardinal importance, *enacts* that religious ideal—the prayer from the depths in the third movement motivates the interplanetary ascent in the finale of one who becomes 'an ember of the Holy Fire . . . an echo of the Holy Voice'. *Herzgewächse* compresses a similar upward movement into three minutes' span: as the text speaks of heartfelt prayer rising to God so does the vocal line soar clear of its accompaniment, higher and higher till it pinnacles softly on an F natural *in alt*, a sound so high and rare that it seems free of all earthly associations. The fragment of *Die Jakobsleiter* breaks off on that same sound, with the voice of the 'Dying One'. But there Schoenberg had intended to go further and actually compose a hymn of Union with God. He went on trying: prayer was a vital escape from the subjectivity of his egocentric temperament, necessary for his own spiritual and emotional clarification. The twelve-note method achieves this for him in the formal sphere, as a means of objectifying and disciplining the riotous inventions of his subjective consciousness. But he never found himself able to compose the explicit music of union with the divine. Of his last choral trilogy, Op. 50, *Dreimal Tausend Jahre* is a far-off glimpse, in the mind's eye, of a Promised Land which Schoenberg, like Moses, was destined never to enter. Yet *De Profundis* and the *Modern Psalm* are dramatic presentations of the *act* of prayer, against all odds: the music never gives up hope.

Schoenberg sought, then, to reassert in his music the traditional romantic and religious values of European civilization. In this sense, he was a conservative composer. But because such a reassertion was not just aesthetic but ethical in intention, it inevitably involved an attack on the bogus traditionalism and intellectual inertia of the decaying society in which he found himself; and in this sense his approach was a critical, even revolutionary one. It is the approach advocated by Moses in

Moses und Aron; in the one passage that he is given to *sing* rather than speak, he exhorts his brother:

> Purify your thinking,
> Renounce what is worthless,
> Make it truthful.

To seek the truths enshrined in tradition and state them anew, freed from unnecessary or obscuring associations—that was Schoenberg's aim; and since the truly essential only reveals itself in extreme situations, the search rapidly carried him into strange and perilous regions. So strange, that at first very few listeners understood the music that resulted, and his dedicated attempts at clarification paradoxically brought confusion in their train. Other, lesser composers, with little for audiences to comprehend in the first place, saw the perfect disguise, plus fame and notoriety, in writing 'incomprehensible' music.

When the society of which Schoenberg's early music had been an implied critique was mortally wounded, if not quite overthrown, by the holocaust of World War I, there was no lack of 'iconoclastic' *avant-gardists* in the arts to condemn the real qualities of that society and its traditions, no less than its failures and hypocrisies. That had never been Schoenberg's intention; he wished to revitalize tradition, not break with it. So since the twelve-note method provided a way of acknowledging and applying his 'revolutionary' stylistic advances, he was able to exercise his 'conservative' instincts in building a whole network of links to the music of the past. Baroque dance-forms, classical variation-forms and sonata-like frameworks; rhythmic structures and melodies never entirely divorced from the vernacular of the Viennese masters; a largely familiar range of register, articulation and flow; reminiscences of traditional tonality; even tonality itself. From this point of view, the most 'revolutionary' gesture in one of his most extreme works—the String Trio—is not the fifty-bar flood of trills, stabbing chords, shrieking dissonances, harmonics, *glissandi* and *col legno, ponticello* effects with which it begins, but the calm bars of pure unsullied A major that follow. Or rather, what is 'revolutionary' is the idea that both passages are necessary parts of the same musical world. Schoenberg seems to have felt that he had transformed the musical language only insofar as the human body is healthily transformed several times in an average lifetime by the death and replacement of its every individual cell, so that we become different flesh, but remain the same person.

Here again his attempt at clarification failed, at least in the short term. Twelve-note music, as is notorious, is important because it uses twelve notes. It was Schoenberg's serial practices that attracted, and still attract, most attention and comment, just as if the beauty of a face were to be judged by examining the structure of the grinning skull beneath. Yet the method's whole *raison d'être*—the emotional and intellectual circumstances in which a composer may find it a necessary path along which to proceed—were hardly discussed or comprehended. The music's traditional features, on the other hand, tend to be played down, and indeed rather offend the sensibilities of many commentators. Schoenberg, they feel, failed to recognize the potential of his own discoveries—he should have gone on to create new forms which spring direct from the seed of the note-row itself, as (so the story goes) Webern did. But Schoenberg's forms are neither old-fashioned nor new-fangled: they are simply those he felt most valid within his conception of the twelve-note method. Such phenomena as the 'total serialism' of the early 1950s would hardly have aroused his sympathy.

Nor might he have supported the view that what he had done offered the 'only way forward' for Western music. Indeed, we know he rejected the proposition as it was stated in Adorno's *Der Philosophie der Neuen Musik*. It could hardly have been a tenable opinion for a man who, for all his egomania, expressed admiration for composers as diverse as Bartók, Gershwin, Ives,

Milhaud, Shostakovich and Sibelius; a man who declared that much good music was still to be written in C major (and wrote some of it himself), who saw many as yet unexplored possibilities between traditional tonality and serialism. Of course he had a strong pride in his own achievement, and attached great importance to it. But in any grave situation there are potentially as many ways forward as there are thinking men to take them.

Consider, for instance, the path trodden—in what seems a diametrically opposed direction—by a man of very similar racial and cultural background. Kurt Weill was a lesser composer than Schoenberg; but he too, in his own way, attempted to revitalize the Austro-German musical tradition through a critique of its forms and idioms. The differences between two masterpieces which preserve that tradition such as Weill's Second Symphony and Schoenberg's Third Quartet are ones of means and personality, not of intention or achievement. And Weill's case should give us cause for thought: *he* cultivated a deliberately accessible musical language—yet his finest works, such as the Symphony and the opera *Die Bürgschaft*, are quite as little known as Schoenberg's. To argue against the latter's music simply because of its difficulty must be to beg at least part of the question. Just as to argue for and about it (as so many seem to) merely from some nineteenth-century historicist notion of cultural 'progress' must be to miss most of the point.

What, then, is the significance of Schoenberg's works—if we lift them clear of their 'historically inevitable' reputation, of misunderstanding or analytical obfuscation? Well: they may bewilder, satisfy or annoy, according to individual taste; they may be disliked, warily respected, or simply loved. But no one can afford to remain indifferent to them, for they raise questions at so many different levels, challenge preconceptions, force us to think, to find reasons for loving or hating them. With their graphic exploration of emotional extremes, their will towards clarification and refusal to entirely despair, they chart a passionate man's twentieth-century pilgrimage and remain, as all life-works should, the last repository of essential information about their creator. They render a complex world and a complex human being as they deserve—complexly. Through them, Schoenberg is seen to embody the ethic of the dedicated artist, in its most uncompromising form. His works are devastatingly free from the condescension implicit in 'writing down' to the audience: they are not intended for children, though I know children to whom they appeal. Sometimes, on the other hand, one feels they were directed at an audience of Arnold Schoenbergs; and that is perhaps a defect, for we may (and with adequate reason) not wish to be Schoenberg ourselves.

In short, the great craggy edifice that was his life's work, with its extraordinary range of style—gothic horrors, gargoyles, calm cloisters, classical forms, unfinished portions and all—cannot and should not be avoided by anyone with the slightest interest in the music of our century. From the vantage-point of his centenary year, it fills at least half the skyline. The shadow it casts, true, is sometimes oppressive. But to wish that its builder had never existed, or that he had built differently, is like wanting to return to the womb. Given the kind of place the world is, it may be natural, even rational, that we should sometimes wish we had never been born. But we have only fully grown up when we have experienced that wish, and come to terms with its utter futility.

Epilogue

Maybe something has been achieved but it was not I who deserves the credit for that. The credit must be given to my opponents. They were the ones who really helped me.

(Message to the American Institute of Arts and Letters, 1947)

On his hundredth birthday, 13th September 1974, Arnold Schoenberg did, in a sense, come home to Vienna. In the course of a centenary congress on his life and work held in his native city, the composer's ashes and those of his second wife Gertrud were re-interred in a grave on the Zentralfriedhof, near the memorials to Mozart, Beethoven and Schubert, while a choir sang, in Hebrew, the chorus *De Profundis*. The event was symbolic of the recognition of his achievement that has come about since his death. In the suburb of Mödling the house on the Bernhardgasse where Schoenberg lived from 1919 to 1925 is now a historical monument, property of the International Schoenberg Society founded in 1972. In Los Angeles, on the campus of the University of Southern California, a Schoenberg Institute is under construction, to house the composer's musical and literary legacy. Since 1966, a handsome and scholarly Complete Edition of his works has begun publication, under the guidance of—among others—such old associates as Rudolf Kolisch, Josef Rufer, Leonard Stein and Eduard Steuermann. The technical aspects of his music seem set fair to provide topics for learned dissertations till the end of time. It is fame of a kind.

As for his influence—one could say, if you seek Schoenberg's monument, look about you. One could, but it would be unfair. The disarray of contemporary music in the West is hardly his fault. The gap between the contemporary composer and his audience had opened long before Schoenberg was born, as far back as Beethoven's late sonatas and quartets. With Schoenberg it certainly widened, but he took care never to go beyond at least hailing distance of those willing to listen. He believed the gulf would eventually close again; for he, after all, had something to communicate from the other side. Plenty of bad twelve-note music has been written, but bad music outnumbers the good in any age. Schoenberg cannot be blamed for the mediocrity of others, or for those who use the method to disguise their poverty of invention. It is more pleasant to consider the composers who have harvested a vital beauty from it: to remember Berg's Violin Concerto and Webern's Cantatas, the symphonic achievements of Roberto Gerhard, Roger Sessions and Egon Wellesz, how Gerhard wed twelve-note technique to the rhythms and colours of Spain, how Nikos Skalkottas did the same for the music of his native Greece, how Luigi Dallapiccola brought to it a specifically Italian lucidity and melodic grace. Twelve-note serialism, which in 1951 almost seemed to have died with Schoenberg, has since spread over the world and become a major musical force. It should be judged by its best results, not by the misunderstandings and barren orthodoxies that are essentially perversions of it.

For the method has grown and changed. Few composers of stature have ever used it strictly: but some have come to it only after long consideration, and employed it in whatever way came most naturally for the expressive ends they had in view. So there is really no single twelve-note method—there are as many methods 'after an idea by Arnold Schoenberg' as there are real creative personalities to apply them. We might instance the symphonies of Frankel, the operas of Henze, the concertos of Petrassi, the chamber works of Busoni's pupil Stefan Wolpe, the

227

music of the Norwegian, Fartein Valen and the Rumanian, Roman Vlad. We might instance the most spectacular convert to serialism, shortly after Schoenberg's death—the late Stravinsky.

But the influence is wider still. There is hardly a major composer in this century whom contact with Schoenberg's work has not forced to re-examine the foundations of music. If in the event he has rejected Schoenberg's path, his own music may have gained in purpose and direction. Hindemith is one example; others are Shostakovich and Britten, who employ twelve-note melodic formations simply as one colour in their palettes. Hanns Eisler, whose enormous output of politically committed Marxist works seems utterly opposed to Schoenberg in spirit and technique, could hardly have become the composer he was had he not studied with Schoenberg and revered his mastery and perfectionism. Even the symphonist Robert Simpson—no friend to Schoenberg's music—has said that one of his cardinal inspirations for the treatment of tonality in symphonic form came, not from his beloved Nielsen or Bruckner, but from listening to Schoenberg's Piano Concerto.

He is thus by now assured of his place in history. Popularity—by which one can only mean the general liking of the mass of music-lovers, for what composer save maybe Beethoven is 'popular' by any universal sense?—eludes his music still. Yet it is a fact that the biggest works—the *Gurrelieder, Die Jakobsleiter* and *Moses und Aron*—have an immediate and dramatic impact on audiences whenever they are performed, and the other works have proved themselves on too many individual pulses for a more general acceptance to be forever withheld. In a world of fracturing values, collapsing traditions and advancing mediocracy—and with, in all probability, harder times ahead, Schoenberg's virtues of idealism, master craftsmanship, intellectual honesty, relationship to tradition, survival (in music as in life) against extreme odds and qualified but real affirmation of human value ought to concern us more and more, and speak to us in

Epilogue

ever clearer tones. Works like the Second Chamber Symphony, the String Quartets, the String Trio, the Concertos, the Op. 35 Choruses, the Orchestral Variations, *Erwartung*, the Orchestral Pieces and *A Survivor from Warsaw* do not just deserve their place in the repertoire: they are necessary to it. There is a story that when he had completed his Violin Concerto, Schoenberg was told it could never be played until human beings developed a sixth finger. 'Well,' he replied, 'I can wait.' Complex human nature needs complex music; and, whatever else it signifies,

Ex.55

Und trotz_dem be _ te ich

is certainly not the end.

Appendix A   Calendar

(Figures in brackets denote the age reached by the person mentioned during the year in question)

LIFE

CONTEMPORARY MUSICIANS AND EVENTS

1874   Arnold (Franz Walter) Schoenberg born on Sept. 13 in Vienna, son of Samuel (44), owner of a small shoe shop, and Pauline (*née* Nachod).

Cornelius (50) dies, Oct. 26; Holst born, Sept. 21; Ives born, Oct. 20; Franz Schmidt born, Dec. 22; Suk born, Jan. 4. Albeniz aged 14; Alkan 61; Balakirev 38; Bantock 6; Bizet 36; Boito 32; Borodin 50; Brahms 41; Bruch 36; Bruckner 50; Busoni 8; Chabrier 33; Charpentier 14; Chausson 17; Debussy 12; Delius 12; Dukas 9; Duparc 26; Dvořák 33; Elgar 17; Fauré 29; Franck 52; Glazunov 9; Godowsky 3; Goldmark 44; Goetz 34; Gounod 56; Granados 7; Grieg 31; Humperdinck 20; d'Indy 23; Janáček 20; Koechlin 6; Lalo 51; Lekeu 4; Leoncavallo 16; Liadov 19; Liszt 63; Loeffler 13; Magnard 9; Mahler 29; Mascagni 11; Massenet 32; Mussorgsky 35; Nielsen 9;

YEAR	AGE	LIFE	CONTEMPORARY MUSICIANS AND EVENTS
			Novák 4; Offenbach 55; Paderewski 8; Parry 27; Pedrell 33; Pfitzner 5; Puccini 16; Rakhmaninov 1; Reger 1; Rimsky-Korsakov 30; Roussel 5; Saint-Saëns 39; Satie 8; Florent Schmitt 4; Sibelius 9; Smetana 50; Ethel Smyth 34; J. Strauss II 48; R. Strauss 10; Sullivan 32; Tchaikovsky 34; Vaughan Williams 2; Verdi 61; Wagner 61; Wolf 14; Zemlinsky 2.
1875	1		Bizet (36) dies, June 3; Coleridge-Taylor born, Aug. 15; Glière born, Jan. 11; Ravel born, March 7; Tovey born, July 17.
1876	2	Birth of sister Ottilie, June 9.	Havergal Brian born, Jan. 29; Falla born, Nov. 23; Goetz (35) dies, Dec. 3; Ruggles born, March 11; Wolf-Ferrari born, Jan. 12. First perfs. of the complete *Ring* cycle, Aug. 13–17; Brahms, Symphony No. 1, Nov. 6.
1877	3		Dohnanyi born, July 27; First perf. of Brahms, Symphony No 2, Dec. 30.
1878	4		Boughton born, Jan. 23; Holbrooke born, July 6; Schreker born, March 23.

YEAR	AGE	LIFE	CONTEMPORARY MUSICIANS AND EVENTS
1879	5		Bridge born, Feb. 26; Ireland born, Aug. 13; Respighi born, July 9; Cyril Scott born, Sept. 27. First perf. of Brahms, Violin Concerto, Jan. 1.
1880	6	Goes to primary school.	Bloch born, July 24; Foulds born, Dec. 2; Medtner born, Dec. 24; Offenbach (61) dies, Oct. 5; F. G. Scott born, Jan. 25.
1881	7		Bartók born, March 25; Enesco born, Aug. 19; Miaskovsky born, April 20; Mussorsgky (42) dies, March 28. First perf. of Brahms, Piano Concerto No. 2, Nov. 9.
1882	8	Birth of brother Heinrich.	Grainger born, July 8; Griffes born, Sept. 17; Kodály born, Dec. 16; Malipiero born, March 18; Stravinsky born, June 17; Szymanowski born, Oct. 6; First perf. of Wagner, *Parsifal*, July 25.
1883	9	Begins learning the violin, and almost immediately begins composing.	Bax born, Nov. 8; Casella born, July 25; Hauer born, March 19; Varèse born, Dec. 22; Wagner (69) dies, Feb. 13; Webern born, Dec. 3.
1884	10		Van Dieren born, Dec. 27; Smetana (60) dies, May 12. First perf. of Bruckner,

YEAR	AGE	LIFE	CONTEMPORARY MUSICIANS AND EVENTS
1885	11	Goes to Realschule; meets Oskar Adler, with whom he beings to play chamber music. During the next few years composes marches, polkas, *ländler*, etc. in the popular style of the day.	Symphony No. 7, Dec. 30. Berg born, Feb. 7; Butterworth born, July 12; Reigger born, April 29; Wellesz born, Oct. 21. First perf. of Brahms, Symphony No. 4, Oct. 25. Liszt (73) composes his *Bagatelle without Tonality*.
1886	12		Liszt (74) dies, July 31; Ponchielli (51) dies, Jan. 17; Schoeck born, Sept. 1.
1887	13		Borodin (53) dies, Feb. 28; Fartein Valen born, Aug. 25; Villa-Lobos born, Feb. 8. First perfs. of Brahms, Double Concerto, Oct. 18; Verdi, *Otello*, Feb. 5. Alkan (74) dies, March 29; Max Butting born, Oct. 6; Vermeulen born, Feb. 8.
1889	15		First perfs. of Strauss, *Don Juan*, Nov. 11; Mahler, Symphony No. 1, Nov. 20. Parry (42) composes his Symphony in E minor.
1890	16	Influenza epidemic in Vienna. Samuel Schoenberg dies of it on Dec. 31, at the age of 60.	Franck (67) dies, Nov. 8; Ibert born, Aug. 15; Frank Martin born, Sept. 15; Martinů born, Dec. 8; Nyström born, Oct. 13. Wolf (30) composes the *Spanisches Liederbuch*.
1891	17	Arnold leaves school on Jan. 22 without taking the	Bliss born, Aug. 2; Prokofiev born, April 23. Brahms

YEAR	AGE	LIFE	CONTEMPORARY MUSICIANS AND EVENTS
		final exams; goes to work for a private bank, Werner & Co. Falls in love with his cousin Malvina Goldschmeid and writes a *Nocturne* for small orchestra.	(58) composes the Clarinet Quintet; Wolf (31) the *Italienisches Liederbuch*.
1892	18		Honegger born, March 10; Howells born, Oct. 17; Kilpinen born, Feb. 4; Lalo (69) dies, April 22; Milhaud born, Sept. 4; Rosenberg born, June 6. First perf. of Bruckner, Symphony No. 8, Dec. 18. Maeterlinck (30) writes *Pelléas et Mélisande*; Albert Guiraud writes *Pierrot Lunaire*.
1893	19	Composes songs; plays cello in the amateur orchestra Polyhymnia and is awarded a composition prize by them for a *Schilflied*. Befriended by Alexander von Zemlinsky (21).	Gounod (75) dies, Oct. 18; Hábá born, June 21; Tchaikovsky (53) dies, Nov. 6. First perfs. of Verdi, *Falstaff*, Feb. 9; Tchaikovsky, *Pathétique* Symphony, Oct. 28. Brahms (60) completes the *Klavierstücke*, Op. 116–19.
1894	20	Composes Three Piano Pieces and (perhaps) a String Quartet in C major; receives encouragement from Josef Labor.	Chabrier (53) dies, Sept. 13; Heseltine born, Oct. 30; Lekeu (23) dies, Jan. 21; Moeran born, Dec. 31; Pijper born, Jan. 20. Debussy (32) composes *Prélude à l'après-midi d'un faune*.

YEAR	AGE	LIFE	CONTEMPORARY MUSICIANS AND EVENTS
1895	21	Loses his job with Werner & Co.; thereon devotes himself exclusively to music — starts conducting workers' choral societies.	Castlenuovo-Tedesco born, April 3; Hindemith born, Nov. 16; Orff born, July 10; First perfs. of Mahler, Symphony No. 2, Dec. 13; Strauss, *Guntram*, Nov. 16.
1896	22	Serenade in D (unfinished).	Bruckner (72) dies, Oct. 11; Gerhard born, Sept. 25; Sessions born, Dec. 28; Vogel born, Feb. 29. Mahler (36) completes Symphony No. 3; Strauss (32) *Also Sprach Zarathustra*. Richard Dehmel (33) writes *Weib und Welt*.
1897	23	Composes String Quartet in D major (performed with success at the end of the year) and songs.	Brahms (63) dies, April 3; Cowell born, March 11; Korngold born, May 29; Saeverud born, April 17.
1898	24	Is converted from Judaism to Protestantism, and baptised on March 25. Begins, but does not complete, a symphonic poem *Frühlings Tod*.	Eisler born, July 6; Gershwin born, Sept. 25; Hannenheim born; Roy Harris born, Feb. 12; Strauss (34) composes *Ein Heldenleben*; first perf. of *Don Quixote*, March 8.
1899	25	Composes the sextet *Verklärte Nacht*. Finds a publisher (Dreililien Verlag of Berlin). Conducts a male chorus in Heiligenstadt.	Baines born, March 26; Chausson (44) dies, June 10; Chavez born, June 13; Poulenc born, Jan. 7; Revueltas born, Dec. 23; Johann Strauss II (73) dies, June 3. First perf. of Elgar, *Enigma Variations*, June 19.

YEAR	AGE	LIFE	CONTEMPORARY MUSICIANS AND EVENTS

Debussy (37) completes his *Trois Nocturnes*.

1900 26 Composes the bulk of the *Gurrelieder*. He conducts workers' choirs and earns the rest of his living scoring operettas. Meets Alma-Maria Schindler, later Mahler's wife.

Antheil born, July 9; Alan Bush born, Dec. 22; Copland born, Nov. 14; Krenek born, Aug. 23; Sullivan (58) dies, Nov. 22; Weill born, March 2. First perfs. of Puccini, *Tosca*, Jan. 14; Charpentier, *Louise*, Feb. 2; Fauré, *Promethée*, Aug. 26; Elgar, *The Dream of Gerontius*, Oct. 3; Zemlinsky, *Es war Einmal*. Strindberg (51) writes *The Dance of Death*.

1901 27 Completes the draft of the *Gurrelieder*, and begins scoring it. Composes the *Brettl-lieder* (cabaret-songs) and meets Ernst von Wolzogen, who invites him to Berlin to work for the *Überbrettl* cabaret in Berlin. He marries Mathilde von Zemlinsky (Oct. 7), and moves to Berlin in Dec.

Ruth Crawford born, July 3; Finzi born, July 14; Rheinberger (62) dies, Nov. 25; Rubbra born, May 23; Verdi (87) dies, Jan. 27. First perf. of Mahler's Symphony No. 4, Nov. 25. Strindberg (52) writes *To Damascus*.

1902 28 Unsatisfied at the *Überbrettl*. Daughter Gertrud born, Jan. 8. *Verklärte Nacht* given a stormy first performance (Vienna, March 18). He breaks off work on the *Gurrelieder*, but continues scoring operettas,

Duruflé born, Jan. 11; Walton born, March 29; Wolpe born, Aug. 25. First perfs. of Debussy, *Pelléas et Mélisande*, April 30; Sibelius, Symphony No. 2, March 8; Grainger (20) completes *Hill-Song No. 1*;

YEAR	AGE	LIFE	CONTEMPORARY MUSICIANS AND EVENTS
		and copies the parts of *Taillefer* by Strauss (38), whom he meets for the first time in April. Strauss helps him financially and professionally, and suggests composing an opera on Maeterlinck's *Pelléas*. Instead, Schoenberg begins a symphonic poem (July 4).	Mahler (42), Symphony No. 5.
1903	29	Completes *Pelleas und Melisande*, Feb. 28, which he shows to Busoni (37). Busoni conducts his orchestration of Schenker's *Syrische Tänze* in Berlin (Nov.). Strauss secures him the Liszt Stipendium for a second year. Returns to Vienna in July. Makes four-hand piano arrangements for Universal Edition. *Verklärte Nacht* played again in Vienna; during a rehearsal Schoenberg meets Mahler (43) for the first time. Teaches harmony and counterpoint at the Music Course in Dr Eugenie Schwarzwald's school.	Berkeley born, May 12; Blacher born, Jan. 3; Khachaturian born, June 6; Wolf (42) dies, Feb. 22. First perf. of Bruckner, Symphony No. 9, Feb. 11.
1904	30	Three songs are performed at an Ansorge-Verein concert, Feb. 11. With Zemlinsky (32), founds 'Society of Creative Musicians' with	Dallapiccola born, Feb. 3; Dvořák (63) dies, May 1; Petrassi born, July 16; Skalkottas born, March 8. First perfs. of Janáček,

YEAR	AGE	LIFE	CONTEMPORARY MUSICIANS AND EVENTS
		Mahler as Honorary President. Composes *Six Orchestral Songs*, Op. 8 (March–Nov.) and begins the String Quartet Op. 7. In financial difficulties; begins teaching composition privately: Webern (21) becomes a pupil in the autumn, soon followed by Berg (19) and Erwin Stein (18).	*Jenufa*, Jan. 21; Puccini, *Madama Butterfly*, Feb. 17; Delius, *Appalachia*, Oct 15; Busoni, Piano Concerto, Nov. 10. Mahler (44) completes Symphony No. 6.
1905	31	Conducts the première of *Pelleas und Melisande* in Vienna, Jan. 26. Egon Wellesz (20) joins the ranks of Schoenberg's pupils in Oct. S. completes String Quartet No. 1 on Sept. 26 at Traunstein near Gmunden; also finishes the *Eight Songs*, Op. 6 (Oct.).	Blitzstein born, March 2; Hartmann born, Aug. 2; Jolivet born, Aug. 8; Lambert born, Aug. 23; Rawsthorne born, May 2; Seiber born, May 4; Tippett born, Jan. 2; Zillig born, May 1. First perfs. of Debussy, *La Mer*, Oct. 15; Strauss, *Salome*, Dec. 9. Mahler (45) completes Symphony No. 7.
1906	32	Completes the First Chamber Symphony at Rottach, Tegernsee, July 25. Begins work on the Second, Aug. 1—destined to stay unfinished for over 30 years. Son Georg born, Sept. 22.	Frankel born, Jan. 31; Lutyens born, July 9: Shostakovich born, Sept. 25; Spinner born, April 26. Elgar (49) completes *The Kingdom*; Mahler (46) his Symphony No. 8.
1907	33	The First String Quartet and Chamber Symphony premièred in Vienna, Feb. 5 and 8 respectively. The Rosé Quartet repeat the former in Dresden in June.	Badings born, Jan. 17; Grieg (64) dies, Sept. 4. First perf. of Sibelius, Symphony No. 3, Sept. 25.

YEAR	AGE	LIFE
		Two Ballads, Op. 12 composed (March–April); *Friede auf Erden*, Op. 13 completed March 9 and String Quartet No. 2 begun the same day. Begins to become active as a painter, and takes lessons from the artist Richard Gerstl (24). Mahler leaves Vienna for the U.S.A., Dec. 9.
1908	34	Mathilde elopes with Gerstl. Schoenberg completes String Quartet No. 2 (dedicated 'to my wife'), works on Chamber Symphony No. 2, begins *Das Buch der hängenden Gärten* and makes the first sketch for *Die glückliche Hand*. Meanwhile Webern (25) eventually persuades Mathilde to return to Schoenberg. Gerstl commits suicide, Nov. 4. On Dec. 21 the Rosé Quartet, with Marie Gutheil-Schoder, give the first performance of String Quartet No. 2, amid scenes of uproar and abuse.
1909	35	In a great creative upsurge, Schoenberg completes *Das Buch der hängenden Gärten*, Op. 15, on Feb. 28; and composes the *Three Piano*

Elliott Carter born, Dec. 11; Messiaen born, Dec. 10; Rimsky-Korsakov (64) dies, June 21. First perfs. of Elgar, Symphony No. 1, Dec. 3; Scriabin, *Poem of Ecstasy*, Dec. 10. Mahler (48) composes *Das Lied von der Erde*; Webern his *Passacaglia*.

Albeniz (48) dies, May 18; Holmboe born, Dec. 20. First perfs. of Strauss, *Elektra*, Jan. 25; Delius, *Mass of Life* (complete),

YEAR	AGE	LIFE	CONTEMPORARY MUSICIANS AND EVENTS
		Pieces, Op. 11 (in Feb. and Aug.), 'Am Strande' (Feb. 8), *Five Pieces for Orchestra*, Op. 16 (June–Aug.) and the monodrama *Erwartung*, Op. 17 (Aug. 27–Oct. 4). Sends the first two of the Op. 11 pieces to Busoni (43) who makes a 'concert edition' of the second; offers the Op. 16 pieces to Strauss (45) for performance; but he turns them down.	June 10; Rachmaninov, Piano Concerto No. 3, Nov. 28; Webern (26) writes *Five Pieces for String Quartet*.
1910	36	Opp. 11 and 15 premièred in Vienna, Jan. 14. Writes *Three Little Pieces* for chamber orchestra, Feb. 8. Begins *Die glückliche Hand*, Sept. 9. Holds his first exhibition of paintings in Oct. (works of this year include 'Christ', 'Red Gaze', 'Gustav Mahler: Vision'). In grave financial straits, is forced to borrow money from Mahler (Aug.); becomes an outside lecturer at the Imperial Academy from June 28—his application supported by Mahler, Löwe, Weingartner and Goldmark. Highly successful second performance of *Pelleas* in Berlin, under Oskar Fried, Oct. 8.	Balakirev (73) dies, May 29; Barber born, March 9; William Schuman born, Aug. 4. Busoni (44) composes the *Fantasia Contrappuntistica* (first version); Debussy (48), *Préludes* Book I; Grainger (28) *Mock Morris*; Mahler (50) completes Symphony No. 9 and begins No. 10; Novák (40), *The Storm*; Scriabin (38), *Prometheus*; Stravinsky (28), *The Firebird* (first perf. June 25); Vaughan Williams (36), *Fantasia on a Theme by Thomas Tallis* (first perf. Sept. 6); Webern (27), *Six Pieces for Orchestra*.

YEAR	AGE	LIFE	CONTEMPORARY MUSICIANS AND EVENTS
1911	37	Composes the *Six Little Piano Pieces*, Op. 19 (Feb.–June), and completes the first edition of *Harmonielehre* in July. After Mahler's death, decides to leave Vienna, and spends much of Sept. near Munich in near-poverty. Meets Kandinsky (45). Reaches Berlin in Oct.; he lectures at the Stern Conservatoire, completes the scoring of the *Gurrelieder* (Nov. 8) and composes *Herzgewächse*. Paintings of this year include the 'Self-portrait from behind'; this, and two 'Visions', are featured in the first 'Blaue Reiter' Exhibition (opened on Dec. 18).	Hovhaness born, March 8; Mahler (50) dies, May 29; Allan Petterson born. First perfs. of Strauss, *Der Rosenkavalier*, Jan. 26; Sibelius, Symphony No. 4, April 3; Elgar, Symphony No. 2, May 24; Stravinsky, *Petruskha*, June 13; Mahler, *Das Lied von der Erde*, Nov. 20. Bartók (30) composes *Bluebeard's Castle*; Ives (37), the *Robert Browning Overture*.
1912	38	Three of the *Five Orchestral Pieces* performed in an 8-hand piano arrangement in Berlin, Feb. 4. Conducts *Pelleas* in Prague, Feb. 29, and gives a lecture there in memory of Mahler, March 25. Teaches composition in Berlin, pupils including Edward Clark (24) and Eduard Steuermann (20), introduced by Busoni. Composes *Pierrot Lunaire* to Albertine Zehme's com-	Cage born, Sept. 15; Massenet (70) dies, Aug. 13. First perfs. of Busoni, *Die Brautwahl*, April 13; Strauss, *Ariadne auf Naxos* (first version), Oct. 25. Debussy (50) composes *Jeux* and *Khamma*; Parry (64), Symphony No. 5 and Nativity Ode; Suk (38), *Zrání*.

mission; premières it in
Berlin, Oct. 16, and tours
the work through Germany
and Austria with success.
Conducts *Pelleas* in Am-
sterdam (Nov. 30) and St
Petersburg (Dec. 21). The
Five Orchestral Pieces are
premièred in London by
Henry Wood, Sept. 3.
Begins sketching a very
large-scale symphony in
Dec.

1913 39 The first performance of the
Gurrelieder (Feb. 23, Vienna
under Franz Schreker) is an
overwhelming success;
but a concert of music by
Schoenberg, Berg, Webern,
Mahler and Zemlinsky
(Vienna, March 31) pro-
vokes riots. Completes *Die
glückliche Hand* on Nov. 20,
and composes 'Seraphita',
Op. 22 No. 1 (completed
Oct. 6).

Britten born, Nov. 22;
Lutoslawski born, Jan. 25.
First perfs. of Fauré, *Péné-
lope*, March 4; Stravinsky,
The Rite of Spring, May 29;
Elgar, *Falstaff*, Oct. 1.
Magnard (48) composes
Symphony No. 4; Scriabin
(41), Piano Sonatas 8–10;
Webern (30) completes *Five
Pieces for Orchestra*, Op. 10.

1914 40 Conducts the *Gurrelieder* in
Liepzig and the *Five
Orchestral Pieces* in London
(both in Jan.). Still sketching symphony, notes down
a twelve-note theme on
May 27. Composes 'Alle
welche dich suchen', Op.
22 No. 2 (Nov.–Dec.).

Liadov (59) dies, Aug. 28;
Magnard (49) dies, Sept. 3;
Panufnik born, Sept. 24.
Ives (40) completes *Three
Places in New England*;
Vaughan Williams (42), *A
London Symphony* (first
perf. March 27).

YEAR	AGE	LIFE	CONTEMPORARY MUSICIANS AND EVENTS

1915 41 Completes 'Mach mich zum Wachter', Op. 22 No. 3, on Jan. 1, and the poem 'Totentanz der Principien' on Jan. 15. Begins the text of *Die Jakobsleiter*. Conducts Beethoven's 9th Symphony in Vienna (April). Moves back to that city in the summer, and is called up for the Austrian Army in Dec.

Goldmark (84) dies, Jan. 2; Scriabin (43) dies, April 27; Searle born, Aug 26. Debussy (53) writes *En Blanc et Noir, Études,* and two sonatas; Ives (41) completes the *Concord* Sonata and *Tone-Roads No. 3*; Strauss (51), *Ein Alpensinfonie.*

1916 42 In camp, composes *Die eiserne Brigade.* Composes 'Vorgefühl', last of the Op. 22 Songs, in July. Suffers from asthma attacks, but is not discharged from the army till Oct. 20. Resumes work on *Die Jakobsleiter,* and tinkers (for the last time for 20 years) with Chamber Symphony No. 2.

Babbitt born, May 10; Butterworth (31) dies, Aug. 5; Dutilleux born, Jan. 22; Ginastera born, April 11; Granados (48) dies, March 24; Reger (42) dies, May 11. First perf. of Nielsen, Symphony No. 4, Feb. 1.

1917 43 Completes text of *Die Jakobsleiter* on May 26 and begins composing the music (stemming from the unfinished symphony). Called up again on Sept. 19, irreparably interrupting this work. Discharged on Dec. 7 because of physical unfitness.

First perfs. of Busoni, *Arlecchino,* May 11; Debussy, Violin Sonata, May 5; Pfitzner, *Palestrina,* June 12; Satie, *Parade,* May 18. Baines (18) composes Symphony in C minor.

1918 44 Begins new composition class in Dr Schwarzwald's School (Jan.–April); moves

Boito (76) dies, June 10; Debussy (55) dies, March 26; von Einem born, Jan.

YEAR	AGE	LIFE	CONTEMPORARY MUSICIANS AND EVENTS
		to Mödling in April. Conducts 10 public rehearsals of Chamber Symphony No. 1 in Vienna (June). Founds the Society for Private Musical Performances, Nov. 23, with Webern (35), Berg (33) and Steuermann (26) as his chief assistants. The first concert, Dec. 29, is of Debussy, Mahler and Scriabin. Josef Rufer (25) becomes a pupil.	24; Parry (70) dies, Oct. 7; Rochberg born, July 5; Zimmermann born, March 18. First perf. of Stravinsky, *The Soldier's Tale*, Sept. 28. Brian (42) completes *The Tigers*.
1919	45	Eisler (21), Rudolf Kolisch (23) and Karl Rankl (21) become pupils. Contributes to Adolf Loos's symposium *Guide-Lines for a Ministry of the Arts*. Paints 'The Victor' and 'The Vanquished' in April.	Leoncavallo (61) dies, Aug. 9; Vlad born, Dec. 29. First perf. of Elgar, Cello Concerto, Oct. 27; Bartók (38) composes *The Miraculous Mandarin*; Satie (53), *Socrate*.
1920	46	Conducts in Amsterdam in March. In May returns there with his family, Webern and Wellesz, to attend the first Mahler Festival; elected President of the International Mahler League. Conducts the *Gurrelieder* in Vienna, June 13. First sketches of the *Serenade*, Aug. In Oct., returns to Holland to conduct and lecture until the following spring.	Bruch (82) dies, Oct. 2; Fricker born, Sept. 5; Griffes (36) dies, April 8. First perf. of Stravinsky, *Symphonies of Wind Instruments*, June 10; Vermeulen (32) completes Symphony No. 2, *Prélude à la nouvelle journée*.

YEAR	AGE	LIFE	CONTEMPORARY MUSICIANS AND EVENTS
1921	47	Conducts the *Gurrelieder* in Amsterdam, March 19, before returning to Vienna. In June, goes to Mattsee for a holiday but is forced to leave because of local anti-semitic discrimination. Spends the summer in Traunkirchen, working on *Die Jakobsleiter* and on Opp. 23–5; he 'discovers' the twelve-note method probably at the end of July. Death of mother Pauline, in Berlin, Oct. 12. Conducts *Pierrot Lunaire* at the 154th and last concert of the Vienna Society for Private Musical Performances, Dec. 5.	Humperdinck (67) dies, Sept. 27; Andrew Imbrie born, April 6; Saint-Saëns (86) dies, Dec. 16; Robert Simpson born, March 2. Berg (36) completes *Wozzeck*; Fauré (76), Piano Quintet No. 2; Weill (21), Symphony No. 1.
1922	48	Conducts *Pierrot* in Prague, May 25, for the first concert of the Prague Society for Private Musical Perform-ances, successor to the Vienna Society. Arranges two Bach chorale-preludes for orchestra (April–June); breaks off work on *Die Jakobsleiter* in July; ar-ranges the *Lied der Wald-taube* in Dec.	Baines (23) dies, Nov. 6; Pedrell (81) dies, Aug. 19; Xenakis born, May 29. First perfs. of Nielsen, Symphony No. 5, Jan. 24; Vaughan Williams, *A Pas-toral Symphony*, Jan. 26.
1923	49	Affected by the raging infla-tion in Austria. Does his best to aid other musicians,	Ligeti born, May 28. First perfs. of Sibelius, Sym-phony No. 6, Feb. 19;

YEAR	AGE	LIFE	CONTEMPORARY MUSICIANS AND EVENTS

notably Berg (38), Eisler (25) and Hauer (40), whom he corresponds with, and meets in Dec. Break with Kandinsky over the anti-semitic tendencies at the Bauhaus; Schoenberg warns him against Hitler in a letter of May 4. Completes *Five Piano Pieces* Op. 23 and *Serenade* Op. 24 in April and the *Suite* for piano Op. 25 in July. Conducts an all-Schoenberg concert in Copenhagen in Jan. Wife Mathilde falls ill in Sept. and dies of a liver complaint on Oct 22. S. writes the poem 'Requiem', Nov. 15. Roberto Gerhard (27) becomes a pupil at the end of the year.

Stravinsky, *Les Noces*, June 13 and Octet, Oct. 18; Foulds, *A World Requiem*, Nov. 11. F. G. Scott (43) composes *Country Life*; Zemlinsky (51), the *Lyric Symphony*.

1924 50 Tours Italy, conducting *Pierrot*, March–April. Premières of *Serenade*, under S., Donaueschingen, May 2; *Erwartung*, under Zemlinsky, Prague, June 6; *Die glückliche Hand*, under Fritz Stiedry, Vienna, Oct. 14. Several other concerts given to mark S.'s fiftieth birthday. Completes the Wind Quintet in Aug.; remarries, to Gertrud, sister of pupil Rudolf Kolisch, on Oct 28.

Busoni (58) dies, July 27 (leaving *Doktor Faust* unfinished): Fauré (79) dies, Nov. 4; Nono born, Jan. 29; Puccini (65) dies, Nov. 29; Scharwenka (74) dies, Dec. 8; Christopher Shaw born, July 30; First perf. of Strauss, *Intermezzo*, Nov. 4.

YEAR	AGE	LIFE	CONTEMPORARY MUSICIANS AND EVENTS
1925	51	Holidays in Italy, Jan.–Feb.; conducts *Pierrot* in Barcelona in April. Attends the ICSM Festival in Venice, Aug.–Sept. Appointed director of the composition Masterclass at the Berlin Academy of the Arts, in succession to Busoni, on Aug. 28. Operation for appendicitis in Nov. Writes the choruses Opp. 27–8 (Sept.–Dec.).	Berio born, Oct. 10; Boulez born, March 25; Satie (59) dies, July 1. First perf. of Varèse, *Intégrales*, March 1. Berg (40) composes the Chamber Concerto; Max Butting (37), Symphony No. 3.
1926	52	Arrives in Berlin, followed by pupils Gerhard (30), Zillig (21) and Rufer (33), whom he makes his assistant. New pupils include Walter Goehr (23). Completes the *Suite* (Septet) Op. 29 on May 1; begins *Variations for Orchestra* on May 2, and works on the play *Der biblische Weg*. Visits Vienna in the autumn.	Henze born, July 1. First perfs. of Hindemith, *Cardillac*, Nov. 9; Janáček, Sinfonietta, June 26; Sibelius, *Tapiola*, Dec. 26; Vaughan Williams, *Sancta Civitas*, May 7.
1927	53	Composes String Quartet No. 3 (Jan.–March, first perf. in Vienna, Sept. 19 by the Kolisch Quartet) and completes *Der biblische Weg* on July 12. Marc Blitzstein (22) becomes a pupil in Jan., Skalkottas (23) in Oct. Conducts in Berlin, Spain	First perfs. of Berg, *Lyric Suite*, Jan. 8; Janáček, *Glagolitic Mass*, Dec. 5; Stravinsky, *Oedipus Rex*, May 30. Brian (51) completes the *Gothic* Symphony; Bridge (48), *Enter Spring*; Krenek (27), *Johnny Spielt Auf*; Varèse

YEAR	AGE	LIFE	CONTEMPORARY MUSICIANS AND EVENTS
		and Paris, and lectures at the Sorbonne in Dec.	(44), *Arcana*; Webern (44), String Trio.
1928	54	Conducts British première of the *Gurrelieder* in London, Jan. 27; also conducts in Basle and Berne. Spends the summer in Roquebrune. Completes *Variations for Orchestra*, Op. 31 (Sept. 20—first perf. in Berlin, Dec. 2, under Furtwängler); orchestrates Bach's Prelude & Fugue in E flat, May–Oct.; writes the libretto of *Moses und Aron* (Oct.); composes *Von heute auf Morgen* (Oct.–Jan. 1, 1929).	Barraqué born, Jan. 17; Janáček (74) dies, Aug. 12; Ronald Stevenson born, March 6; Stockhausen born, Aug. 22. Bartók (47) writes String Quartet No. 4; Webern (45), Symphony Op. 21.
1929	55	Composes 'Verbundenheit' in April. In Oct. begins *Begleitungsmusik zu einer Lichtspielszene*; and Norbert von Hannenheim (31) becomes a pupil.	Edison Denisov born, April 6. First perf. of Weill-Hindemith, *Der Lindbergh-flug*, July 27. Foulds (49) composes *Dynamic Triptych*.
1930	56	First perf. of *Von heute auf Morgen* (Frankfurt, Feb. 1). Completes *Begleitungsmusik* on Feb. 14 and the Six Pieces for Male Chorus in March. Begins composing *Moses und Aron* on May 7.	Heseltine (36) dies, Dec. 17. First perfs. of Stravinsky, *Symphony of Psalms*, Dec. 13; Vaughan Williams, *Job*, Oct. 23; Weill, *Aufsteig und Fall der Stadt Mahagonny*, March 9, and *Der Jasager*, June 23; Eisler, *Die Massnahme*, Dec. 10.
1931	57	Conducts *Erwartung* for the BBC in London, Jan. 9. For	d'Indy (80) dies, Dec. 2; Nielsen (66) dies, Oct. 2.

YEAR	AGE	LIFE	CONTEMPORARY MUSICIANS AND EVENTS
		health reasons, spends May–Sept. in Territet (Montreux), then moves on to Spain; spends the winter with Gerhard (35) in Barcelona, working on *Moses und Aron*.	Bridge (52) composes *Phantasm*; Szymanowski (48), *Harnasie*.
1932	58	First perf. of the Op. 22 Orchestral Songs (Berlin, Feb. 21). Completes Act 2 of *Moses und Aron* on March 10. Daughter Nuria born, May 7. Returns to Berlin (June) and winters there despite poor health and bad political situation. Begins Cello Concerto in Nov.	Goehr born, Aug. 10; Hugh Wood born, June 27. First perf. of Weill, *Die Bürgschaft*, March 10. Brian (56) completes Symphony No. 3.
1933	59	Completes the Cello Concerto, Jan. 4 and composes Three Songs, Op. 48 (Jan.–Feb.). After the Nazis attain power (Jan. 30) S. becomes *persona ingratissima* at the Berlin Academy because of his race and teaching. Leaves Berlin for Paris, May 17, where he formally rejoins the Jewish religion, July 24. Completes the String Quartet Concerto on Aug. 16. Sails for the U.S.A. on Oct 25; arrives New York on Oct. 31 and settles in Boston to teach at the Malkin Conservatoire.	Justin Connolly born; Duparc (85) dies, Feb. 13; Penderecki born, Nov. 23. Brian (57) completes *Das Siegeslied*; Koechlin (66), the *Seven Stars Symphony*; Franz Schmidt (59), Symphony No. 4; Strauss (69), *Arabella* (first perf. July 1). First perf. of Weill, *Der Silbersee*, Feb. 18.

YEAR	AGE	LIFE	CONTEMPORARY MUSICIANS AND EVENTS
1934	60	Conducts *Pelleas* in Boston on March 16, and lectures at the University of Chicago. Poor health forces him to move to New York (March), then Chautauqua (summer) and finally Los Angeles (autumn). Composes *Suite in G* for strings (Sept.–Dec.).	Birtwistle born, July 15; Peter Maxwell Davies born, Sept. 8; Durkó born, April 10; Delius (72) dies, June 10; Elgar (76) dies, Feb. 23; Holst (60) dies, May 25; Schnittke born, Nov. 24; Schreker (55) dies, March 21. Hindemith (39) composes *Mathis der Maler*; Varèse (51) *Ecuatorial*; Webern (51), Concerto op. 24; Weill (34), Symphony No. 2.
1935	61	Arranges Chamber Symphony No. 1 for orchestra (April); begins the Violin Concerto. Lectures at the University of Southern California in Sept. Health and financial position improve. Gives private lessons to—among others—John Cage (22).	Berg (50) dies, Dec. 24; Dukas (69) dies, May 18; Loeffler (74) dies, May 19; Suk (61) dies, May 29. First perfs. of Vaughan Williams, Symphony No. 4, April 10; Walton, Symphony No. 1 (complete), Nov. 6. Berg completes the Violin Concerto and leaves *Lulu* unfinished. Zemlinsky (63) composes *Psalm 13*.
1936	62	Composes String Quartet No. 4, April–July 26 and completes Violin Concerto on Sept. 23. Appointed Professor at the University of California, Los Angeles. Settles in Brentwood Park, Hollywood. Becomes friendly with Gershwin (38).	David Blake born, Sept. 2; van Dieren (51) dies, April 24; Glazunov (70) dies, March 21; Respighi (56) dies, April 18.

Schoenberg

YEAR	AGE	LIFE
1937	63	All four of S.'s quartets performed by the Kolisch Quartet at U.C.L.A., Jan. 4–8. Sketches a 'Jewish Symphony' (Jan.–Feb.); orchestrates Brahms's G minor Piano Quartet. Birth of son Ronald, May 26. Begins a textbook (later *Fundamentals of Musical Composition*). Teaches and travels.
1938	64	Composes *Kol Nidre*, Op. 39 (Aug.–Sept. 22, first perf. Oct. 4 in Los Angeles).
1939	65	Completes Chamber Symphony No. 2, Op. 38, on Oct. 21—thirty-three years after beginning it.
1940	66	Conducts *Pierrot Lunaire* for a recording (Sept.–Oct.). First perf. of Violin Concerto (Dec. 6, Philadelphia, played by Louis Krasner).
1941	67	Birth of son Lawrence, Jan. 27. Assumes American citizenship on April 11. Leaves an Organ Sonata unfinished (Aug.) but completes *Variations on a Recitative* on Oct. 12. Brother Heinrich dies, poisoned in a

Gershwin (38) dies, July 11; Ravel (62) dies, Dec. 28; Roussel (68) dies, Aug. 23; Szymanowski (54) dies, March 29. First perfs. of Bartók, *Music for strings, percussion and celesta*, Jan. 21; Rachmaninov, Symphony No. 3, Nov. 6; Shostakovich, Symphony No. 5, Oct. 21.

Franz Schmidt (64) completes *Das Buch mit sieben Siegeln*; Webern (55), String Quartet Op. 28.

Foulds (58) dies, April 24; Godowsky (68) dies, Nov. 21; Franz Schmidt (64) dies, Feb. 11. Koechlin (72) composes *Les Bandar-Log*; Webern (56), Cantata No. 1.

Revueltas (40) dies, Oct. 5; Tovey (64) dies, July 10. Eisler (42) composes the *Deutsche Sinfonie*; Webern (57), the *Variations* for orchestra Op. 30.

Bridge (61) dies, Jan. 10; Paderewski (75) dies, June 29; Dallapiccola (37) completes *Canti di Prigionera*; Petrassi (37) composes *Coro di Morti*. First perf. of Weill, *Lady in the Dark*, Jan. 23.

YEAR	AGE	LIFE	CONTEMPORARY MUSICIANS AND EVENTS
		Nazi hospital in Salzburg.	
1942	68	Composes *Ode to Napoleon* (March–July 12) and Piano Concerto (July 5–Dec. 31). Also writes textbook *Models for Beginners in Composition* (completed Sept. 12).	Zemlinsky (70) dies, March 16. First perf. of Strauss, *Capriccio*, Oct. 28. Hindemith (47) completes *Ludus Tonalis*.
1943	69	Completes *Theme and Variations* for wind band (or orchestra) on Aug. 24.	Hannenheim (45) dies, (?); Rachmaninov (69) dies, March 28. Bartók (62) composes Concerto for orchestra; Skalkottas (39), Suite No. 2; Shostakovich (37), Symphony No. 8; Webern (60), Cantata No. 2.
1944	70	Health deteriorates badly in Feb., and on Sept. 13 S. is compelled by statute to retire from U.C.L.A. on a pitifully small pension. His 70th birthday celebrated by many perfs. of his works. Begins, but does not persist in, a revision of *Die Jakobsleiter* (Oct.–Dec.).	Havergal Brian (68) completes *Prometheus Unbound*; Copland (44), *Appalachian Spring*; Koechlin (77), Symphony No. 2; Messiaen (36), *Vingt Regards sur l'Enfant Jésus*; Wolpe (42), *Battle Piece*.
1945	71	Financial straits compel S. to continue giving private lessons. The Guggenheim Foundation refuse his application for monetary assistance to complete *Moses und Aron, Die Jakobsleiter*, and textbooks.	Bartók (64) dies, Sept. 26; Mascagni (81) dies, Aug. 2; Webern (62) dies, Sept. 15. Skalkottas (41) composes *The Return of Ulysses*; Strauss (81), *Metamorphosen*; Vogel (49) completes *Thyl Claes*.

YEAR	AGE	LIFE	CONTEMPORARY MUSICIANS AND EVENTS
		Composes *Prelude*, Op. 44 (Sept.).	
1946	72	Lectures at the University of Chicago. Suffers a near-fatal heart attack on Aug. 2; composes String Trio (Aug. 20–Sept. 23).	Bantock (78) dies, Oct. 16; Falla (69) dies, Nov. 14; Ethel Smyth (86) dies, May 9.
1947	73	Health improves. Elected to the American Academy of Arts and Letters (April). Composes *A Survivor from Warsaw*, Aug. 11–23 (first perf. Nov. 4 in Albuquerque), and works on essays and the textbook *Structural Functions of Harmony*.	Casella (63) dies, March 5; Pijper (52) dies, March 19. Gerhard (51) composes *The Duenna*; Prokofiev (56), Symphony No. 6; Seiber (42), *Ulysses*; Spinner (41), Piano Concerto; Grainger (65) completes his *Jungle Book Cycle* (begun in 1898); Thomas Mann writes *Doktor Faustus*.
1948	74	Quarrels with Thomas Mann over his novel *Doktor Faustus*. Arranges *Three Folksongs* for chorus, Op. 49, in June.	Wolf-Ferrari (72) dies, Jan. 21. Havergal Brian (72) composes Symphony No. 7; Dallapiccola (44), *Il Prigioniero*; Messiaen (40), *Turangalîla-Symphonie*.
1949	75	Composes *Phantasy* for violin, Op. 47, March 3–22; *Dreimal Tausend Jahre* Op. 50A (completed April 20), and works on *Israel Exists Again* (March–June) which remains unfinished. Poor health prevents his attending 75th birthday celebrations in Europe.	Novák (78) dies, July 18; Pfitzner (80) dies, May 22; Skalkottas (45) dies, Sept. 19; Strauss (85) dies, Sept. 8.
1950	76	Composes *De Profundis*,	Koechlin (83) dies, Dec. 31;

254

YEAR	AGE	LIFE	CONTEMPORARY MUSICIANS AND EVENTS

Op. 50B (June–July); writes the texts of the 'Modern Psalms' and composes music for the first, Op. 50C (begun Oct. 2, not completed). Ill again. Essay-collection *Style and Idea* published.

Miaskovsky (69) dies, Aug. 9; Weill (50) dies, April 3. Korngold (53) completes Symphony in F sharp.

1951 76 Elected Honorary President of the Israel Academy of Music in Jerusalem (April). Continues writing psalm-texts until his death at Brentwood Park, July 13.

Lambert (43) dies, Aug. 21; Medtner (71) dies, Nov. 13. Antheil aged 51; Babbitt 35; Berio 25; Berkeley 48; Birtwistle 17; Blacher 48; Blake 15; Bliss 59; Bloch 70; Boulez 26; Brian 75 (completes *Turandot*, May 18); Britten 37; Bush 50; Cage 38; Carter 42 (completes String Quartet No. 1); Castelnuovo-Tedesco 55; Charpentier 90; Chavez 52; Connolly 17; Copland 50; Cowell 54; Ruth Crawford 50; Dallapiccola 47; Davies 17; Denisov 22; Dohnanyi 74; Dutilleux 35; Egk 51; von Einem 33; Eisler 53; Enesco 69; Finzi 49; Frankel 45; Fricker 30; Gerhard 54; Ginastera 35; Glière 76; Goehr 19; Grainger 69; Hábá 58; Harris 53; Hartmann 45; Hauer 68; Henze 25; Hindemith 55 (completes Sym-

YEAR	AGE	LIFE

CONTEMPORARY MUSICIANS
AND EVENTS

phony, *Die Harmonie der Welt*); Holbrooke 72; Holmboe 41; Honegger 59; Hovhaness 40; Howells 58; Ireland 71; Ives 76; Jolivet 45; Khachaturian 47; Kilpinen 59; Kodaly 68; Korngold 54; Krenek 50; Ligeti 28; Lutoslawski 38; Lutyens 45; Malipiero 69; Martin 61; Martinů 61; Maw 16; Messiaen 42 (completes *Livre d'Orgue*); Milhaud 58; Nono 27; Nyström 61; Orff 56; Panufnik 36; Penderecki 18; Petrassi 46; Petterson 40; Piston 57; Pizzetti 70; Poulenc 52; Prokofiev 60; Rawsthorne 46; Riegger 66; Rochberg 33; Rosenberg 59; Rubbra 50; Ruggles 75; Saeverud 54; Schmitt 80; Schnittke 16; Schoeck 64; Schuman 40; Cyril Scott 71; F. G. Scott 71; Searle 35; Seiber 46; Sessions 54; Shaw 27; Shostakovich 45 (completes *24 Preludes & Fugues*); Simpson 30; Spinner 45; Stevenson 23; Stockhausen 22; Stravinsky 69 (completes *The Rake's Progress*, April 7); Tippett 56; Valen 63; Varèse 67; Vaughan

YEAR	AGE	LIFE	CONTEMPORARY MUSICIANS AND EVENTS
			Williams 78 (first perf. of *The Pilgrim's Progress*, April 26); Vermeulen 63; Villa-Lobos 64; Vlad 31; Vogel 55; Walton 49; Wellesz 65; Wood 19; Wolpe 48; Xenakis 29; Zillig 46; Zimmermann 33.

Appendix B   Catalogue of works

The following list of works excludes all 'juvenilia' (pre-1897) unless they have been mentioned in the main text; and includes all completed works after that date—whether or not they have been performed—as well as all substantial unfinished compositions that have either reached performance, or publication, or been alluded to in the text. For a fuller catalogue the reader is referred to *The Works of Arnold Schoenberg* (London, 1962) by Josef Rufer; for yet fuller listing of the works up to 1933, in greater and more authoritative detail, to Volume I of *Studien zur Entwicklung des dodekaphonen Satzes bei Arnold Schönberg* (Copenhagen, 1972) by Jan Maegaard. Reasons of space have led me to omit details of publication; but it is expected that most, if not all, of the material here catalogued will eventually appear in the Complete Edition which since 1966 has begun to be issued under the joint imprint of B. Schotts Söhne, Mainz and Universal Edition AG (Vienna).

Texts of vocal works, where not otherwise indicated, are Schoenberg's own.

STAGE WORKS

Erwartung, Op. 17. Monodrama in one act, libretto by Marie Pappenheim (1909)

Die glückliche Hand, Op. 18. Drama with music in one act (1910–13)

Von heute auf Morgen, Op. 32. Opera in one act, libretto by Gertrud Schoenberg ('Max Blonda') (1928–9)

Moses und Aron. Opera in three acts. *Unfinished* (1930–2)

VOICES AND ORCHESTRA

Gurrelieder (Jacobsen) for soprano, contralto, tenor, baritone, bass, reciter, chorus and orchestra (1900–11)

Symphony (Dehmel, Tagore, Schoenberg, the Bible) for soli, chorus and orchestra. *Unfinished* (1912–14)

Die Jakobsleiter. Oratorio for soli, chorus and orchestra. *Unfinished* (1917–22, 1944; performing version by Winfried Zillig, 1958)

Kol Nidre, Op. 39 for speaker, chorus and orchestra (1938)

A Survivor from Warsaw, Op. 46 for speaker, male chorus and orchestra (1947)

Israel Exists Again for chorus and orchestra. *Unfinished* (1949)

Modern Psalm, Op. 50c for speaker, chorus and orchestra. *Unfinished* (1950)

SOLO VOICE AND ORCHESTRA

Six Orchestral Songs, Op. 8 (1903–5)
    1. *Natur* (Hart); 2. *Das Wappenschild*; 3. *Sehnsucht* (Das Knaben Wunderhorn); 4. *Nie ward' ich, Herrin, müd*; 5. *Voll jener Süsse*; 6. *Wenn Vöglein klagen* (Petrarch)

Four Orchestral Songs, Op. 22 (1913–16)
    1. *Seraphita* (Dowson trs. George); 2. *Alle, welche dich suchen*; 3. *Mach mich zum Wächter deiner Weiten*; 4. *Vorgefühl* (Rilke)

CHORUS WITH OR WITHOUT ENSEMBLE

Ei du Lütte (Groth) for male chorus a cappella (undated; late 1890s?)

Friede auf Erden (Meyer), Op. 13 for mixed chorus a cappella (1907; optional accompaniment of wind instruments added 1911)

Four Pieces for mixed chorus, Op. 27—with clarinet, mandolin, violin and cello in No. 4 (1925)
    1. *Unentrinnbar*; 2. *Du sollst nicht, du musst*; 3. *Mond und Menschen* (Bethge, after Tschan-Jo-Su); 4. *Der Wunsch des Liebhabers* (Bethge, after Hung-so-Fan)

Three Satires, Op. 28 for mixed chorus—with viola, cello and piano in No. 3 and an Appendix for mixed chorus and string quartet (1925–6)

 1. *Am Scheideweg*; 2. *Vielseitigkeit*; 3. *Der neue Klassizismus*; Appendix: 1. *Ein Spruch und zwei Variationen über ihn*; 2. Canon for string quartet; 3. *Legitimation als Canon*

Three Folksongs for mixed chorus (1929)

 1. *Es gingen zwei Gespielen gut*; 2. *Herzlieblich Lieb, durch Scheiden*; 3. *Schein uns, du liebe Sonne*

Six Pieces for male chorus, Op. 35 (1929–30)

 1. *Hemmung*; 2. *Das Gesetz*; 3. *Ausdrucksweise*; 4. *Glück*; 5. *Landsknechte*; 6. *Verbundenheit*

Three Folksongs, Op. 49 for mixed chorus (1948)

 1. *Es gingen zwei Gespielen gut*; 2. *Der Mai tritt ein mit Freuden*; 3. *Mein Herz in steten Treuen*

Dreimal Tausend Jahre (Runes) for mixed chorus, Op. 50A (1949)

De Profundis (Psalm 130) for mixed chorus, Op. 50B (1950)

SOLO VOICE AND ENSEMBLE

Nachtwandler (Falke), *Brettl-lied* for voice, piccolo, trumpet, snare-drum and piano (1901)

Herzegewächse (Maeterlinck), Op. 20 for high soprano, harp, celesta and harmonium (1911)

Pierrot Lunaire (Guiraud trs. Hartleben), Op. 21: three times seven melodramas for reciter, piano, flute (piccolo), clarinet (bass clarinet), violin (viola) and cello (1912)

Lied der Waldtaube (Jacobsen) for mezzo-soprano, seventeen instruments and percussion (arr. 1922 from *Gurrelieder*)

Ode to Napoleon Buonaparte (Byron), Op. 41 for reciter, piano and string quartet (1942; also version with string orchestra, Op. 41B)

SONGS WITH PIANO

Eclogue (?)
Lied der Schnitterin (Pfau)
Mädchenlied (Heyse)
Mannesbangen (Dehmel) } (undated; probably late 1890s)
Nicht doch! (Dehmel)
Waldesnacht (Heyse)
Mädchenfruhling (Dehmel) (1897)

Two Songs (von Levetzow), Op. 1 for baritone (*c.* 1898)
    1. *Dank*; 2. *Abscheid*
Die Beiden (Hofmannsthal) (1899)
Four Songs, Op. 2 (2 and 4 undated; 1 and 3 dated 1899)
    1. *Erwartung*; 2. *Schenk mir deinen goldenen Kamm*; 3. *Erhebung* (Dehmel); 4. *Waldsonne* (Schlaf)
Gruss in die Ferne (Lingg) (1900)
Breitl-lieder (1901)
    Der genügsame Liebhaber (Salus); *Einfältiges Lied* (Salus); *Jedem das Seine* (Colly); *Mahnung* (Hochstetter); *Galathea* (Wedekind); *Gigerlette* (Bierbaum); *Aus dem Spiegel von Arcadia* (Schikaneder)
Six Songs, Op. 3 (1899–1903)
    1. *Wie Georg von Frundsberg von sich selber sang* (Das Knaben Wunderhorn); 2. *Die Aufgeregten* (Keller); 3. *Warnung* (Dehmel); 4. *Hochzeitslied* (Jacobsen); 5. *Geübtes Herz* (Keller); 6. *Freihold* (Lingg)
Deinem Blick zu mich bequemen (Goethe) (1903)
Eight Songs, Op. 6 (1903–5)
    1. *Traumleben* (Hart); 2. *Alles* (Dehmel); 3. *Mädchenlied* (Remer); 4. *Verlassen* (Conradi); 5. *Ghasel* (Keller); 6. *Am Wegrand* (Mackay); 7. *Lockung* (Aram); 8. *Der Wanderer* (Nietzsche)
Gedenken (?) (undated; mid-1900's?)
Two Ballads, Op. 12 (1907)
    1. *Jane Grey* (Amman); 2. *Der verlorene Haufen* (Klemperer)
Jeduch. Ballad (Löns). *Unfinished* (1907) [1]
Mignon (Goethe). *Unfinished* (1907) [1]
Two Songs, Op. 14 (1907–8)
    1. *Ich darf nicht dankend* (George); 2. *In diesen Wintertagen* (Henckel)
Friedesabend (George). *Unfinished* (1908) [1]
Das Buch der hängenden Garten, Op. 15. Song-cycle on fifteen verses from Stefan George's 'The Book of the Hanging Gardens', for high voice (1908–9)

---

[1] Portions of these quite substantial fragments are published in Maegaard, *op. cit.*

Am Strande (?Rilke) (dated 1909; possibly 1908)
Four German Folksongs (1929)
    1. *Der Mai tritt ein mit Freuden*; 2. *Es gingen zwei Gespielen gut*;
    3. *Mein Herz in steten Treuen*; 4. *Mein Herz ist mir genenget*
Three Songs (Haringer), Op. 48 for low voice (1933)
    1. *Sommermüd*; 2. *Tot*; 3. *Mädchenlied*

ORCHESTRA, CHAMBER ORCHESTRA, STRING ORCHESTRA

Serenade in D major, for small orchestra. *Unfinished* (1896)
Gavotte and Musette, for string orchestra (1897)
Frühlings Tod: Symphonic Poem, after Lenau. *Unfinished* (1898)
Adagio in A flat, for string orchestra and harp (undated: late 1890s?)
Pelleas und Melisande, Op. 5. Symphonic Poem, after Maeterlinck
    (1902–3)
Chamber Symphony No. 1 in E major, Op. 9, for fifteen instruments
    (1906; version for full orchestra, 1922; second, revised version
    for full orchestra, Op. 9B, 1935)
Five Orchestral Pieces, Op. 16 (1909; revised 1922; revised again, for
    slightly reduced orchestra, 1949; version of Nos. 1, 2, 4 and 5 for
    chamber ensemble by Schoenberg and Felix Greissle *c.* 1919)
Three Little Pieces for chamber orchestra (1910)
Variations for orchestra, Op. 31 (1926–8)
Begleitungsmusik zu einer Lichtspielszene, for orchestra, Op. 34 (1929–
    1930)
Suite in G major, for string orchestra (1934)
Chamber Symphony No. 2 in E flat minor, Op. 38, for medium
    orchestra (1906–16, 1939; version for 2 pianos, Op. 38B, 1941)
Theme and Variations in G minor, for wind band, Op. 43A (1943; also
    version for full orchestra, Op. 43B)
Prelude to the *Genesis* Suite, Op. 44, for orchestra with wordless choir
    (1945)

SOLO INSTRUMENT(S) AND ORCHESTRA

Cello Concerto in D major (after a harpsichord concerto by G. M.
    Monn) (1932–3)

Concerto for string quartet and orchestra in B flat (after Handel's
Concerto Grosso Op. 6, No. 7) (1933)
Violin Concerto, Op. 36 (1935–6)
Piano Concerto, Op. 42 (1942)

CHAMBER MUSIC

Presto in C major, for string quartet (undated: perhaps 1894)
Scherzo in F major, for string quartet (1897)
String Quartet in D major (1897)
Verklärte Nacht. String Sextet, after Dehmel, Op. 4 (1899; versions
for string orchestra arr. 1917, 1943)
String Quartet No. 1 in D minor, Op. 7 (1904–5)
Ein Stelldichein, for oboe, clarinet, violin, cello and piano. *Unfinished.*
(1905)
String Quartet No. 2 in F sharp minor, Op. 10, with soprano (1907–8;
version for string orchestra, ? 1919)
Serenade, Op. 24, for clarinet, bass clarinet, mandolin, guitar, violin,
viola and cello, with baritone (1920–3)
Wind Quintet, Op. 26 (1923–4)
Suite (Septet), Op. 29, for piano, 3 clarinets, violin, viola and
cello (1925–6)
String Quartet No. 3, Op. 30 (1927)
String Quartet No. 4, Op. 37 (1936)
String Trio, Op. 45 (1946)
Phantasy, Op. 47, for violin with piano accompaniment (1949)

ORGAN

Sonata. *Unfinished.* (1941)
Variations on a Recitative, in D minor, Op. 40 (1941)

PIANO

Lied ohne Worte (c. 1890)
Three Piano Pieces (1894)
    1. Andantino; 2. Andantino grazioso; 3. Presto
Six Pieces for piano duet (1896)

Alla Marcia in E flat (probably not originally intended as a piano piece)
(undated; mid to late 1900s?)
Three Piano Pieces, Op. 11 (1909)
    1. Mässig; 2. Mässig; 3. Bewegt
Six Little Piano Pieces, Op. 19 (1911)
    1. Leicht, zart; 2. Langsam; 3. Sehr langsam; 4. Rasch, aber
    leicht; 5. Etwas rasch; 6. Sehr langsam
Five Piano Pieces, Op. 23 (1920–3)
    1. Sehr langsam; 2. Sehr rasch; 3. Langsam; 4. Schwungvoll;
    5. Walzer
Suite for piano, Op. 25 (1921–3)
    1. Präludium; 2. Gavotte & Musette; 3. Intermezzo; 4. Menuett
    & Trio; 5. Gigue
Piano Piece in G. *Unfinished* (1925)
Piano Piece, Op. 33A (1928–9)
Piano Piece, Op. 33B (1931)

OCCASIONAL WORKS

Der Deutsche Michel (Kernstock). War-song for male chorus (1915?)
Der eiserne Brigade. March for piano and string quartet (1916)
Allein Gott in der Höh' sei Ehr. Chorale-setting for alto, violin, cello
    and piano (between 1918 and 1925)
Weihnachtsmusik for 2 violins, cello, harmonium and piano (1921)
Gerpa. Variations for horn, 2 violins, piano and harmonium. *Un-
    finished* (1922)
30 Canons for voices or instruments (1905–49)

ARRANGEMENTS AND ORCHESTRATIONS

(The following list omits the 'several thousand pages' of operettas
which Schoenberg is said to have scored in the late 1890s and early
1900s: so far none of the pieces in question have been identified with
complete certainty.)

Zemlinsky: *Sarema* (libretto reportedly by Schoenberg), vocal score
    (1897)
Heinrich van Eycken: *Lied der Walküre*, arrangement for voice and
    orchestra (1901)

Bogumil Zepler: *Mädchenreigen*, arrangement for 3 voices and orchestra (1902)

Heinrich Schenker: *Syrische Tänze*, arrangement for orchestra (1903)

Lortzing: *Der Waffenschmied von Worms*, pianoforte arrangement for four hands (?1904)

Rossini: *Il barbiere di Seviglia*, pianoforte arrangement for four hands of Overture and fifteen numbers (?1904)

Schubert: *Rosamunde*, pianoforte arrangement for four hands of Entr'actes and Ballet Music (?1904)

Carl Löwe: *Der Nock*, arrangement for voice and orchestra (1912)

Beethoven: *Adelaïde*, arrangement for voice and orchestra (1912)

Schubert: Three Songs, arrangement for voice and orchestra (1912)

G. M. Monn: Cello Concerto in G minor, arrangement for cello and piano with cadenza by Schoenberg (1912)

Zemlinsky: String Quartet No. 2, pianoforte arrangement for four hands (1915)

Johann Strauss: *Roses from the South* and *Lagunenwalzer*, arrangement for piano, harmonium and string quartet (1921)

Schubert: *Ständchen*, arrangement for clarinet, bassoon, mandolin, guitar and string quartet (1921)

Denza: *Funiculi, funiculá*, arrangement for clarinet, mandolin, guitar and string trio (1921)

Anon.: Short piece, arrangement (?) for clarinet, mandolin, guitar and string trio (1921) [1]

Busoni: *Berceuse Élégiaque*, arrangement for flute, clarinet, harmonium, piano and string quartet (*c.* 1921)

Bach: *Komm, Gott, Schöpfer, Heiliger Geist*, arrangement for large orchestra (1922)

Bach: *Schmücke dich, o liebe Seele*, arrangement for large orchestra (1922)

Johann Strauss: *Kaiserwalzer*, arrangement for flute, clarinet, string quartet and piano (1925)

Bach: Prelude and Fugue in E flat (from *Clavierübung*), arrangement for large orchestra (1928)

Brahms: Piano Quartet No. 1 in G minor, arrangement for orchestra (1937)

[1] This tiny piece (a polka with a waltz-time trio) could be by Schoenberg himself.

EDITIONS (realization of figured basses)

G .M. Monn: Symphonia a QuattroinA major
            Cello Concerto in G minor
            Harpsichord Concerto in D major
J. C. Mann: Divertimento in D major
Franz Tuma: Sinfonia a Quattro in E minor   1911–12
            Partita a Tre in C minor
            Partita a Tre in A major
            Partita a Tre in G major

LITERARY WORKS AND TEXTBOOKS

Harmonielehre (Vienna 1911; revised and enlarged, Vienna 1922; much abridged English version, *Theory of Harmony*, New York 1948)

Texte. Poems and texts intended for musical setting, including *Totentanz der Prinzipien, Die Jakobsleiter,* and *Requiem* (Vienna 1926)

Models for Beginners in Composition (New York 1942)

Style and Idea. Essays and lectures (New York 1950, ed. Dika Newlin; new greatly enlarged edition, ed. Leonard Stein, London 1975)

Structural Functions of Harmony (London 1954)

Preliminary Exercises in Counterpoint (London 1963, ed. Leonard Stein)

Schöpferische Konfessionen. Essays, aphorisms etc. (Zürich 1964, ed. Willi Reich)

Testi poetici e drammatici. Italian translations including the first publication of the play *Der biblische Weg* (Milan 1967)

Fundamentals of Musical Composition (London 1967, ed. Gerald Strang and Leonard Stein)

The above lists all publications in book form. The remainder of Schoenberg's literary estate (published and unpublished) is very extensive: further details may be found in Rufer, *op. cit.* Mention should also be made of the Selected Letters (Mainz 1958, ed. Erwin Stein; enlarged English edition, London 1964) and of the 'Berlin Diary' of 1912 (Berlin, 1974).

Appendix C Personalia

Adler, Guido (1855–1941), Austrian musicologist, a pupil of Bruckner and friend of Mahler. He founded and became first director of the Institute for Musical History at Vienna University, where he was professor of musicology in succession to Hanslick (1898–1927). He helped Schoenberg find his feet in Vienna on his return from Berlin in 1903, and encouraged his own students (e.g. Webern and Wellesz) to study with him. He was editor of the *Denkmäler der Tonkunst in Österreich*, for which Schoenberg contributed editions of works by eighteenth-century Viennese composers in 1912.

Adorno, Theodor Wiesengrund- (1903–69), German post-Hegelian, semi-Marxist philosopher, polymath, composer and *Kultur-Kritik*; pupil of Berg in Vienna and a member of Schoenberg's circle there and in Berlin. Emigrated to the U.S.A. in 1934; was Thomas Mann's musical adviser in the writing of *Doktor Faustus*. Returned to Germany in 1950 and taught at Frankfurt University. His musicological writings, which have been highly regarded on the Continent, include studies of Berg and Mahler, and above all *Die Philosophie der neuen Musik* (1949), a volume principally devoted to Schoenberg and Stravinsky which profoundly influenced the emergence of post-Webern serialists such as Boulez and Stockhausen. Schoenberg strongly disapproved of it.

Bahr, Hermann (1863–1934), Austrian novelist, dramatist and critic, influenced by the French symbolists and a member of the Expressionist movement in literature. He was a friend of Schoenberg; his wife, the singer Anna Bahr-Mildenburg, was a member of the Court Opera company during Mahler's tenure in Vienna, and gave some of the earliest performances of Schoenberg's songs.

267

Blitzstein, Marc (1905–64), American composer and pianist, pupil of Nadia Boulanger and Schoenberg. He was best known for his light operas and musicals (of pronounced left-wing political stance) *The Cradle will Rock*, *No for an Answer* and *Regina*.

Brian, William Havergal (1876–1972), British composer and musical journalist. The most prolific symphonist of the twentieth century (he wrote thirty-two, as well as five operas and many other works) and one of the most under-valued. He was a spirited advocate of Schoenberg's music in British journals between the wars, and met him in 1928.

Clark, Edward (1888–1962), British conductor and writer on music; pupil of Schoenberg in Berlin before World War I. A dedicated campaigner for new music, he played a very active role as head of the Music Department in the early days of the B.B.C., not only for Schoenberg's circle but also for Bartók, Busoni, Stravinsky and others. Conducted the British première of Schoenberg's First Chamber Symphony and the world première of the Cello Concerto. Husband of the composer Elisabeth Lutyens.

Dehmel, Richard (1863–1920), from Brandenburg, was perhaps the most discussed lyric poet in Germany before World War I. Schoenberg set several of Dehmel's poems; derived inspiration for *Verklärte Nacht* from a poem in his *Weib und Welt* (1896); and invited him to write the libretto for a proposed choral symphony (the final result was *Die Jakobsleiter*, to a text of Schoenberg's own).

Eisler, Hanns (1898–1962), son of the Austrian philosopher Rudolf Eisler, was a pupil of Schoenberg 1919–23; they frequently quarrelled over Eisler's left-wing political affiliations. By 1927 his works began to reflect the aspirations of the revolutionary workers' movement, and he became one of Bertolt Brecht's chief collaborators in political songs, films and stage music. He moved to the U.S.A. in 1938 and wrote many film scores (as well as a classic book on the subject), but was forced to leave the country by the Un-American Activities Committee. Settled in East Berlin in 1950. He wrote an enormous amount of music of all kinds in a vast variety of styles, ranging from the simplest diatonicism to the twelve-note method.

George, Stefan (1868–1933), Rhineland poet. Much influenced by the French Symbolists. By his own example and through his periodical *Blätter für die Kunst* he brought about a purification of German poetic diction. Died in voluntary exile, having refused honours from the Nazis. Schoenberg set several of his poems, above all in *Das Buch der hängenden Gärten* and the Second String Quartet.

Gerhard, Roberto Juan Rene (1896–1970), probably the greatest Spanish composer of the twentieth century. A pupil of Granados and Pedrell, he studied with Schoenberg in Vienna and Berlin from 1923 to 1928, and was host to Schoenberg in 1931–2, during the composition of much of *Moses und Aron*, in Barcelona. After the Spanish Civil War, because of his connections with the Republican Government, he went into exile and settled in Cambridge. Like many Schoenberg pupils he came late to twelve-note composition, but applied it for very personal, exploratory ends. His works include four symphonies, an opera, the ballet *Don Quixote*, and much chamber music; it can justly be said that he contributed some of the finest music written anywhere in the two decades after Schoenberg's death.

Gerstl, Richard (1883–1908), Austrian Fauvist painter, born in Vienna. Virtually self-taught, he was greatly influenced by the work of Edvard Munch and began painting in 1903, producing mainly portraits and landscapes. He gave lessons to Schoenberg, whose own paintings show signs of his influence, and was the cause of Schoenberg's matrimonial crisis in 1908. He committed suicide the same year. In recent years Gerstl has come to be recognized as one of the most original and underrated painters of the early Expressionist period.

Goehr, Walter (1903–60), German conductor, born in Berlin, where he studied with Schoenberg. He came to Britain in 1933. He did much work with German radio and with the B.B.C. Father of the composer Alexander Goehr.

Gutheil-Schoder, Marie (1874–1935), dramatic soprano who was one of the outstanding singer-actresses of the Vienna Opera during

Mahler's reign; famous for her interpretation of the title-role in Strauss's *Elektra*. She was the soloist in the premières of Schoenberg's Second String Quartet and *Erwartung*.

Hannenheim, Norbert Han von (1898–1943), Transylvanian composer, born in Vienna; pupil of Schoenberg in Berlin 1929–32, and highly regarded by him. He wrote symphonies, chamber and choral music, employing the twelve-note method to some extent, but most of his works seem to have been destroyed in the war. He was killed in Berlin during an air-raid.

Hauer, Josef Matthias (1883–1959), eccentric self-taught Austrian composer and theorist who was writing freely chromatic music as early as 1908 and by 1919, independently of Schoenberg, had evolved a method of twelve-note composition involving forty-four 'tropes'—divisions of the 479,001,000 possible combinations of the twelve chromatic pitches, each twelve further divided into two six-note groups. The method has never been mastered by anyone else. Schoenberg was interested in Hauer at a decisive period of his own development (they were in contact around 1918–25), although Schoenberg had arrived at his own twelve-note method before Hauer began to issue a series of theoretical pamphlets in the early 1920s. Hauer's output was voluminous (all his works after 1939 being titled simply *Zwölftonspiel*); his music has an individual sound, but little variety or lasting interest.

Jacobsen, Jens Peter (1847–85), Danish poet, novelist and storywriter, much concerned with liberating thought from Romantic dreams. His best-known works are the novels *Fru Marie Grubbe* (1876) and *Niels Lyhne* (1880). The *Gurresange*, set by Schoenberg as the *Gurrelieder*, is an early poetic cycle.

Kandinsky, Wassily (1866–1944), Russian painter, playwright and art theorist; one of the principal leaders of the Expressionist movement in art, and one of the first Abstract painters. Studied in Munich. With Franz Marc, organized the *Blaue Reiter* Exhibitions there (which included paintings by Schoenberg), and edited the *Blaue Reiter* Almanac, for which Schoenberg composed *Herzgewächse*. His drama *Der gelbe Klang* (1909) had some influence on Schoenberg's *Die glückliche Hand*. His friendship with Schoenberg was long-lasting, though his post-war involvement with the Bauhaus in Weimar provoked a serious rift between them because of anti-semitic tendencies there, and occasioned one of Schoenberg's most famous letters (of 4th May 1923) on the subject of politics, racial discrimination and human rights.

Kokoschka, Oskar (b. 1886), Austrian painter, poet and playwright, a leader of the Expressionist movement. Active first in Vienna and then in Berlin before the Great War at roughly the same times as Schoenberg. He had a stormy affair with Alma Mahler and was a friend of Schoenberg, of whom he painted a famous portrait in 1924. Gravely wounded during the war, he was later professor of the Dresden Academy of Art, and has continued painting to the present day. His early Expressionist dramas probably influenced Schoenberg in *Die glückliche Hand*.

Kolisch, Rudolf (b. 1896), Austrian violinist, also a composition pupil of Schoenberg, who married his sister Gertrud in 1924. Founder (in 1922) and leader of the Kolisch Quartet, which gave the premières of Schoenberg's Third and Fourth Quartets and String Quartet Concerto; leader (from 1942) of the Pro Arte Quartet.

Kraus, Karl (1874–1936), Australian poet and satirist, founder and virtually sole contributor of the social and literary periodical *Die Fackel* (the Torch) which he published from 1899 until his death. He was the leading spokesman for the most advanced wing of the creative generation that included Schoenberg. Deeply distressed by what he saw as the collapse of Western cultural values, he was obsessed with the rejuvenation of language ('the crystallized tradition of the spirit of man') through the rejection of all cliché, ornament or falsity; and his work inhabits the sounds and rhythms of German so completely as to be virtually untranslatable. He wrote essays, poetry and plays, the greatest of which is the ironic epic *The Last Days of Mankind* (1919). Schoenberg's literary style was deeply influenced by Kraus, with whom he was on friendly terms.

Labor, Josef (1842–1924), Austrian composer and organist (blind), pupil of Simon Sechter. He encouraged the young Schoenberg to devote himself to music, and later collaborated with him on a volume of the *Denkmäler der Tonkunst in Österreich*. Labor's own

Schoenberg

works include music for organ and orchestra. He is said to have been Wittgenstein's favourite composer.

Pappenheim, Marie (1882–1966), doctor (specialist in skin diseases) and poet, born in Bratislava. She became part of Schoenberg's circle about 1908, while a medical student in Vienna. She wrote the libretto for *Erwartung* in 1909, and her poems were published in Karl Kraus's *Die Fackel*. She served in cholera epidemics in Istanbul and Bulgaria before the Great War, and later worked in Mexico.

Rankl, Karl (1898–1968), Austrian conductor and composer, was a pupil of Schoenberg in the early 1920s. He came to Britain in 1939 and was musical director of Covent Garden 1946–51 and conductor of the Scottish National Orchestra 1952–7. His own works, which include five symphonies and an opera on J. M. Synge's *Deirdre of the Sorrows*, incline in style towards that of Mahler.

Rosbaud, Hans (1895–1962), Austrian conductor, noted for his interpretations of contemporary music. His recordings of Schoenberg's Variations for Orchestra and *Moses und Aron* (whose world première he conducted in a concert in Hamburg on 12th March 1954, and the stage première in Zürich on 6 June 1957) are classics.

Rosé, Arnold (1863–1946), Austrian violinist, Mahler's brother-in-law, leader of the Vienna Philharmonic and Opera orchestras for fifty-seven years. He founded and led the Rosé Quartet, which gave the premières of Schoenberg's *Verklärte Nacht* and First and Second String Quartets. He died in London, having fled there after the *Anschluss* in 1938.

Rufer, Josef (b. 1893), Austrian musicologist, pupil of Zemlinsky and Schoenberg, and the latter's chief assistant in Berlin from 1925 to 1933. His *Composition with Twelve Notes* remains perhaps the best introduction, in a perilous field, to Schoenberg's twelve-note method; his catalogue of *The Works of Arnold Schoenberg* is the volume with which all who seriously wish to explore the *œuvre* must begin.

Scherchen, Hermann (1891–1966), German conductor, self-taught, who made his debut sharing the conducting of *Pierrot Lunaire* with Schoenberg in 1912 and championed contemporary music, especially the 'Second Viennese School', throughout his life. Founded the periodical *Melos* in 1920. His recordings of Schoenberg vary in quality but are of great interest.

Schreker, Franz (1878–1934), Austrian composer, conductor and teacher, best known for his stage works, especially the operas *Der ferne Klang* and *Der Schatzgräber*, in a highly coloured post-Straussian and post-Puccinian idiom. He founded the Vienna Philharmonic Choir in 1911, with whom he conducted the world première of Schoenberg's *Gurrelieder* in 1913. Became Director of Music at the Berlin Academy in 1920; dismissed by the Nazis in 1933.

Shilkret, Nathaniel ('*Nat*') (b. 1895), American conductor, arranger and composer, mainly of popular and film music, at one time director of Victor Recordings Inc. His ambition to 'put the Bible on records' resulted in the composite *Genesis Suite* (1942–5) with movements by Castelnuovo-Tedesco, Milhaud, Schoenberg, Shilkret, Stravinsky, Tansman and Toch. Schoenberg provided the Prelude.

Skalkottas, Nikos (1904–49), Greek composer and violinist. Studied with Schoenberg in Berlin from 1927 to 1930, after being a pupil of Kurt Weill and Philipp Jarnach. He returned to Athens in 1933, where he composed in obscurity for the rest of his life. His compositions (which are still too little known) are very numerous, and wed the intonations of Greek folk-music to a highly individual form of twelve-note technique: they range from the thirty-six *Greek Dances* to large-scale concertos and symphonic works. One of the major composers among Schoenberg's later pupils.

Stein, Erwin (1885–1958), Austrian musicologist, one of Schoenberg's earliest pupils. Worked much in music publishing, especially with Universal Edition in Vienna. Settled in London after the *Anschluss*, and was founder and first editor of the modern music review *Tempo*.

Steuermann, Eduard (1892–1964), internationally known concert pianist and composer, born in Poland. He was a pupil in Berlin of Busoni, Schoenberg and Humperdinck. He championed modern piano music, especially that of the 'Second Viennese School', and was the soloist in the première of Schoenberg's Piano Concerto in 1944. Emigrated to the U.S.A. in 1936. His own music, influenced by twelve-note procedures, has affinities with Busoni, Webern and Schoenberg.

Stiedry, Fritz (1883–1968), Austrian conductor, noted in Wagner and in twentieth-century music. Between 1907 and 1958 he held posts in Dresden, Berlin, Vienna, Leningrad and New York (he emigrated to the U.S.A. in 1938). A friend of Schoenberg, he conducted the premières of *Die glückliche Hand* and the Second Chamber Symphony. His wife, the singer Erika Stiedry-Wagner, was a noted interpreter of *Pierrot Lunaire*, and recorded it under Schoenberg's direction.

Strang, Gerald (b. 1901), American composer and acoustics expert, studied with Schoenberg in California, 1935–6, and was his editorial assistant 1936–50. His own works include music for orchestra as well as computer-music and works for electronic tape.

Ullmann, Viktor (1898–1944), Bohemian composer, pupil of Schoenberg 1919–21 and a founder-member of both the Vienna and Prague Societies for Private Musical Performances. He spent most of World War II in a concentration camp in Czechoslovakia (where he wrote much music, including the opera *Der Kaiser von Atlantis*) before being sent to his death at Auschwitz.

Weiss, Adolph (1891–1971), American composer, bassoonist and conductor; he studied with Schoenberg 1924–7 and was the first American to compose music in the twelve-note method. His works include the cantata *The Libation Bearers* and much chamber music.

Wellesz, Egon (1885–1974), Austrian composer and musicologist, became a pupil of Schoenberg in 1905, and in 1921 wrote the first book-length study of him (it is still among the best). He taught at Vienna University till 1938, when he emigrated to Britain and taught at Oxford. He was one of the world's leading authorities on Byzantine music. His own compositions, many of which employ various forms of twelve-note technique, are numerous: they include *Alkestis* and six other operas, ballets, chamber and vocal music, and an important series of nine symphonies.

Zehme, Albertine (1857–1946), Viennese actress, reciter, *diseuse* and singer who specialized in melodrama. She commissioned several works in this form from different composers, the most famous being Schoenberg's *Pierrot Lunaire* (1912). She toured Europe performing *Pierrot* under his direction, and remained on friendly terms with the Schoenbergs until 1924, when her interests strayed into other fields.

Zemlinsky, Alexander (von) (1872–1942), prominent Austrian opera conductor and gifted composer: one of Schoenberg's closest friends, his only formal teacher, and his brother-in-law. Conductor at the German Theatre in Prague 1911–27 (where he gave the première of *Erwartung* in 1924) and at the Krolloper in Berlin 1927–32; died in the U.S.A. He was best known in his own day for his operas; nowadays it is the (regrettably infrequent) performance of his chamber works and the fine *Lyric Symphony* (from which Berg quotes in his *Lyric Suite*) that principally keep his name alive.

Zillig, Winfried (1905–63), German composer and writer on music, pupil of Schoenberg 1923–7, and highly regarded by him. He made the performing version of *Die Jakobsleiter* which has been given in concert since 1961. His own works include *Troilus und Cressida* and other operas, *Osterkonzert* for orchestra, choral and chamber music and songs.

Appendix D   Bibliography

The following is no attempt at a general bibliography of the available material on Schoenberg; nor does it indicate more than a fraction of my own reading in the course of writing this book. The range of Schoenberg literature (in article, if not book form) is vast; a very large proportion of it, however, is to some degree polemical in intention, and needs therefore to be approached with care. My aim here has been to provide the basis of a useful further-reading list for the interested explorer of Schoenberg, classified under a few general (and by no means mutually exclusive) headings. Naturally, in a book for English-speaking readers, I have concentrated on English-language publications, but have indicated some of the most necessary material in other languages as well. It is almost inevitable in a list of this kind that the selection of items should appear somewhat arbitrary; for a much fuller bibliography the reader is referred to the forthcoming article (noted below) by O. W. Neighbour in the new edition of *Grove's Dictionary of Music and Musicians*.

IN GENERAL

Armitage, Merle (ed.), *Schoenberg* (New York, 1937).

Neighbour, O. W., 'Schoenberg'—article in *Grove's Dictionary of Music and Musicians* (6th ed., London, 1978?).

'In defence of Schoenberg' (*Music & Letters*, January 1952).

Newlin, Dika, *Bruckner-Mahler-Schoenberg* (New York, 1947).

Rosen, Charles, *Schoenberg* (New York, 1975; London, 1976).

Stuckenschmidt, Hans Heinz, *Arnold Schönberg* (Zürich, 1951, 1957); Translation (London, 1959).

Wellesz, Egon, *Arnold Schönberg* (Vienna, 1921); translated (London, 1925); new English edition, as *A.S.: the Formative Years* (London, 1971).

Arnold Schoenberg: an appreciative monograph (Oxford, 1945).

MAINLY BIOGRAPHICAL; NON-MUSICAL TOPICS

Black, Leo, 'Schoenberg's Pupils' (*The Listener*, May 1968).

Keller, Hans, 'Schoenberg: Problems of Translation' (*Books and Bookmen*, July, August, September 1974).

Lessem, Alan, 'Schönberg and the Crisis of Expressionism' (*Music & Letters*, October 1974).

Meyerowitz, Jan, *Arnold Schönberg* (Berlin, 1967).

Nachod, Hans, 'The Very First Performance of Schoenberg's *Gurre-lieder*' (*Music Survey*, Summer 1950).

Reich, Willi, *Schönberg oder der Konservativ Revolutionär* (Vienna, 1968); translated as *Schoenberg: a critical biography* (London, 1971).

Ringer, Alexander L., 'Schoenbergiana in Jerusalem' (*Musical Quarterly*, January 1973).

Rubsamen, Walter H., 'Schoenberg in America' (*Musical Quarterly*, October 1951).

Stein, Leonard, 'The *Privataufführungen* Revisited', in *Paul A. Pisk: Essays in his Honour* (Austin, Texas, 1966).

Stuckenschmidt, Hans Heinz, *Schönberg: Leben, Umwelt, Werk* (Zürich, 1974).

Warren, C. Henry, 'Schoenberg and his English critics' (*The Sackbut*, January 1932).

Whitford, Frank, 'Arnold Schoenberg as Painter' (*The Times Literary Supplement*, 13 July 1973).

THE MUSIC IN GENERAL; INDIVIDUAL WORKS

Boretz, Benjamin and Cone, Edward T. (ed.), *Perspectives on Schoenberg and Stravinsky* (Princeton, 1968).

Brian, Havergal, 'Arnold Schönberg' (*Musical Opinion*, September 1937).

'Schönberg: Triumph at the B.B.C. National Concerts' (*Musical Opinion*, March 1928).

Crawford, John C., '*Die glückliche Hand:* Schoenberg's *Gesamtkunst-werk*' (*Musical Quarterly*, October 1974).

Crowson, Lamar, 'Playing Schoenberg's Op. 29' (*RCM Magazine*, 1962, No. 3).

Goehr, Alexander, 'Schoenberg's Late Tonal Works' (*The Listener*, January 1964).

Jalowetz, Heinrich, 'On the Spontaneity of Schoenberg's Music' (*Musical Quarterly*, Vol. XXX, 1944).

Keller, Hans, 'A Survivor of Warsaw' (*Music Survey*, June 1951).
    '*Moses und Aron*' (*The Score*, June, October 1957).
    'Schoenberg's last work' (*Music Review*, August 1957).
    'Moses, Freud and Schoenberg' (*The Monthly Musical Record*, Jan.–Feb., March–April 1958).
    'Schoenberg and the String Quartet' (*The Listener*, April 1960).
    'Schoenberg as Music' (*The Listener*, January 1965).
    'Whose Fault is the Speaking Voice?' (*Tempo*, Winter 1965–6).
    'Schoenberg's Four Concertos' (*The Listener*, February 1967).
    'Schoenberg and the Crisis of Communication', in the programme-book of the London Sinfonietta Schoenberg/Gerhard series (London, 1973).

Leibowitz, René, *Schoenberg et son École* (Paris, 1947).

Mason, Colin, 'Schoenberg and the Orchestra' (*The Listener*, September 1961).

Neighbour, O. W., 'A talk on Schoenberg for Composers' Concourse' (*The Score*, June 1956).
    '*Moses and Aaron*' (*Musical Times*, June 1965).

Nelson, Robert U., 'Schoenberg's Variation Seminar' (*Musical Quarterly*, April 1964).

Payne, Anthony, *Schoenberg* (London, 1968).

Perle, George, 'Schoenberg's Late Style' (*Music Review*, November 1952).

Rachhaupt, Ursula von (ed.), *Schoenberg, Berg, Webern: the String Quartets—a Documentary Study* (Hamburg, 1971).

Rufer, Josef, *Das Werk Arnold Schönbergs* (Kassel, 1959); translated as *The Works of Arnold Schoenberg* (London, 1962).

Sessions, Roger, 'Schoenberg in the United States' (*Tempo*, December 1944; reprinted with additions in *Tempo*, Winter 1972).

Spies, Claudio, 'The Organ Supplanted: a Case for Differentiations' (*Perspectives of New Music*, Spring–Summer 1973).

Steiner, Ena, 'Schoenberg's Quest: newly discovered works from his early years' (*Musical Quarterly*, July 1974).

Whittall, Arnold, *Schoenberg Chamber Music* (London, 1972).

Wörner, Karl H., *Gotteswort und Magie* (Heidelberg, 1959); translated as *Schoenberg's 'Moses und Aron'* (London, 1963).

Zillig, Winfried, 'Notes on *Die Jakobsleiter*' (*The Score*, June 1959).

'ATONALITY' AND THE TWELVE-NOTE METHOD

Gerhard, Roberto, 'Tonality in Twelve-note Music' (*The Score*, May 1952).

Goehr, Alexander and Goehr, Walter, 'Arnold Schönberg's Development towards the Twelve-Note System', in *European Music in the Twentieth Century*, ed. Howard Hartog (London, 1957).

Herschkowitz, Filipp, 'Le Fonti Tonali della Dodecaphonia di Schoenberg' (*Rivista Musicale Italiana*, October–December 1974).

Hicken, Kenneth L., 'Schoenberg's "Atonality": Fused Bitonality?' (*Tempo*, June 1974).

Hopkins, G. W., 'Schoenberg and the Logic of Atonality' (*Tempo*, Autumn 1970).

Maegaard, Jan, *Studien zur Entwicklung des dodekaphonen Satzes bei Arnold Schönberg* (Copenhagen, 1972).

Neighbour, O. W., 'Dodecaphony in Schoenberg's String Trio' (*Music Survey*, June 1952).

Perle, George, *Serial Composition and Atonality: An Introduction to the music of Schoenberg, Berg and Webern* (Berkeley, 1962).

Rufer, Josef, *Die Komposition mit Zwölf Tönen* (Berlin, 1952); translated as *Composition with Twelve Tones* (London, 1954).

Samson, Jim, 'Schoenberg's "Atonal" Music' (*Tempo*, June 1974).

Sessions, Roger, 'Some notes on Schoenberg and the "Method of Composing with Twelve Tones"' (*The Score*, May 1952).

Webern, Anton, *The Path to the New Music*, ed. Willi Reich (Pennsylvania, 1963).

Wellesz, Egon, *The Origins of Schönberg's Twelve-Tone System* (Washington, 1958).

A NOTE ON RECORDINGS

Schoenberg's music benefits enormously from the familiarity of repeated hearings. In view of the infrequency of performance, recordings are especially valuable: and Schoenberg is in the apparently fortunate position that practically his entire *œuvre*, some unpublished and/or unfinished works included, has been committed to disc (at the time of writing the only major gap is *Die Jakobsleiter*). Though some important records have been deleted, most of these can be obtained through specialist record shops. However, many Schoenberg recordings have been first and only ones; and a variety of circumstances (notably the lack of a real performing tradition for his music) makes it difficult to give unqualified recommendation to all but a very few.

Three large sets claim the attention. The eight-volume 'Music of Arnold Schoenberg' under the direction of Robert Craft (CBS, 16 discs) provides an admirable cross section of the music in performances that range from good to indifferent. The documentation in the early volumes is impressive, and makes a useful supplement to our Bibliography. Most recommendable are Volume I, which includes *Erwartung, Die glückliche Hand* and *A Survivor from Warsaw*, and Volume 3 (with the Op. 22 Orchestral Songs, Op. 16 Orchestral Pieces and both Chamber Symphonies). The Lasalle Quartet's set of the complete String Quartets of Schoenberg, Berg and Webern (DGG, 5 records) is very serviceable. The London Sinfonietta's set of most of Schoenberg's other chamber music (Decca, 5 records) is variable: the performances of *Herzgewächse*, the *Serenade* and the Op. 29 Suite are especially fine, however.

Three recordings exist of *Moses und Aron*: those of Gielen (Philips) and Boulez (CBS) have exemplary clarity and drama, but the original cast under Rosbaud (Columbia) is still, for me, the greatest performance. Likewise the *Gurrelieder* under Kubelik (DGG) still seems preferable to more recent performances. Rosbaud's account of the Orchestral Variations (Wergo) was undoubtedly the finest until the recent appearance of Karajan's new recording, which with the same conductor's *Pelleas und Melisande* (both are part of a 4-record DGG set) sets an entirely new standard of Schoenberg performance and is highly recommended as an introduction to the composer. Perhaps the best version of the Op. 16 Orchestral Pieces is that of Dorati (on Philips); while no collector should be without Alfred Brendel's peerless account of the Piano Concerto (DGG). Maurizio Pollini's is perhaps the best version of the solo piano music (also DGG). Two interesting and valuable records deserve mention: the Chamber Symphony No. 2 under Frederik Prausnitz coupled with the Six Pieces for male chorus (on HMV); and the String Trio coupled with the Concerto for String Quartet and Orchestra, played by the Lenox Quartet (Desto). There have been many recordings of *Pierrot Lunaire*: the London Sinfonietta's (Decca) is most beautifully played; but, for my money, the most characterful performance is Schoenberg's own, recorded in 1943 with Erika Stiedry-Wagner, Kolisch, Steuermann and others (CBS).

Index

Index

285

Index

Index

DATE DUE

JUN 8 '10 JUN 5 '10	JUN 6 '10		